Reluctant Pioneer
a life of Elizabeth Wordsworth

T. Binney Gibbs.
1922

Georgina Battiscombe

RELUCTANT PIONEER

a life of Elizabeth Wordsworth

Constable London

First published in Great Britain 1978
by Constable and Company Ltd
10 Orange Street London WC2H 7EG
Copyright © 1978 by Georgina Battiscombe
ISBN 0 09 461200 5
Set in Monotype Fournier 12pt, 2 pt leaded
Printed in Great Britain by The Anchor Press Ltd
and bound by Wm Brendon & Son Ltd
both of Tiptree, Essex

Contents

Illustrations

Foreword

IN the late nineteen-thirties Evelyn Jamison began collecting material for a biography of Elizabeth Wordsworth. She would have been the ideal author for such a book, having known and loved Miss Wordsworth and worked with her for many years. Unfortunately she found herself hindered by the many other demands upon her time and energy and when she died in 1972 she had completed only the first chapter. No better account could be given of Elizabeth Wordsworth's childhood and youth, but it is too long to fit into the scheme of a much shorter book than the one she had planned. It is therefore printed here in an Appendix so that it may be enjoyed by Evelyn Jamison's old pupils and admirers or consulted by those who wish to know more details about Elizabeth Wordsworth's early years. The present book is based almost entirely upon the material collected by Evelyn Jamison and is to that extent her work.

I would wish to thank most warmly the many people who have helped me with reminiscences or with the loan of letters and papers, in particular the late Mrs Dorothea Smeeton who kindly allowed me to use her large collection of papers relating to Elizabeth Wordsworth. I am especially grateful to the Principal and staff of Lady Margaret Hall and in particular to Miss Susan Reynolds; without her unfailing help and interest this book could not have been written.

Chapter 1

Elizabeth Wordsworth
and her Background

ELIZABETH WORDSWORTH is one of the great figures in
the women's movement, a cause in which she took not the
faintest interest. She had no friends among the leaders of that
movement, and she felt herself to be out of sympathy with those
of her own students—Kathleen Courtney, for example, or
Maude Royden—who joined actively in the struggle for
women's rights. No one would wish to belittle the part played
by such pioneers as Annie Rogers or Bertha Johnson but the
fact remains that from the moment of her appointment as
first Lady Principal of Lady Margaret Hall, Elizabeth Wordsworth occupied an extraordinary and unique position at Oxford.
At Cambridge no one person came to embody the cause of the
higher education of women; in Elizabeth Wordsworth both
the University and the outside world saw 'the Oxford woman'
personified.

How came it that University women were to be represented
by someone who cared nothing for the emancipation of women
and who took a minimal part in their struggle for admittance
to degrees and to full membership of the University? Elizabeth
Wordsworth's unique position was in part due to purely
factual causes: she was Principal of L.M.H.[1] for the abnormally
long period of thirty years and after her retirement she lived
on in Oxford for another thirty-three, old indeed but by no
means a spent force. As head of L.M.H. and founder of St
Hugh's she stamped her impress upon two out of the five

---

1. From earliest days Lady Margaret Hall has been known as L.M.H.

women's colleges now in existence. It was, however, not merely the unusual length and breadth of her influence which accounted for her special position in Oxford, but rather the peculiar nature of that influence, depending as it did not at all on scholarship or organizing ability but solely on the force of her personality. 'I suppose Miss Wordsworth could be described as a splendid personality,' someone once remarked to Dame Kathleen Courtney. 'No,' came the quick reply, 'simply a *personality*.'

Here it is that the would-be biographer runs up against an almost insuperable difficulty. Evelyn Jamison declared with truth that no one who had not known Elizabeth Wordsworth personally was qualified to write about her. As Elizabeth herself wrote, 'One cannot draw the outlines round an influence.' Reminiscences abound but none of them provide more than a passing glimpse of this elusive personality. The impression is always of someone moving so quickly and in so unpredictable a direction that it is only possible to draw a lightning sketch, never a finished portrait. A contributor to the Wordsworth memorial number of the *Brown Book*[1] puts the problem in a nutshell: 'How can one catch a breeze and fix it on a piece of paper?'

Lack of material is no hindrance. Besides the many written reminiscences and the personal recollections of people still alive there are all Elizabeth Wordsworth's own writings, a mass of letters, speeches, notes for addresses (though, alas, only one short, incomplete diary) as well as her published pamphlets, novels, plays and poetry. All this written material is, however, of a curiously baffling nature. She did not possess the art of putting herself on paper; even her book of autobiographical memoirs conceals rather than reveals its central character. Maybe this deficiency of hers was due not so much

1. L.M.H. Old Students' magazine.

to lack of ability as deliberate intention; she chose not to admit other people into the secret places of her personality.

Those who had the good fortune to know Elizabeth Wordsworth personally may well protest that reserve is the very last word which should be used in connection with her. They remember her as a witty, outspoken, openly-affectionate person, with an embarrassing but ineradicable habit of saying the first thing that came into her head. How could anyone so spontaneous ever be described as reticent? Yet an uneasy suspicion persists that all this witty inconsequence, this quick flitting from point to point and from position to position might have been a refusal to allow herself to be pinned down, a deliberate effort to avoid capture. Though she frequently speaks and acts on impulse she is never caught off guard nor does she ever give herself away. She uses her brilliant humour as a shield against any too-close contact. 'She put her wits between herself and me,' says a character in one of Stella Benson's novels, 'a shining armour.'

This fundamental reserve was at least in part due to the peculiar nature of Elizabeth Wordsworth's religious upbringing. Her parents belonged to a group of old-fashioned High Churchmen, Tractarians rather than Anglo-Catholics, who looked to John Keble as their leader and inspiration. Keble had equated reserve with reverence, elevating it almost to the position of a Christian virtue. Religion was the most important thing of all to Elizabeth, and religion, as she had been taught to understand it, inculcated a decent reserve rather than an uninhibited 'sharing'.

By temperament as well as by training Elizabeth Wordsworth was inclined to keep herself to herself and to avoid any disclosure of her private feelings. She would fling her arms around a girl's neck but she would never tell that girl the secrets of her heart. On the whole the Wordsworths were an undemonstrative race. In this respect Elizabeth took after her great-uncle

William, whom she highly revered, rather than after her more demonstrative great-aunt Dorothy. In Wordsworth's poetry 'feeling' is a key-word, but it is not to be read as 'feelings'. And, like his great-niece, he is more interested in *agape* than in *eros*.

One supreme quality Elizabeth certainly inherited from her Wordsworth forebears. The spark which burnt so brightly in William and Dorothy flared up again in their great-niece. The word 'genius' occurs over and over again; Vera Brittain, for instance, writes, 'Her genius may have had Victorian roots but genius it was none the less,' and the anonymous author of her obituary in *The Oxford Magazine* declares, 'She has been herself an instance of what was said of Wordsworths in more than one generation, "They all have a touch of genius".' That touch was not apparent in her writings, though such a distinguished critic as the philosopher J. A. Stewart seriously described them as 'Wordsworthian'. Elizabeth Wordsworth's genius is to be perceived not in her poetry but in her personality.

This remarkable woman's work for the higher education of women was achieved, as some bishops are said to have been appointed, 'by divine inadvertence'. According to both Vera Brittain and Kathleen Courtney, Elizabeth Wordsworth was no feminist, yet she presided over one women's college, founded another, and became the first woman to receive the signal honour of an Oxford honorary degree of Master of Arts. To quote Evelyn Jamison's comment, 'as has been said of St Louis, she accomplished all this almost *sans le savoir et sans le vouloir*'.

Elizabeth Wordsworth neither opposed nor supported the movement for the emancipation of women: she simply left it on one side as uninteresting to herself personally and irrelevant to her work at L.M.H. Her views on the position of women were feminine rather than feminist in character; she would, for instance, have approved the modern custom of women dining at high table in men's colleges and vice versa not because she believed that women should be treated as men's equals but because she enjoyed masculine company at dinner-time. Today a woman who devoted herself to the education of women while disapproving of the struggle for women's rights appears a baffling contradiction; in Elizabeth Wordsworth's day, or at least in her earlier years, such a position was a comprehensible and natural one. Unlike their twentieth-century counterparts, few or none of the Victorian reformers wished to make a radical change in the existing order of society; instead they planned to improve the condition of affairs within the bounds of that order. Wilberforce and Shaftesbury, the two greatest figures in the history of nineteenth-century social reform, both sat in Parliament as Tories. So, in her lesser sphere, Elizabeth Wordsworth did not believe that women should be educated in order that they might take a different position in the world to the one they already occupied, but she saw an educated woman as a person who could play with more intelligence, and therefore with more efficiency and pleasure, her accepted role in the existing order of society. Education was not a means to an end but something to be enjoyed for itself. In her own youth learning had been her greatest delight; now she wished to give to other girls a share in this supreme pleasure.

In her attitude towards women's rights and women's education Elizabeth Wordsworth differed fundamentally from the pioneers of the higher education of women at Cambridge. Through her friendship with the pioneer woman doctor Elizabeth Garrett, afterwards Mrs Garrett-Anderson, Emily Davies, the founder of Girton College, became deeply involved in the struggle to open the professions to women. One evening at the Garretts' house, Emily, Elizabeth, and Elizabeth's young sister Millicent (who was to become a

leading suffragette and to marry the blind statesman, Henry
Fawcett) sat discussing their future as they brushed their hair
beside the bedroom fire. 'I must devote myself to securing
higher education,' said Emily, 'while you, Elizabeth, open the
medical profession to women. After that we must see about
getting the vote.' She turned to Millicent—'You are younger
than we are, Millie, so you must see to *that.*'

In pursuance of her concern with education Emily Davies
fought to get the Cambridge Local Examinations opened to
women, organized the London Headmistresses' Association,
gave evidence before a Government Commission on schools,
and became one of the first women members of the London
School Board before founding the Ladies' College at Hitchin
which was later to move to the neighbourhood of Cambridge
and become Girton. She saw that college in the larger context of
the women's movement as a whole. If women were to be
emancipated they must be educated; hence the sudden growth
of girls' schools such as Cheltenham and Queen's College.
Schools required teachers, and teachers must themselves be
taught, preferably up to University level. The official historian
of Girton writes of Emily Davies that 'for her, education was a
means to an end; that end was the admission of women to full
equality.'

Though a very different character from Emily Davies, Anne
Clough, the first Principal of Newnham, had also been a friend
of a famous woman pioneer—in her case Josephine Butler—and
had herself taken an active part in the women's movement,
organizing lectures and courses for women in north country
provincial cities. According to Dame Mary Agnes Hamilton
both Anne Clough and the founder of Newnham, Henry
Sidgwick, 'sought to meet the needs of large numbers of young
women to get some adequate training for themselves which
would enable them to go out into the schools and remove them
from the blight of the drawing-room.' Roughly three-quarters

of the girls leaving Newnham went into the teaching profession.

Elizabeth Wordsworth, on the contrary, played no part in the struggle for the emancipation of women and deeply distrusted what is now described as vocational education. She had seldom felt in the least blighted in any drawing-room and she did not expect the majority of her students to become teachers. Her object was to give women the chance to share with men in the intellectual pursuits and pleasures which she herself had enjoyed in her own scholarly home, and she believed passionately that the best form of education was one which had a religious basis.

The difference in outlook between Elizabeth Wordsworth and the Cambridge pioneers was in part due to a difference in upbringing and circumstances. In her history of Girton, M. C. Bradbrook writes that Emily Davies 'would not have felt at ease in the society to which the founders of Newnham naturally belonged.' She was the daughter of a poor Tyneside parson; her intellectual roots were in London and she had no previous connection with Cambridge. Both Anne Clough and Elizabeth Wordsworth belonged to a different stratum of society, coming from scholarly, well-to-do, well-connected families. Anne Clough, however, had been brought up in the West Indies and returned to England to find herself in straitened circumstances and obliged to make money by running a school. When Elizabeth Wordsworth described herself as coming from 'the class . . . which, while obliged to depend upon its own exertions, is nevertheless rarely exposed to the shifts and struggles of poverty,' she was thinking of the men as far as exertions were concerned. No one supposed that any of the five Wordsworth sisters would ever have to earn their own living. In early days at Stanford money was not too plentiful but there was never any real shortage. Later, the considerable income enjoyed by a nineteenth-century bishop allowed Christopher

Wordsworth to maintain a large house and grounds and to
keep his wife and daughters in circumstances which could be
described as very comfortable indeed, with a carriage and pair
and a large staff of domestic servants. Elizabeth's habits of
thrift, her small economies in bus fares and envelopes, sprang
from ingrained 'carefulness' inherited from her north country
forebears rather than from any experience of poverty.

This deep sense of social and financial security naturally
affected both her opinions and her outlook on life. It is easy to
take a high view of the purpose of education and to despise its
vocational aspect if you know that you yourself will never be
under the necessity to earn a living. Elizabeth Wordsworth
was very well aware of the needs of less well-off young women,
and of poor parsons' daughters in particular, as she showed by
her action in founding St Hugh's but, unlike Emily Davies
and to a lesser degree Anne Clough, she had no personal
experience of their plight. Because she herself had been free
to enjoy such education as came her way without thought of its
practical usefulness she lacked any instinctive understanding
of the attitude of those who of necessity used education as a
means of obtaining work or qualifications.

Because of Emily's own achievements and those of other
members of her family today the name Llewelyn Davies is a
very well-known one. Emily's father was a person well respected in his own northern neighbourhood but his name meant
nothing in the Cambridge of the 1860s. This lack of social
background combined with her natural shyness to make
Emily Davies a prickly personality. She was a great woman
but, unlike Elizabeth Wordsworth, she was not ideal company
at the dinner-table, and in consequence she shunned the social
life of Cambridge both for herself and for the girls who came
under her supervision. She had indeed little time or inclination
for frivolity. Being wholly dedicated to the women's cause, she
believed so passionately in the ideal which she had set before

herself that she was unable or unwilling to compromise. Elizabeth Wordsworth, who had no such clear conception of the end, could take many more liberties with the means at her disposal. Vera Brittain describes her as having 'the courage to take a new road when she saw it'; she did not, however, waste much time in speculating as to the exact shape of the object which might lie at the end of that road. When she opened L.M.H. with a tiny handful of students she did not plan, or even foresee, that this family party would grow into a large and formally organized college famous throughout the world. This freedom from preconceptions meant that she could grasp each opportunity as it arose and make the most of it; she could wait on events and follow the path they presented rather than attempt to force events along a path which she herself had previously mapped out. In flexibility combined with force of personality lay the secret of her strength; when pragmatism and a touch of genius go hand-in-hand the result can be both successful and surprising.

The influence of early upbringing and childhood surroundings is very apparent in the development of Elizabeth Wordsworth's personality;[1] home and family were always to remain a central interest in her life. She was the eldest of the seven children of Christopher Wordsworth, son of another Christopher who was Master of Trinity College Cambridge and brother to the poet. The second Christopher married Susannah Frere, a member of a family distinguished in many fields including scholarship and diplomacy. Elizabeth was born on 23 June 1840, to be followed by Priscilla, John, Mary, Susan, Christopher and Dora. At the time of her birth her father was headmaster of Harrow but in 1844 he was appointed Canon of Westminster and moved to a house in Little Cloister. In 1851

1. A longer and more detailed account of E.W.'s ancestry and early years will be found in the Appendix.

he was presented to the living of Stanford-in-the-Vale, which he held in plurality with his canonry so that although the Wordsworths retained the London house and lived in it for part of the year they had a second home in a country parsonage in Berkshire.

When she was an elderly lady Elizabeth wrote a little pamphlet entitled *Only a Feather* in which she described the nursery as 'the very nicest room in the house'. Her account of life in that very nicest room is surely coloured by memories of the Wordsworth nursery which was presided over by a loving and beloved Scottish nannie called Janet McCraw. 'There is no hushing up or stiffness or constraint,' Elizabeth wrote, 'but everything goes on as usual, naturally and pleasantly, and the children are taught good manners, even from their cradles.'

From nursery days onwards the person who counted most with Elizabeth was her father, a saintly and scholarly man of great simplicity of character. 'Dear old man,' said Bishop Magee of him, 'there's very little of him in the nineteenth century; most of him is in the ninth and the rest is in Heaven.' When a clergyman complained about the small attendance at an early communion service Christopher Wordsworth asked, 'Have you counted in the angels?' He never talked down to his children but discussed with them all his own interests and pre-occupations. This admirable habit of treating them as intellectual equals had some drawbacks. In his official biography, written by Elizabeth in conjunction with Canon J. H. Overton, 'a member of the family', probably Elizabeth herself, is quoted as speaking of 'his highly susceptible nervous system', and stating that 'the agonies of neuralgia which he used to suffer and the nervous depression which accompanied it have left a very strong impression on our memories.' He was a man who worried profoundly about the state of the world in general and the Church of England in particular, and he passed on his anxieties to his children. Labouring under the weight of problems and difficulties beyond their understanding it was not surprising that they grew up, as Elizabeth put it, 'with a rather uneasy sense of some sort of crisis hanging over our heads.'

If from a very early age the Wordsworth children suffered from a feeling of over-strain they had the ideal antidote close at hand in their mother's calm imperturbability. Her unobtrusive affection complemented and to some extent counteracted the demands their father made upon them and the too-great pressure he placed upon their intellects. In later life Elizabeth was to declare that she believed it had been a real advantage to her family to be able to let their minds relax in the company of a mother whom she described as 'a soft cushion'. In her girlhood, however, she did not find her mother either sympathetic or congenial. Essentially she was her father's child, a Wordsworth rather than a Frere. 'I never did understand the Freres,' she admitted, and in turn she believed that her mother had never properly understood her.

Though she was an affectionate and conscientious parent Susannah Wordsworth's life revolved round her husband rather than her children. In later years, when Christopher Wordsworth became a bishop, she always accompanied him on such occasions as Confirmation tours. Janet Courtney gives a charmingly ludicrous description of her as 'the dearest little old lady, entirely wrapped up in the Bishop, very precise in her requirements for him, the early tea and fire because he rose at 6 a.m., the cup of beef-tea before he went into Church for the Confirmation, with her safety-pins ready to fasten up his robes if it was wet.' Although she was very good-looking Susannah Wordsworth never attempted to shine in society; perhaps because she was a little deaf she refused to put herself forward, preferring to remain quietly in the background. Herself an intelligent and well-informed person, she nevertheless deprecated any show of interest in scholarship as something highly unbecoming in a woman. Elizabeth's insatiable

thirst for knowledge was a constant source of friction between
mother and daughter. Christopher Wordsworth, on the contrary, thoroughly approved Elizabeth's intellectual pursuits
and gave her much-needed help and support. If it cannot be
said that he actually taught her Greek, Latin and Hebrew—
'our dear father's mind was much more intent on theology
than on grammar which he seemed to expect one to know by
instinct'—he certainly encouraged her studies and made use of
her knowledge of these languages when compiling his great
commentary on the Bible. Their shared interest in learning of
all sorts formed a special bond between father and daughter;
she never ceased to be grateful to him for his help and encouragement in this direction.

'I feel what a *rare* blessing it has been to have a united home
life,' Elizabeth wrote on 7 December 1898, looking back over
past years. Yet, though the Wordsworths formed a united and
loving family circle, it was not a particularly intimate one.
Elizabeth's letters to her brothers and sisters are curiously
impersonal; she does not seem to differentiate between her
correspondents and what she writes to one she could equally
well have written to all, with the possible exception of John,
who stood to her in a rather more close relationship. Though
the more private letters may well have been destroyed the tone
of those which survive clearly indicates that fond as the brothers
and sisters were of one another they did not think to share their
inmost thoughts and feelings.

Other more distant relatives played a considerable part in
Elizabeth's life. She took great interest in the doings of aunts
and uncles, nephews, nieces and cousins, counting herself a
member of a closely-knit family connection, almost a clan. To
her grief she could remember nothing of a visit paid to the
house in Little Cloister by her great-uncle William when she
was about seven years old, but she had clear recollections of
great-aunt Dorothy in her sad dotage, and of that dedicated

and self-effacing woman, Mary Wordsworth. Of her Frere relations the nearest and dearest was her mother's unmarried sister, 'Aunt Lissie' who was for many years a close neighbour, first in London and then at Stanford.

When the Wordsworths were 'in residence' at Little Cloister there would be much entertaining of a serious, ecclesiastical kind, visits to galleries, exhibitions, museums and an occasional theatre and, brooding above the daily comings and goings, the tremendous presence of Westminster Abbey. At Stanford life consisted of 'some lessons and a good deal of parish', to use Elizabeth's own phrase. 'Parish' included amateur concerts, clothing clubs, the distribution of food and clothes to the needy, and—what Elizabeth most enjoyed—regular teaching in Sunday school. 'Lessons' were presided over by a series of governesses, all of them sensible, intelligent women who were treated as members of the family and who bore little or no resemblance to the ignorant, down-trodden governesses of Victorian fiction. In her late teens Elizabeth spent a rather profitless year at boarding-school but her real education she acquired for herself, reading every book she could lay hands on, borrowing Greek, Latin and Hebrew grammars from her brother John, and picking up information by listening to the conversation of her father and his learned friends. The arts were not neglected. Most of the family were musical and there was much singing and playing at home and occasional concerts in London. All through her life Elizabeth drew and painted with enormous enjoyment, though with little talent to judge from surviving specimens of her art. Above all, she wrote, but unfortunately none of her early stories and verses have escaped destruction.

Predominant over every other influence in the upbringing of the Wordsworth family was the influence of religion. They were reared in a Tractarian tradition, reverent, reticent, and deeply imbued with the consciousness of the Church's historic

past. These children did not have religion forced upon them;
they grew up to it just as naturally as a farmer's child grows up
to a love and understanding of crops and animals, a soldier's
child to a pride in regimental tradition, a musician's child to a
knowledge and appreciation of good music. Religion had been
all around them from their birth, taken as much for granted as
the air they breathed. An interest in what might be called the
technical side of religion was specially marked in Elizabeth,
perhaps because she was of them all the one closest to their
father. She made his interests her own, filling her letters with
long accounts of such functions as Church Congresses, and
endless discussion of current ecclesiastical problems and con-
troversies, but writing always with a touch of humour and
sometimes with the faintest hint of self-mockery. Although all
the members of the family who could read Greek or Hebrew
were pressed into service to help check references or look up
quotations, Elizabeth was always her father's chief assistant in
the enormous task of writing a commentary on the entire
Bible.

Thus almost imperceptibly Elizabeth Wordsworth grew up
from child to girl and from girl to grown-up young lady with
little or no change in her interests, occupations or surroundings.
Except for the fairly frequent holidays abroad which were
perhaps her greatest pleasure, her life could not be described
as an exciting one, yet she was neither unhappy nor discontented nor, it would seem, bored. The ten years between
her eighteenth and her twenty-eighth birthday were a singu-
larly uneventful period in Wordsworth family history; no one
died, no one married, no one even fell seriously ill. Then,
in the late summer of 1868, an important event occurred;
Christopher Wordsworth was offered and after some
hesitation accepted the see of Lincoln.

Her father's elevation to the episcopate meant a move from
the old house at Westminster, which had been Elizabeth's

home for as long as she could remember, and from the spartan discomforts of Stanford Vicarage to the comparative splendours of Riseholme Palace, some two or three miles out of Lincoln, 'a handsome modern house, much grander than anything we have lived in before.' Built in solid classical style, it stood on a little rise surrounded by lawns sloping down to a large lake. Canon Overton's description of the Bishop's private chapel as 'a square room of somewhat un-ecclesiastical aspect' aptly conveys the atmosphere of the house as a whole. That plain, regular exterior, those large, well-lit rooms conveniently grouped around a central hall with a domed skylight, bore no resemblance to the uncomfortable but romantic bishop's palace of tradition. The ethos of Riseholme was essentially secular; even the sweep of lawn beyond the *porte-cochère* seemed better suited to a meet of the Burton foxhounds than to a garden-party for clergy and their wives. Edward King, Christopher Wordsworth's saintly successor in the bishopric, found the place so uncongenial that he insisted on moving back into the old medieval palace in Lincoln. Christopher Wordsworth himself seems to have had doubts as to the suitability of Riseholme as an episcopal residence, for shortly after her arrival there Elizabeth was writing to her sister Dora that 'it seems likely we shall have to live here for a couple of years as there is really at present no place in Lincoln.' In the event they were to remain at Riseholme for all the eighteen years of Christopher Wordsworth's episcopate.

Elizabeth's summary of her own objections to Riseholme is a perfect period piece—'No poor people, no broth, no flannel; we must begin our district at Lincoln soon, but as yet can only practice the charity which begins at home.' In the grounds was a little church designed by that notable designer of ugly churches, S. S. Teulon, where the regular congregation consisted of the Bishop's family and 'two rows of nodding housemaids'. Lincoln, however, was within easy reach; and there the Wordsworth girls could attend cathedral services and find plenty of scope for charitable work in the poor district of the city known as 'downhill'. Elizabeth was soon back at her favourite work of teaching, finding herself considerably shocked by the ignorance of her pupils—'It is terrible to think that not one of them seems to know who King Jeroboam was.' As well as teaching in Sunday school and organizing classes for working girls, once a week she taught a group of 'damsels', to use her brother John's word, who came from a more educated background. One or two of them were assistant teachers and, according to Elizabeth, 'had done something or other in the Cambridge examinations.' She herself was to achieve more than 'something or other' in these same examinations. A certificate headed 'University of Cambridge, lectures and classes in Populous Places, Lincoln, Michaelmas Term, 1875' states that 'Elizabeth Wordsworth has attended a course of instruction in English Constitutional History consisting of weekly lectures for a period of eleven weeks and in the examination held by the syndicate has been placed by the examiners in the division of Merit, with special distinction.'

Apart from good works Elizabeth was kept busy helping her mother with the considerable entertaining expected of a bishop's wife, and acting as her father's unofficial private secretary while at the same time quietly taking upon herself more and more of the routine work on the Bible commentary. In a letter dated 3 April 1869 and written shortly after his consecration as bishop her father gratefully acknowledges the debt he owes to her: 'You know how much I need your help in these things now that I have no time for them myself; and I am never unthankful, my dear daughter, to Almighty God for the great blessing He has given me of your help in these important matters.' It is typical of Bishop Wordsworth that he should express his thanks not to his daughter but to the Almighty.

Though she appeared happy enough at the time, fifty years later Elizabeth was to hint that these years at Riseholme had been for her a period of doubt, stress, and difficulty. In the course of a memorial address on her friend Minnie Benson she described the trials of life in a bishop's household in terms which suggest that she herself was all too familiar with these trials:

The women who belong to a bishop's family cannot fail to see a good deal of the weaker side of ecclesiastical life, the little rivalries, intrigues, personal feelings, the gossip and mutual criticism, the small ambitions and misunderstandings which will always exist. And when a woman is exceptionally shrewd and has a dangerous sense of humour, and keen critical power, the temptation to her cannot but be strong to forget the pricelessness of the treasure which, after all, is really hid in some of the poorest earthen vessels. It would have been difficult for a woman of such a temperament to have lived through this particular form of trial and to have gone on being religious, in spite of what one might have called 'religiosity'.

Herself a remarkably shrewd woman gifted with an irreverent and irrepressible sense of humour, she must have found much to mock at and little to admire in the aspect of Church life which was now exposed to her critical gaze. The pettiness of Church people may even have shaken her faith in the Church itself. But though inwardly she may have felt slightly dis-illusioned and dismayed she remained a dutiful and devoted Church-woman, keenly concerned in all ecclesiastical affairs. Her life continued in much the same way as at Stanford and Westminster, though of course on a larger scale. The groove had widened but it was still the same groove, and it seemed improbable that she would ever succeed in climbing out of it, even if she should wish so to do. What she needed was someone or something which could bring a new element into her life and teach her to look on familiar faces and surroundings with a new vision. This she found in her friendship with the Benson family and in particular with Edward Benson.

Chapter 2

Friendship

LIKE the Wordsworths, the Bensons were of north country origin. Again like the Wordsworths, some of the Bensons were scholars, others had literary gifts, all of them—at this date—were devoted members of the Church of England. There the resemblance ended; no two families could have been less alike in temperament or in character. The difference between them was the difference between sense and sensibility. Though a strain of pleasant eccentricity marked their outward behaviour, the Wordsworths were essentially sensible, normal people. They might even be called hard-headed. William Wordsworth, for instance, had none of the peculiarities of manners, morals or appearance usually associated with poetic genius; his family life was a happy one and, given the circumstances of his age and class, his one recorded love affair was a perfectly natural, almost conventional episode. The modern theory of an incestuous relationship between William and Dorothy is basically improbable because it would be out of character for a Wordsworth to do anything so abnormal as to to fall in love with his own sister.

About the Bensons, however, there was hardly anything that could be described as normal, least of all where their love affairs were concerned. At the age of twelve Minnie Sidgwick found herself engaged to Edward Benson, a grown man many years her senior. Ignorant, and a little unwilling—'Oh, how my heart sank—I daren't let it, no wonder, a mere child'—she was married at eighteen, and bore her husband four sons and two daughters in quick succession. None of these six children married. One daughter died in her twenties; a second became insane; the eldest and most promising son died of meningitis at the age of sixteen; the other three sons, all of them well-known and successful authors, were with some reason suspected of homosexual tendencies. The mother of this curious but attractive brood was herself in the habit of falling in love with other women. At the beginning of the Wordsworth–Benson friendship she had been attracted to Elizabeth and had been under the delusion that her feelings were returned—'Oh, my vanity! I thought she was looking at and thinking of me when far other and nobler things occupied her.' In startling contrast to the objective, solid and reticent Wordsworths the Bensons were introspective, volatile, and highly articulate. Scorning the middle way, they rushed from the heights to the depths; charming they certainly were but it must be admitted that they were also a little second-rate.

Edward White Benson, the father of the family, summed up in himself most of these Benson characteristics. Tall, with long, light-brown hair and protuberant blue eyes, he was startlingly handsome in a slightly obvious manner. Years later Elizabeth Wordsworth was to record that she had often seen him blush for pleasure like a school-boy. 'This characteristic,' she added, 'together with the unusual flexibility of the lower part of the face, gave a great range of expression, and was, when combined with a rich, deep, sonorous and often very affecting voice, a splendid outfit from nature for such a career as his was to be.' In 1859 Edward Benson had been chosen as first headmaster of Wellington College, the new public school established under the aegis of the Prince Consort. Benson's rule at Wellington was a successful if somewhat stormy dictatorship. Whether he was teaching, preaching, conducting innumerable services—the Prince Consort himself was moved to protest

against the amount of chapel-going expected of the boys—
wrestling spiritually with recalcitrant pupils or haranguing
the staff on their sad lack of zeal he was all the time at fever-
pitch. Even his beatings were more intense, and very much
more painful than those inflicted by lesser men. When things
were going well with the school he was ecstatic; when they
went badly he burst into tears.

In 1868 John Wordsworth took up a temporary teaching
post at Wellington and there made friends with the headmaster
and his family. In November of that year Christopher Wordsworth, with his wife and his daughters Elizabeth and Susan,
arrived at Wellington to stay for a few days with the Bensons.
When out for a walk with his host Christopher remarked that
he had that day written a letter to Disraeli refusing the offer of
a bishopric. Edward Benson turned back immediately,
extracted the letter of refusal from the school letter-box and
insisted on his guest writing a letter of acceptance in its
place.

This first momentous visit to Wellington was followed by
many others. As sometimes happens, the two families, Wordsworths and Bensons, fell collectively in love with each other.
The religious, intellectual Bensons were delighted to find new
friends as religious and intellectual as they were themselves,
while for the undemonstrative Wordsworths the effervescent
Bensons spelt excitement and romance. Minnie Benson, though
a headmaster's wife and the mother of five children, was a year
younger than Elizabeth who, long afterwards, wrote an
excellent description of her as she appeared to the other
members of that group of gay and lively young people:

> She had the spirits of a girl. Unconventional, rather
> regardless of externals and proprieties, and, as always,
> mercilessly argumentative, she was as unlike a typical
> headmaster's wife as anyone could be.

Writing to one of Minnie's sons Elizabeth recorded memories of Wellington, telling how Minnie would be 'on the look out for us, with a volume of Browning in her hand, a corner of the green velvet sofa kept vacant,' while elsewhere, with less politeness, she recalled 'the peculiarly uncomfortable green velvet drawing-room furniture . . . in the pretty room with its pinewood wainscoting and the beautiful prints, and your father would be coming in to insist on our hurrying out to see the new mosaics, Saint Matthew, Daniel, or Melchizedek, in the chapel.' To those mosaics Bishop Wordsworth added as his own gift a figure of St Hugh, patron saint of the diocese of Lincoln.

When Edward Benson had persuaded Christopher Wordsworth to accept a bishopric he had promised that he himself would ultimately give up his post at Wellington and come to work in his friend's diocese. He first visited Lincoln in March 1869 on the occasion of Wordsworth's enthronement as bishop, when he found much to criticize in the inefficiency of the arrangements and the all-too-apparent lethargy of the Dean and Chapter. Appointed Examining Chaplain to the new Bishop and presented to a prebendal stall with the peculiar name of Heydour-cum-Walton, he threw himself zealously into the business of reform and reorganization. Noting the contrast between the Trollopeian atmosphere of Lincoln Close and the other-worldliness of the Wordsworth household at Riseholme he commented, 'Certainly if Deans and Canons lead this life of elevated gossip it is very different from the earnest life of the Bishop's house.' At the back of his mind was a vision of what he described as a 'coenobium', a pseudo-monastic establishment of married clergy living a simple life of prayer and study —the type of life which he could have wished his own family might live in company with their new friends, the Wordsworths.

Intimacy between the two families grew quickly. In the

Family group taken in 1880 at the wedding of Dora Wordsworth and Edward Tucker Leeke. Mary Wordsworth, Chr. Wordsworth, P. A. Steedman, J. J. Trebeck, E. T. Leeke, Mary Trebeck, Priscilla Steedman, Susan Wordsworth, Mrs Wordsworth, S. E. Wordsworth, John Wordsworth, Dora Leeke, Bishop of Lincoln, Elizabeth Wordsworth

Elizabeth Wordsworth and her first nine students, taken outside 21 Norham Gardens, now Old Hall, L.M.H. Mary E. E. Smith, E. Dorothy Bradby, E. Laura F. Jones, M. Evelyn Anstruther, Edith M. Argles, Charlotte M. Ward, Miss Wordsworth, Edith A. Pearson, Winifred L. Cobbe and L. D. La Touche

Edward White Benson
when Headmaster of
Wellington College, 1867

Annie Moberly, Principal of
St Hugh's College, with a
group of early St Hugh's
students. Jessie Emmerson,
Charlotte Jourdain, Mitchell,
Miss Moberly, Constance
E. Ashburner, Grace Parsons

summer of 1869 Bensons and Wordsworths spent a memorable holiday together at Whitby. They chipped fossils out of the cliffs, hunted out Roman inscriptions, and tramped miles over the moors, deep in discussion of Keble's poetry. On the last day of the holiday they paid a farewell visit to 'the dear old Abbey which seems to have become part of ourselves', and, walking arm-in-arm through the ruined aisles, recited the Magnificat and some favourite psalms: 'an evening none of us will, I think, ever forget.' The Whitby visit seemed touched with a light not altogether of this world. In a curious discourse which he entitled a 'Concio' and addressed to the three Wordsworth sisters who had shared those happy days with him (Priscilla had left home to train as a hospital nurse) Edward Benson wrote, 'We too have wondered, and have spoken of our wonder, that the purple of the moors, and twilight on the river while the northern sea lay all gold, and the living beauty of stately trees and waving branches should have such power to make us forget the world's trouble and labour, and send us home stronger at evening than when we arose in the morning.' Then, after speaking of God's presence with them, he added, 'For, as well as the teaching of Nature under His presence, they had too the conversation of friends.'

Years later Elizabeth was to describe 'that happy September' as 'almost the high water mark of our enthusiasm'. Enthusiasm was indeed the key-note of the hour. The Whitby holiday was crowned by a week at Riseholme which, as Minnie Benson expressed it 'sealed the *geschwister bund*'. Deeply devoted to Bishop Wordsworth, and passionately concerned with everything to do with cathedrals and cathedral life, Edward Benson was bubbling over with excited interest in all he saw about him. His eagerness communicated itself to his friends, who found themselves looking at their surroundings with a new and more romantic vision. 'Doctor Benson's enthusiasm for the cathedral and city life and it would be unfair not to add for

B

the Bishop, had a reflex action upon ourselves,' Elizabeth wrote; 'we viewed the life there in the light of his vivid and poetical imagination.' What she described as 'this extraordinary vitality of his that enabled him to throw a glamour over everything he touched,' was one of the qualities which most attracted her to him. (She herself had the opposite gift, being expert in the art of 'de-bunking'.) Nearly sixty years later she was to write to an old friend, 'We women, who get so tired and feel so dull sometimes, know how to value a man who seems to brighten and cheer existence like a clear blazing fire on a dreary day.' Such a man she found in Edward Benson, and with him she was soon on such familiar terms that she could agree to break the rigid convention which forbade the use of Christian names between men and women.[1] Immediately after his departure from Riseholme she wrote him a letter beginning, 'My dear Edward, this is a nice name to give you on Sundays', and adding a comment typical of Wordsworth reticence, 'It would be a sad state of affairs if we did not always feel *a great deal* more than we said, even in so small a matter as names.' Benson replied with an enormously long letter; for the next nine months they were to write to one another nearly every week.

They were certainly not consciously in love. In 1869 the daughter of a bishop did not fall in love with a clerical headmaster who was already a married man and the father of five children. Such a preposterous idea could never cross anyone's mind. Because a love affair was a ludicrous impossibility the situation was a perfectly safe one; and Edward Benson took advantage of that safety to conduct what can best be called an intellectual flirtation. Though Elizabeth was his foremost object he extended his range, as it were, to include the other

1. Mary Anne Moberly, wife of George Moberly, headmaster of Winchester and Bishop of Salisbury, in the course of fifty years of married life was only once heard to call her husband 'George'.

Wordsworth sisters. Unfortunately the letters he wrote to Susan and to Mary (Priscilla was away from home and Dora little more than a school-girl) have not survived for comparison with those to Elizabeth. To her he writes that 'the expectation of letters from you has changed my view with regard to the post.' He declares that 'somehow you tempt me to be sentimental and I am never quite sure that when I am sentimental I am not laughable, and if I am I know *you* will laugh'—a remark which shows how well he understood his Elizabeth. He says he has no right to bother her with his troubles—'it is an odd sign of love but it is one.' One letter begins, 'Dearest Elizabeth, don't be offended please. But I have already torn off one sheet which began to you *so* yesterday.' Another ends thus: 'Best love to all. And I love you. Your ever affectionate brother Edward.' (The Wordsworths and Bensons had adopted one another as brothers and sisters.)

Today a woman receiving such letters would immediately see the warning light. For Elizabeth there was no warning because there was no danger. How could she see anything wrong in a relationship which she shared with the whole family and one which was based on a mutual love for all that was beautiful and good? She summed up her feelings on this subject in a letter written to Benson soon after the Whitby holiday: 'It is, I think, a fortunate circumstance when one can associate a friendship with things that one's memory would love to dwell upon on other accounts—cliffs—waves—moors —grey stones and heath—ruins—sunsets—psalms—cathedrals—and last, not least, the recollections of the week before you left us.' This sentence does not read in any way like an extract from a love-letter, but neither does it express feelings normally associated with a brother or sister or with a woman friend. Elizabeth Wordsworth was a perfectly normal young woman, reasonably pretty, gay, approachable, supremely good company, and with an admitted liking for men's society.

She was indeed so gifted that some young men may have fought shy of her. To the query 'I wonder why Miss Wordsworth never married', one of her successors at Lady Margaret Hall replied, 'What had any man to offer such a lady?' There should, however, have been no lack of suitors; yet the fact remains that in no surviving letter is there even the faintest reference to any sort of love affair. (This, of course, is not proof positive that she had none.) Now, at twenty-nine, she had reached an age when the nineteenth-century unmarried woman counted herself an old maid. A handsome, charming, and brilliant man appears on the scene who is obviously though innocently attracted to her; she blossoms and expands in the warmth of his openly expressed admiration.

Elizabeth's letters to Edward Benson are shorter and more matter-of-fact than his letters to her; they are, however, very much more lively than the colourless screeds she was in the habit of writing to her own family. These letters are concerned with the many interests she had in common with Edward Benson; art, archaeology, history, literature and, of course, Church affairs and religion. Greek and Latin quotations abound, with an occasional excursion into French or Italian. They also record daily events or encounters of special interest. Remembering what the future held for her, Elizabeth's comment on a hard case of clerical poverty is of particular significance:

> The boys in such a family might have got scholarships and done pretty well but what would have become of their poor little sisters with Mamma washing the tea-cups and no chance of a governess? One does not feel the hardship of being uneducated in itself but when the brothers grew up and went to college they must have felt their home very different.

Both Edward Benson and Elizabeth were in the habit of writing verses—in partnership with her brother John Elizabeth had already published a small book of ballads—so it was natural that they should send each other poems to be admired, criticized and read aloud in the family circle. Neither letters nor poems were in any sense private. Since Elizabeth habitually acted as her father's secretary her letters were often more full of the Bishop's affairs than of her own. Occasionally she would write a letter addressed jointly to Edward and Minnie, or an affectionate one to Minnie alone, without Edward. Very rarely, Edward Benson would write a phrase or a paragraph which he must have expected Elizabeth to keep to herself, as when he described Minnie's unhappy reaction to his refusal of the headmastership of Rugby. Again, referring to the controversial but in no way personal question of Frederick Temple's appointment to the see of Exeter, he wrote 'I said to *you* something which I think I never said to anyone else about my own feelings.' Such instances, however, are so rare as to be negligible. Throughout the whole of this long correspondence only two or three sentences are carefully obliterated, something which was presumably done before the letters were passed on to A. C. Benson for inclusion in his official biography of his father. In that age of innocence no one thought to imagine that these letters might lead readers to suppose that Edward Benson and Elizabeth Wordsworth were in love with one another.

In the summer of 1870 Wordsworths and Bensons enjoyed another holiday together, this time at Ambleside. But the magic of Whitby could not be recalled; Minnie Benson described this Lake District holiday as 'a sad time' full of 'unlovingness, bickerings, jealousies', presumably between herself and her husband. Already ill and unhappy, she was not cheered when five months later she found herself pregnant yet again, and after the birth of her sixth child, Robert Hugh, she

broke down completely. Suffering from headaches, sleepless-
ness, 'utter misery, dreading I knew not what,' she took refuge
with her kind friends at Riseholme. Now, perhaps for the first
time, Elizabeth Wordsworth had reason to be a little dis-
illusioned by Edward Benson's overbearing and insensitive
behaviour. Minnie was so unwell that both Mrs Wordsworth
and the doctor were moved to protest strongly when Benson
insisted that his wife must return to Wellington in time for
the school speech-day. Back, however, she had to go, with the
not surprising result that she suffered an even worse breakdown
and was obliged to spend the whole of the next year abroad.

Minnie's collapse came at a most inconvenient moment for
Edward Benson. In fulfilment of his promise to come to Bishop
Wordsworth's help in November 1872 he resigned from the
headmastership and accepted the post of Chancellor of Lincoln. He was now faced with the business of moving his family
into their new home and taking up unfamiliar work in surroundings which at first he found uncongenial except for the
presence of his friends at Riseholme. Not surprisingly he fell
into one of his black fits of depression which afflicted him at
intervals all through his life. Even after Minnie's return in
September 1873 the domestic situation remained difficult; the
husband remained in the depths of depression and the wife was
bored and discontented with the almost exclusively clerical
society of Lincoln. Gradually, however, matters improved;
Edward Benson found plenty to interest and occupy him in
the affairs of the cathedral and diocese while Minnie experienced
a religious 'conversion' which genuinely altered her outlook on
life, making her more tolerant both of her husband and her
neighbours.

During the three years spent at Lincoln Minnie played
almost as important a part as her husband in the relationship
between the Wordsworth and the Benson families. Elizabeth
and her brothers and sisters were at this period 'trying to

arrive at some equation between what we considered "the modern spirit" and our own traditional beliefs.' It was a quest in which the young Wordsworths could expect no help or guidance from their parents, whose views were those of a generation even earlier than their own and whose attitude of mind was entirely alien to the climate of thought in the sixties and seventies. Though no one could describe Edward Benson as an advanced theologian he was at least slightly more liberal-minded than Bishop Wordsworth. In 1860 a storm of controversy had been aroused by the publication of *Essays and Reviews*. Nine years later Gladstone selected Frederick Temple, one of the essayists, for the bishopric of Exeter, a choice which drove Bishop Wordsworth and other conservative churchmen to furious protest. Edward Benson, on the contrary, while dreading any disagreement with the Bishop (whom he referred to as '*my* Lord'), admired and approved Frederick Temple, even going so far as to write to *The Times* in support of his appointment.

On the whole, however, Benson's religious views were the conventional ones of his day and generation, though expressed with slightly unconventional fervour. Minnie's instinctive attitude and opinions were very different; born a Sidgwick, she had been brought up at Rugby, the centre of what was then considered to be an ultra modern and dangerously liberal school of religious thought. Both as philosopher and economist her brother Henry was one of the most advanced thinkers of the day. Reared in such an atmosphere, she naturally differed from the Wordsworths on many points; she did not, for instance, venerate a priest as such, regarding the man as more important than the office, and she took no interest whatsoever in the Church's historic past. Contact with such an attitude was little less than a revolution to Elizabeth; as she herself put it, 'the situation seemed to call for a certain re-adjustment of one's own values.' Fortunately, the two found common ground in their mutual conviction that any Christian worthy the name was of necessity profoundly concerned with the poor and the distressed 'in mind, body, or estate'. In Lincoln religion must not stop short with the cathedral 'uphill' but must take the form of teaching and visiting in the slums and schools of the 'downhill' town. Here Minnie and Elizabeth could work together and thus learn to respect and understand each other's point of view.

The correspondence between Elizabeth and Edward Benson noticeably slackened after the 1870 holiday in the Lake District and, of course, ceased completely with the arrival of the Benson family in Lincoln. It was not renewed when in 1877 Benson left Lincoln for Cornwall on his appointment to the newly-established see of Truro. Though she was to remain on the best of terms with his family, Elizabeth's friendship with Edward Benson himself was finished. Why it should have come to such a complete and final end it is impossible now to say. Maybe one or other of the two felt that the situation was growing too intense; more probably in the close neighbouring proximity of Lincoln and Riseholme Elizabeth found the Benson charm wearing a little thin.

At the height of the Benson–Wordsworth involvement Elizabeth chanced to meet and make another new friend. John Wordsworth had been for some time much in love with Esther, daughter of Bodley's Librarian, Henry Coxe, a well-known Oxford character. In June 1870, just before the pair announced their formal engagement, Wordsworths and Coxes made one big family party for Commemoration week at Oxford which was to include the installation of Lord Salisbury as Chancellor and the opening of Keble College. Elizabeth stayed at the Warden's Lodgings in New College, where she found herself a fellow-guest with Charlotte Mary Yonge.

Though the last thirty years have seen a considerable revival of interest in Miss Yonge and her writings it still comes

as a slight surprise to discover that in her own day she was
regarded as a literary star of the first magnitude, especially
among that group of High Church Anglicans to which the
Wordsworths belonged and whose manner of life and thought
her stories reflect with such vivid accuracy. Elizabeth was in
fact a Miss Yonge heroine come to life. Miss Yonge specialized
in stories of large families like the Wordsworths in which the
father was the dominant figure. As a good Miss Yonge
heroine should, Elizabeth devoted herself to her father, never
thinking to question his demands upon her time and attention.
The heroine whom Elizabeth resembles most closely is the
best-loved of them all, dear Ethel May of *The Daisy Chain*.
Elizabeth herself was to make this plain in a description of
intellectual girls—'born scholars' she calls them—which is
clearly a picture of her own youthful self:

> They are to be found in the schoolroom, peering like our
> old friend Ethel May into their brothers' books, trying their
> hands at Greek and Latin, or it may be at mathematics or
> science, picking up crumbs of knowledge from beneath the
> tables of their male belongings, and blushing beautifully
> when detected.

Elizabeth's conversation, like Ethel's, was filled with literary
quotations and historical allusions, and spiced with scholarly
jokes. Like Ethel, she saw school-teaching both as a duty and
a delight whose claims upon her attention were second only
to those of her father and family. Again like Ethel, she was by
nature disorderly, but she was a good needlewoman and clever
with her fingers while poor Ethel was afflicted with what she
described as 'two left hands'.

Elizabeth resembled a Miss Yonge heroine not only in
character but in the circumstances and events of her life. Like
Geraldine Underwood, she watched a great choral service from

a vantage-point in the cathedral organ-loft and marvelled at the sight of 'the white-robed multitude who seemed to fill the whole chancel.' Her sister Mary, like Ethel's sister Flora, had a pronounced taste for 'county' society; the Wordsworths played the same character-guessing game as the Underwoods play in *The Pillars of the House* and the Kendals in *The Young Stepmother*; even her account of dining with John 'off boiled mutton and one of Mary's sago puddings' is reminiscent of Doctor May's pleasure in 'the perfect lack of pretension in the plain leg of mutton' served for dinner at Vale Leston. Similar likenesses are constantly turning up to delight the Miss Yonge addict.

The fundamental link between Elizabeth Wordsworth and Charlotte Yonge was, of course, their religious faith. For both of them religion was not merely the most important thing in life but the substance of life itself, yet neither of them spoke easily about religious experience. Keble warned the fifteen-year-old Charlotte against 'too much talk or discussion of Church matters'; Elizabeth wrote to Edward Benson that 'these are subjects one would rather dwell on than talk of.' On the surface neither of them was unduly earnest or sanctimonious, but underneath was a deep seriousness which showed itself chiefly in small acts of self discipline such as attendance at weekday services, or a ban on novel-reading on Sundays or fast-days. It was typical of Elizabeth's general outlook on life that she should regard small austerities as incumbent on her not only as a Christian but also as a lady, speaking of 'those trifling self-denials which mark the real gentlewoman.'

Not surprisingly, Elizabeth Wordsworth and Charlotte Yonge took to each other at first sight. The elder by seventeen years and reputedly slow to make friends, Miss Yonge was clearly much pleased with this eager, intelligent young woman whose tastes were so nearly akin to her own; while for Elizabeth the congenial companionship of this well-known author added greatly to the pleasures of 'Commem', as she recounted them in a long and interesting journal-letter to her mother's sister, Aunt Lissie. After describing the installation of the new Chancellor—'Since the days of Vandyke there surely never was a more dignified and picturesque specimen of an English nobleman than Lord Salisbury in his black and gold, supported by his two little boys, said to be little pickles but behaving on this occasion in a most exemplary manner'—and the behaviour of the audience at this ceremony—'there is evidently a strong Tory feeling in the University; the Prince of Wales' name was badly received—also Mr Gladstone's—Bob Lowe's and the Bishop of Exeter's dubious to say the least of it'—she goes on to tell of her arrival at the Warden's Lodgings and her first meeting with Miss Yonge:

Miss Yonge (*the* Miss Yonge) who was like ourselves to be his guest had just arrived and went with us to chapel. We had been always told she was shy but I can only say no one could have been pleasanter or more natural. There are some people one instinctively feels one can get on with, and she is one. Such a handsome woman, handsomer now, I dare say, because softer-looking, than when young. She looks, and is, Devonshire all over with the most beautiful bright brown eyes, brown cheeks, and plenty of white hair which contrasted with such a healthy complexion makes her like the picture of some powdered but not rouged Madame la Marquise of the *ancien régime*, an impression which is strengthened by her tall, plump graceful figure. Her voice is not ugly but provincial—I suppose it is the way they talk down in Devonshire![1] Altogether she gives one a feeling of country and out-of-doors, and looks as if she ought always

1. Though a member of a Devonshire family Miss Yonge was born and lived all her life in Hampshire.

to be giving you syllabubs out of beautiful old china in a
nice old-fashioned garden . . . We ladies sat down to high
tea, with open windows beyond filled with crimson geraniums, and grey walls beyond them again. I made Miss Yonge
change her place in order to be opposite them (and beside
me, but I *really* think I didn't do it from secondary motives).
However, as strangers came in afterwards she seemed to be
rather thankful to hide her shyness in a tête-à-tête, and we
chatted away about my new one-and-sixpenny Algerian
brooch, Turkish coins, Ionian islands, the ship of the
Phaeacians turned to stone, snuff-boxes, smoking caps,
travelling scenes that make the most impression on you being
often those about which you can convey fewest ideas to
others, etc. We ate our strawberries, drank our tea, and sat
about in the Warden's private garden until dusk.

The next day the whole party attended the Encaenia to see
Bishop Wordsworth receive an honorary degree, 'Esther Coxe,
Pris, Miss Yonge and I all very snug in an embayed window
somewhere behind the Chancellor's head':

> Papa's name was well received, though of course it was
> nothing like the enthusiasm about Canon Liddon, who is so
> much better known in the Oxford world. It was interesting
> to watch the faces, Mr Lowe, who was dubiously received,
> screwing up his white eyebrows,[1] the Bishop of Peter-
> borough pale and nervous, Mathew Arnold I don't like to
> say conceited, Liddon gently smiling, Lord Lyttelton
> irritated by the bad Latin, Landseer calm and socratic, Lord
> Cowley like a man of the world. We had great fun over the
> recitations. I am afraid Miss Yonge did not find the real

1. Robert Lowe, afterwards Viscount Sherbrooke, Chancellor of the
Exchequer 1868–73, was an albino.

Newdigate equal to her imaginary one in *The Daisy Chain*,[1] oddly enough it was about Margaret of Anjou with some allusion to her namesake flower ... Miss Yonge was cheered, or at least someone said so afterwards, but I think she professed to believe it was 'the ladies'.

Later in the day Bishop Wordsworth, Elizabeth and Miss Yonge had a quiet talk together, the Bishop explaining various difficult Bible passages. When he was called away Miss Yonge remarked, 'How I wish I could hear more of those good words,' recalling earlier talks with John Keble.

On the last day of all came the opening of Keble College. Miss Yonge and Elizabeth walked together to the early communion service in the temporary chapel: 'It was a curious fate for me to be with the person who perhaps cared for him more than any other survivor at such a time and to be beside her all through the service.' At the end of the long and tiring outdoor ceremony of the actual opening the party broke up, Miss Yonge bidding Elizabeth 'quite an affectionate farewell'.

At this same Commemoration Elizabeth had also met Anna Sewell, author of *Black Beauty*. Comparing the two women, Elizabeth especially noted in Anna Sewell 'the charm of extreme womanliness, which Miss Yonge lacks.' She went on to define this quality: 'I take it that it lies a good deal in the fineness of nervous susceptibility, or what might be called the *musical* side of human nature, and in certain delicacy of organization rather than in any part of the moral character.' The criticism is a perceptive one, not inapplicable to Elizabeth herself.

Before saying good-bye Elizabeth had plucked up courage to invite Miss Yonge to Riseholme. Though the proposed

1. Norman May in *The Daisy Chain*, wins the Newdigate Prize poem and recites it in the Sheldonian. Four characters in the book are called Margaret, a name whose double meaning is 'daisy' and 'pearl'.

visit never took place, in the course of the next few years
Elizabeth twice stayed with Miss Yonge at her home at Otterbourne. Her first visit in May 1872 began inauspiciously.
Describing the drive from Winchester station to Otterbourne
Elizabeth wrote to her sister Mary, 'We both of us talked hard,
as shy people are apt to do, and I confess my feeling was "What
shall I do if she goes on in that voice for the next three or four
days?"' Elizabeth's warmly expressed admiration of a fine
Dürer print hanging in Miss Yonge's drawing-room served to
break the ice. For the next four days the two women talked
incessantly and enthusiastically of history, pictures and, of
course, books, exchanging views on Scott, Spenser, Ruskin,
Keble, Jean Ingelow, John Keble, George Eliot and the
Brontës—'How wrong it was letting the brother stay at home
and coarsen those girls' minds!' Miss Yonge, who was putting
the finishing touches to *The Pillars of the House*, knew of no
comic song—'I am not in the way of hearing such things'—
which might be sung by Angela Underwood on a boating
excursion. Elizabeth promptly produced an innocuous little
ditty popular with child patients in Nottingham Hospital
which she described as 'dreadfully vulgar'. There were drives
and walks in the neighbouring woods, a visit to Winchester
cathedral and St Cross, and, as in so many of Miss Yonge's
stories, the absorbing business of Church decoration for the
festival of Ascension Day. 'Miss Wordsworth hardly let me do
anything for talking,' Miss Yonge wrote to her friend Marianne
Dyson at the end of this pleasant visit. 'I have not taken to a
person so much for a great while past; she is so good and so
sensible and, what I was far from expecting, so funny, and her
fervent love and devotion to her father are so very charming,
and her last evening she made such a sweet outpour to me of
her Bild worship[1] of him and her happy home, which has never

---

1. Miss Yonge's usual term for 'hero-worship'.

had a sorrow in it for thirty-two years, and I suppose she took to me, for she ended by saying she never thought she could get to love any one so much in four days.' To Elizabeth herself Miss Yonge wrote a letter calling her by her Christian name 'at the risk of appearing to you both a gushing and an impertinent old lady,' and stressing the same point that she had made in her letter to Marianne Dyson. 'Somehow I did seem to get on with you in a wonderful way; I think the deep spirit of veneration made me feel you were like the dear ones I grew up with.'

From now onwards until her death in 1901 Charlotte Yonge was to be a good friend to Elizabeth, who visited her frequently at Otterbourne and set great store by her opinions both on life and on literature.

Chapter 3

Oxford Encounters

FROM 1870 till 1875 Elizabeth Wordsworth kept a fairly full diary which has luckily survived, though in a mutilated condition and missing several pages. She did not write in it every day, the entries for the last two years being particularly scanty. Dating is erratic and inaccurate, and some passages are so cryptic as to be unintelligible. What, for instance, can be made of this record of a conversation with Edward Benson?

> Settled to read Dante if ever he went to Bolton. 'Couple of muffs.' College clock. 'Finish' about it. Very different from Rugby.

At times the entries are so laconic as to be alarming: 'Minnie went. I nearly run over by a train. Suicide at Reading.' Fortunately the next statement is more reassuring. 'Got all right to Stanford.' Yet incomplete though it is and tantalizingly elliptical, the diary succeeds in giving an impression of a busy and satisfying life, full of visits and visitors, old friends and new faces, meetings with well-known people, attendance at interesting functions, a stream of comings and goings to be somehow combined with a steady routine of teaching, writing, study and home duties.

At Riseholme the Wordsworths entertained some unusual and interesting visitors. In 1870 they were hosts to a Greek Orthodox bishop and a party of Greek clergy. Fortunately most of the family could make themselves understood by using classical Greek since none of their guests had a word of English. A visitor from a more remote region was a Mr Magnusson from Iceland, with much talk of Icelandic customs, seals, eider-duck, and ancient sagas. Bishop Steere, missionary and linguist, fascinated everyone by citing Zanzibar sayings and customs to explain and illustrate various obscure passages in the Old Testament. Another guest was an old family friend, Bishop George Selwyn, who had recently returned from New Zealand to become Bishop of Lichfield. Much visiting went on between Selwyns and Wordsworths. Elizabeth had a special liking and admiration for Bishop Selwyn—'He *is* a man! One minute he will be talking in the most learned way about the Athanasian Creed, and the next describing how they all sat on deck making trousers for the newly-caught savages.'

Most of the visitors to Riseholme were clerics, and doubly welcome on that score. Today it is difficult to realize how intense was the interest and, indeed, the pleasure which women like Elizabeth Wordsworth and Charlotte Yonge took in Church affairs. The social life of a bishop's daughter was more rather than less enjoyable because it revolved round such occasions as the meetings of Synods and Church Congresses. Elizabeth was always to feel herself more closely concerned with Church matters, including even those of lesser interest, than with the more obviously important matters of state, to which, of course, she was by no means indifferent. Her tongue may have been in her cheek when she wrote to Susan in 1868, 'The Deceased Wife's Sister's Bill was thrown out by the Commons the night before last by a majority of eighteen. Who cares for the Reform Bill after that?' Her feeling of satisfaction was, however, a genuine one. The Church of England obstinately opposed marriage with a deceased wife's sister but cared little or nothing for electoral reform, hence Elizabeth's more personal interest in the first measure.

Not all her gaieties had an ecclesiastical flavour. The diary records a visit to Windsor Castle and to the Fourth of June at Eton. She mentions her special enjoyment of the procession of boats and the fireworks and comments on 'the aristocratic and refined faces that meet you at every turn.' There was a long stay in London when she met Dean Stanley and his wife Lady Augusta, listened to a debate in the House of Lords, and attended a Mansion House dinner, dressed for this grand occasion in 'white silk with little red and black spots, and cerise trimming and head-dress,' an outfit run up for her by the old family nurse, Janet McCraw. After the Ambleside holiday of 1870 she went on to stay in Wales near Rhyader. Recording what would seem to have been an enjoyable visit she makes the uncharacteristic and laconic comment, 'low in our minds'—almost the only occasion when she admits to feeling sad or depressed. She stayed at Salisbury with Bishop Moberly and his family, writing to Edward Benson of a visit to 'the quiet, ladylike cathedral, as ladies are, a little lacking in spontaneity.' She went sight-seeing to Wilton and to George Herbert's church at Bemerton, and she visited a teachers' training college newly established in one of the houses in the cathedral close. 'I envied them their pretty views and old-fashioned rooms,' she wrote; 'it must, I think, be a help in moulding the girls' characters'—an interesting comment in view of the very unromantic character of the house in which she was to establish her own college. In the early summer of 1872 she paid another and most successful visit to Miss Yonge at Otterbourne, spending a whole evening in talk about Jane Austen, discussing such questions as Mr Knightley's Christian name or the colour of Fanny Price's eyes. 'I don't think I shall ever be shy of you again,' Elizabeth remarked when saying good-bye, to which Miss Yonge replied with better feeling than grammar, 'It's so nice when people do take to one.'

Back at home, Elizabeth was busy taking a women's Confirmation class and organizing teas and bible study for factory girls, in addition to her usual Sunday-school work, bible classes and home duties. Garden-parties, dances, games of whist or croquet, boating or skating on Riseholme lake lightened the round of more serious occupations. Reading, of ourse, was a constant pleasure, the books mentioned in the diary including a Life of Napoleon, Hans Andersen's fairy stories, poetry by Rossetti, Matthew Arnold, Coventry Patmore and Walt Whitman—'one can only charitably hope he is out of his mind'—and a novel entitled *Hedged In,* 'one of those vigorous, dubious, end-justifying-the-means books which now abound.'

Encouraged by Miss Yonge, Elizabeth herself was taking seriously to the business of writing. From 1871 onwards she sent poems and stories to Miss Yonge for criticism and sometimes for inclusion in the magazine, *The Monthly Packet.* She also wrote two little pious tracts, *Thoughts for the Chimney Corner* (1873) and *Short Words for Long Evenings* (1875) and, in 1876 under the pseudonym Grant Lloyd,[1] she published her first novel, *Thornwell Abbas.* In it she made the fundamental mistake of building a story of everyday life round a wildly melodramatic plot, which hinged on that situation beloved by the writers of operatic libretti, the fortunes of two babies interchanged in their cradles. The book contains some slight but pleasant character sketches, such as the picture of the not-very-successful country parson, who 'did not care for gardening nor—in his heart of hearts—for fishing,' or the plump and puzzled girl who, when questioned about a possible moral meaning in *Hamlet,* replies, 'I suppose that we shouldn't be frightened of ghosts.' This same girl makes the splendid remark, 'But I thought everyone, except quite common people, had plenty of money.' Otherwise, such slight interest as the book

1. E.W.'s paternal grandmother was a Lloyd, and her maternal grandmother a Grant.

still holds lies in the passages written from personal experience such as the charming account of an Oxford Commemoration week or the description of the feelings aroused in the mind of a romantically-inclined adolescent by a first visit to Westminster Abbey. Perhaps Elizabeth expresses a personal preference when she makes one of her characters admit to a dislike of Virgil because 'you can always guess what he is going to say next,' and surely she speaks with her own voice when she describes how 'in a small room, two women, each determined on having her own subject and her own audience, are enough to fatigue anyone's nerves.'

Bearing in mind what the future held for Elizabeth Wordsworth, the most interesting entries in her diary are those which record her frequent visits to Oxford and her increasing involvement in Oxford life and society. Her brother John, now a Tutor of Brasenose, married Esther Coxe in December 1870. The pair established themselves in a new house in Keble Terrace, which was then on the edge of the city. Here Elizabeth was a frequent visitor, sometimes coming to take charge of the housekeeping if Esther were obliged to be away from home. John was the nearest and dearest to her of all her relations; and Esther had been a friend since Stanford days, someone to whom she would speak and write more freely than ever she did to her own sisters.

The wind of change was blowing through the Oxford which Elizabeth Wordsworth came to know so well during the years of the 1870s. In 1872 a brilliant young historian called Mandell Creighton[1] took advantage of a new statute passed by Merton College and married Louise Glehn, thus becoming the first married Fellow at Oxford. Other colleges quickly followed Merton's example; and soon the meadows north of Keble were covered with a growth of houses in vaguely Venetian-Gothic style, the homes of this new race of married dons.

1. Bishop of London 1897–1901.

The young women living in these picturesque but inconvenient dwellings were in complete contrast to the dignified,
old-fashioned ladies, the wives of professors or Heads of
Houses who had hitherto formed the only feminine element in
University society. The newcomers were determinedly *avant-
garde*; they furnished their homes with Morris wallpapers,
Liberty cretonnes, oak furniture, and blue and white Japanese
pots. Their taste in dress was equally aesthetic; at a period
when fashion was all for boned corsets, high necks, elaborately
draped skirts and tightly fitted bodices they wore smocks or
shapeless garments of blue-green serge, hand-embroidered
with sunflowers or marigolds. For jewellery they preferred
long amber chains to the conventional dog-collar of pearls and
diamonds; Elizabeth remarked that every lady of culture of
necessity owned an amber necklace. She was a person who
always took a keen interest in dress—'My dear,' she exclaimed
to one dowdy L.M.H. student, 'I do wish you would let me
trim your next hat for you'—and now she filled her letters
home with drawings of blue serge dresses and patterns for
flower-designs in crewel-work. She herself embroidered a blue
serge 'chimney border' in a pattern of strange animals taken
from the illuminations in a medieval bestiary. Her charming
sketches of frocks show that in defiance of the aesthetic cult of
sloppiness she still clung to a more or less fitted style.

At no time have the ladies of north Oxford even remotely
resembled a fashion-plate. The first generation of don's wives
were no exception to this rule; they had neither the inclination
nor the opportunity to spend much money on dress. The
income of a junior Fellow was hardly sufficient to maintain the
type of household, employing at least two servants, which was
then considered obligatory. It is interesting to note that in the
seventies Louise Creighton reckoned six hundred pounds as
the lowest income on which a young couple could set up house,
whereas fifty years later, when money had at least halved in

value, L.M.H. students could and did marry on four hundred a year. Perhaps because money was short the standard of house-keeping was not high. There was much entertaining but none of it on a lavish or luxurious scale; at a typical north Oxford dinner-party the food would be badly cooked and not over-plentiful. These occasions, however, had a charm of their own; in a letter written to Esther from Riseholme Elizabeth, who greatly enjoyed such parties, gives a sketch of the preliminaries they entailed:

> As I write John is (let us hope) going down to the cellar after his best claret, and you are putting ivy-leaves from Wytham into the dessert dates and crystallized fruit, and Ada Benson[1] is doing up for herself some little bit of finery in which blue ribbon is the chief ingredient, and the great guns who shall be nameless are saying what a bore it is to have to dine with college tutors and their wives.

Oxford soon discovered that Elizabeth was excellent company, and she was much in demand as a party guest. She could be annoyed when at one dinner Miss Sewell monopolized 'a charming right-hand neighbour, and threw me over to the Bursar, who is a Liberal and a great smoker,' but for dinner-party company she normally preferred the heretics to the orthodox. On another occasion she was delighted to find herself sitting next to 'a pleasant Mr Warren, who was strong on Mr Jex-Blake and the rights of women—give me the Broad Church folks for a good talk!' Unfortunately she does not record her own reactions to women's rights or to the head-master of Rugby whose daughter was one day to succeed her as Principal of Lady Margaret Hall.

Among the young wives of Oxford plain living was matched

---

1. Edward Benson's sister.

by much high thinking. Living as they did in a place of learning these eager young women were determined to acquire some of this learning for themselves. As early as 1866 Eleanor Smith, sister of the Savile Professor of Geometry, organized a series of lectures for women, an experiment in which she was supported by Mark Pattison, the famous Rector of Lincoln, and his young and good-looking wife. Frances Pattison dressed beautifully, smoked cigarettes and was altogether more sophisticated than other Oxford wives. Men found her very attractive; the historian Taine described her as *'charmante, gracieuse, à visage frais et presque mutin'*. In spite of, or perhaps because of, the Pattisons' backing—they were not a popular couple—the lectures were a failure; seven years were to pass before another and similiar scheme was to be started, this time with a better chance of success.

In 1873 Ruskin visited Oxford to give a course of lectures on Italian art which were to be open to the general public. The young women who flocked to hear him banded themselves together under the leadership of Louise Creighton to form a committee to promote lectures and classes for women in Oxford. These lectures, given by various distinguished dons, proved an immediate success. John and Esther Wordsworth were not concerned with this new development, Esther being what her sister-in-law described as 'one of those women to whom Nature had been so prodigal that one never *wanted* her to be especially well-informed'; Elizabeth, however, while staying at Keble Terrace found time to attend at least two courses given by the historian Robert Laing, who judged her essay on the Crusades to be on a higher level than any other submitted to him.

Through her attendance at these lectures she met and made friends with men and women who were to be the pioneers of the movement for the higher education of women at Oxford. One of the most enthusiastic of the younger women was

Matthew Arnold's niece Mary, who in 1872 married Humphry Ward, a colleague of John Wordsworth's at Brasenose. As a girl Mary had lived in Oxford for some years, and when only seventeen she had been allowed by Bodley's Librarian to read in the Bodleian, where she had wandered at will and absolutely alone, taking down from the shelves any book she wished. In later years she was to record that as a girl still in the school-room, 'regions of the Bodleian were open to me which no ordinary reader sees now.' She had made the most of her opportunities and had already become expert on Spanish history.

Another supporter of the lecture scheme was Clara Pater, sister of the famous author and critic Walter Pater, who, like John Wordsworth and Humphry Ward, was a Fellow of Brasenose. Brother and sister lived together in a house which was regarded as the high-water-mark of Oxford aestheticism. Because of his agnostic opinions Walter Pater and his sister were regarded with suspicion by certain sections of Oxford society. At one of their dinner-parties the wife of a High Church professor indiscreetly goaded her host into remarking that no reasonable person could govern their lives by the opinions or actions of a man who died eighteen centuries ago, whereupon both professor and wife rose to their feet and hurried from the room in great agitation. Though feeling did not run quite so high as it had done in the previous decade, it would seem that in the seventies Oxford dinner-parties still held dangerous pitfalls for the unwary.

Two young women whose friendship was to be of great importance to Elizabeth were Charlotte Toynbee and Bertha Johnson. Charlotte was married to Arnold Toynbee of Balliol, philosopher, economist and social reformer, and perhaps the most brilliant of the younger generation of Oxford men; Bertha to Arthur Johnson, Fellow of All Souls, who delivered the very first of the lectures for women, and was still coaching pupils from L.M.H. as late as 1926. Another young man interested in the lecture scheme was Robert Bridges, then studying medicine but already determined to devote his life to literature and the arts. Among the wives of senior members of the University the lectures had the backing of Mrs Max Muller, niece of Charles Kingsley, Mrs T. H. Green, wife of the philosopher, and Mrs Kitchin, whose husband was later to become Dean of Durham; but since Frances Pattison, who was in poor health and preoccupied with the failure of her marriage, this time stood aside, the only supporter among the wives of Heads of Houses was the twenty-four-year-old Lavinia Talbot.

Lavinia's husband Edward Talbot had been friendly with John Wordsworth ever since their undergraduate days at Christ Church and New College. At the age of twenty-five he had been appointed first Warden of the new Keble College. At Keble the Talbots were near neighbours to the Wordsworths, so that Elizabeth naturally saw much of them during her visits to Oxford. The friendship thus begun was to be long and fruitful, but it was never to be a particularly intimate one. Elderly ladies shook their heads because the young women of north Oxford had adopted the new-fangled habit of calling one another by their Christian names; Elizabeth, however, was never to write to Mrs Talbot as 'Lavinia'.

Lavinia Talbot came from one of the most remarkable of English families, and one which formed part of the great Cavendish and Spencer 'cousinry'. Her father was George, Lord Lyttelton, afterwards Lord Cobham; her mother Mary Glynne was sister to Mrs Gladstone. Had she not died young of typhoid fever Lavinia's sister May would have married Arthur Balfour. Her niece, Elizabeth Alington, married Alec Douglas-Home, thus adding a third Prime Minister to the family circle. Of Lavinia's brothers and sisters Neville became a general, Arthur a bishop, Edward headmaster of Eton, Lucy married Lord Frederick Cavendish, the Irish Secretary murdered in Phoenix Park, Hester married Edward's successor at Eton, and Lavinia herself married the head of an Oxford college who was later to become bishop first of Rochester, then Winchester. The Lytteltons were aristocrats who went their own witty eccentric way, caring nothing at all for fashion or other people's opinion but very much indeed for religion and morals. They were possessed of charm, brains, and a very pungent wit, but their most notable characteristic was goodness. Of all Elizabeth Wordsworth's writings in prose and verse the only one remembered today is the ditty beginning, 'If all the good people were clever, And all clever people were good.' The Lytteltons were the answer to her prayer.

Talbots and Lytteltons had been brought up together and now formed a closely-knit family group, Edward Talbot's brother John having married Lavinia's eldest sister Meriel. At the Warden's Lodgings at Keble Edward and Lavinia entertained such varied notabilities as Newman, Salisbury, Gladstone, Balfour, Curzon, Acton, Burne-Jones, Paul Bourget and Octavia Hill. The young Warden and his wife were people who counted in University circles and their support was of the greatest value to those pioneers who had launched the women's lecture scheme.

As well as paying frequent visits to his home at Oxford Elizabeth would often go on holiday with John, sometimes without Esther whose health was precarious. In the spring of 1876 all three of them made a memorable Italian tour, the high spot, in Elizabeth's judgement, being Verona. In the summer of that same year, Esther being ill, Elizabeth was at Rydal in the Lake District keeping house for John and a reading party of undergraduates. 'I can't think why I don't feel more odd, being the only lady,' she wrote home to Susan. Her position, however, was not without its problems; she found herself in combat with the landlady who was ungracious enough to refuse to give them tapioca pudding for dinner, and worse still she discovered the undergraduates talking and laughing at the top of their voices with a pretty laundress. Perhaps she had her tongue slightly in her cheek when she reported, 'John and I try very hard to improve our young men, even to reading them Doctor Mozley's sermons on Sunday, but what can you expect with the thermometer at ninety?'

These excursions were pleasant interludes in a life which still centred on Riseholme. One by one her brothers and sisters were leaving home. In 1874 Christopher married Mary Reeve, and in the same year Mary Wordsworth married James Trebeck. Of him Elizabeth wrote that 'he inherited all the instincts of the English country gentleman, and though a reverent and earnest Christian, belonged to that good old-fashioned type of clergy who are full of interest in human life.' Four years later Priscilla, who had been working for some time as a hospital nurse, married a doctor called Percy Steedman. The youngest sister, Dora, did not marry until 1880. With five daughters on his hands Bishop Wordsworth, usually so other-worldly, adopted a surprisingly down-to-earth attitude towards matrimony. When a would-be suitor, probably James Trebeck, came timidly to ask for leave to pay suit to the beloved of his choice he was shocked and astonished by the Bishop's cheerful reply, 'Yes! Yes! I quite approve, most suitable. It's time the girls were weeded out a bit.'

In after years Elizabeth was to admit openly that when she was young she would have liked to marry, but at the time she gave no sign that she found it difficult to reconcile herself to the position of a spinster. She was no Florence Nightingale to kick against the lot of a daughter at home, perhaps because, unlike Florence Nightingale, she was not overwhelmed by a sense of unfulfilled vocation or teased by a pointless round of social duties. The social duties which came her way were to her far from pointless, because they were connected with her father's position as bishop, a dignitary who is bidden by St

Paul to be 'given to hospitality'. Apart from the social duties
required of a bishop's daughter, her work as her father's
secretary and chief helper with his bible commentary provided
her with intellectual stimulus and interest, while on her own
account she was busy teaching, reading, sketching, and, above
all, writing both prose and verse.

In 1873 she sent Miss Yonge a completed novel which met
with much approval. Gertrude Walter, an invalid who lived
with Miss Yonge, remarked, 'You seem to have fallen in love
with that story as you did with Miss Wordsworth.' One or
two points, however, came in for criticism: 'I think it should
be made quite clear that she was quite respectable . . . The
Andromeda is rather too horrid a notion of exposure to connect
with her. One thinks of Andromeda as less than lightly clad.'
In a second letter Miss Yonge again brings up the question of
respectability: 'I should not think that there was anything not
desirable in the part about Emma Barker, provided you note
her perfect respectability early enough.' This novel with its
intriguing reference to the nude Andromeda remained unpublished till 1883.

Among Elizabeth Wordsworth's papers is a manuscript of
a play dated July 1878. *The Shadow of the Sphinx* is a strange
effort. Most of her other plays are slight comic sketches, half
masque, half pantomime, suitable for performance by school-
girls or by village clubs. Their humour has not worn well;
today even the least sophisticated Women's Institute would
demand something stronger than these innocuous playlets,
but in their own time they exactly suited the actors and audiences for whom they were intended. *The Shadow of the Sphinx*
is suited to no stage and to no audience. Everything about it is
wrong, even its title, which should surely have been *The
Secret of the Sphinx*. Elizabeth herself may have realized its
deficiencies, because although she had clearly spent much time,
thought, and care on the writing of it, she left it in rough

manuscript form, never troubling to make a fair copy. (She did, however, send it for criticism to a family friend called Mrs Barter, who gave it rather tempered praise.) Part fantasy, part morality-play, it is a fairy-tale version of the Gospel story of Christ's Passion. The scene is set in Egypt, but an Egypt as vague and improbable as Shakespeare's Bohemia. The characters, who speak Elizabethan English, seem to belong to some undefinable period between the beginning of the sixteenth and the end of the eighteenth century. The play is written in the blankest of blank verse, with here and there a hardly discernible echo from *The Prelude*. Yet abysmally bad though it is, *The Shadow of the Sphinx* is not altogether unimpressive; the high seriousness of its theme sometimes shines through the ludicrous, even laughable nature of the *mise en scène*.

One of the characters in the play is a pedlar who sings a song which might have been called charming had it not been so obviously copied from Christina Rossetti's *Goblin Market*:

Buy O buy of me,
Ladies and gentlemen,
Here are good pennyworths,
Porcelain and pottery
Just as you fancy them.

Elizabeth Wordsworth had a remarkable gift of literary mimicry; she could imitate Shakespeare's comic scenes, she could imitate her own great-uncle William, she could imitate W. S. Gilbert; in fact she was a parodist *manquée*. Nobody ever played Stevenson's 'sedulous ape' with more efficiency or with greater damage to their own literary style. Whereas in speaking she was incisive and original, in writing she always fell back on borrowed tones and never found the use of her own voice.

With so much to occupy her time and with a constant stream

of guests coming and going, Elizabeth's life at Riseholme was
a busy one. There were, however, periods of pleasant leisure,
summer days of 'a calm sort of luxury here, strawberries and
cream, green peas, doves cooing, sun shining, and few events
except the post,' or winter evenings when the Bishop dozed
beside the fire while the rest of the family, fearful of disturbing
him, kept so quiet that a little mouse would emerge from its
hole and scuttle across the room to eat the fallen crumbs under
the tea-table. If Elizabeth ever felt that such an existence did
not adequately meet all her aspirations and abilities, she gave
no hint or sign of dissatisfaction nor, to judge from her letters
which are all we have to go on after the diary ceases, did she
display any interest in the movement for the higher education
of women which was now making headway at Oxford.

Chapter 4

A College for Women

THE EXPERIMENT of lectures and classes having proved successful, the supporters of women's education were ready to take another step forward. Since 1867 the Oxford Local Examinations had been opened to girls as well as to the school-boys for whom they were originally intended. In 1873 Annie Rogers, daughter of Thorold Rogers who was a keen supporter of women's education, gained top marks in Senior Locals and thus qualified for an exhibition both at Balliol and at Worces-ter, colleges which gave awards on the result of these examin-ations. (In her letters of this date the only hint which Elizabeth gives of any interest in the progress of women's education at Oxford is a brief, oblique reference to Annie Rogers' achieve-ment.) Two years later the Delegates for Local Examinations were given statutory premission to hold special examinations for women which were to be of a higher grade than Senior Locals, and which were to correspond both in standard and subject to University Finals. There were also to be examin-ations in English and Modern Languages, not at this period recognized subjects at Oxford, and a preliminary examination equivalent to 'Smalls' but without compulsory Latin or Greek. No time limit was imposed and residence in Oxford was not required.

In spite of this last provision the supporters of women's education were determined that these examinations should not merely provide a qualification similar to the London External

Degree, but that girls should be able to live and study at Oxford, enjoying the intellectual atmosphere of the place and taking advantage of such educational facilities as lectures and libraries. Halls of residence for women had already been opened at Cambridge; why should Oxford lag behind?

Throughout 1877 the little band of pioneers discussed this possibility and came to the conclusion that the first move must come from someone connected with Oxford, and not from an outsider, however generous or enthusiastic. The following year, 1878, Moncure Conway, an American Rationalistic preacher who was a friend of Charles Bradlaugh and Annie Besant, came forward with an offer of a large sum of money to to found a women's Hall. The proposal caused considerable perturbation among the leaders of the women's movement who, according to Bertha Johnson, 'felt that any scheme evolved by these special promoters, who were persons of views little acceptable to the Oxford world, would hardly commend a women's College to the University.' Only one course seemed open to them: steps must be immediately taken to forestall any such undesirable scheme by the provision of a better and more acceptable one of their own.

Edward and Lavinia Talbot were to be the prime movers in this new venture. During a visit to Cambridge they had been greatly impressed by what they had seen of Girton, and they were convinced that the higher education of women was something which had come to stay and which would become an important element in the life of the nation. 'Why should the Church not be for once at the front instead of behind in this new development?' Edward Talbot asked of his wife. The pair returned to Oxford full of the idea of starting a hall for women to be run on definite Church principles. From the very first, however, they found this matter of Church principles a major stumbling-block in the way of their scheme. The University was split into what the young Mrs Humphry Ward described

Old Hall, L.M.H. showing the original villa and the Basil Champneys addition, 1892

Punting in the Cherwell backwater in L.M.H. garden, 1896

as the Christ Church camp and the Balliol camp. At Christ
Church the aged Dr Pusey embodied authority and tradition-
alism; at Balliol Benjamin Jowett stood for the new thought
and criticism. The supporters of women's education were
divided between these two groups; in the Christ Church camp
were the Talbots and their friends Henry Scott-Holland,
Francis Paget and Edward King; in the Balliol one were Mr
and Mrs T. H. Green, William Sidgwick, the Paters and Mary
Ward. At a meeting held at Keble on 4 June 1878 it became
clear that no compromise could be arrived at which would be
acceptable to both sides; the supporters of 'Church principles'
therefore decided to proceed with their own scheme for 'a
small Hall or Hostel in connexion with the Church of England
for the reception of women desirous of availing themselves
of the special advantages which Oxford offers of higher
education.' A committee of eight was formed, under the
chairmanship of Edward Talbot, to discuss and promote
the plan.

The Balliol camp replied by forming another committee under
John Percival, President of Trinity, which was charged with
the business of founding a second, undenominational Hall.
The two sides thus agreed to differ, but to differ amicably, and
to work not in opposition but in friendly cooperation. A link
between them was created by the formation of the Association
for the Higher Education of Women in Oxford, which included
people of every shade of religious opinion. Since the Halls were
to be purely residential in character, the A.E.W. (as it was
always called) was in charge of the educational side, dealing
with all such matters as lectures, classes and examinations, as
well as taking complete charge of those students not resident
in a Hall.

Elizabeth Wordsworth's first reference to these happenings
is in an undated letter to her sister Dora, written during a visit
to Oxford some time in the summer of 1878. 'The great

C

excitement just now,' she writes, 'is the proposed College for
Ladies—or rather, the question whether there should be two,
an "undenominational" one and a Church of England one. I
should like to hear what Papa thinks about this when I get
home as John is on one side and Esther and I on the other.'
Unfortunately she does not say who was on which side. It is
impossible now to discover who may have suggested Elizabeth's own name for the headship of the Church Hall, or when
the proposal was first made. The official letter offering her the
post was written by Edward Talbot and dated 19 November
1878. 'I think John has mentioned to you our Ladies' Scheme,'
it begins, 'and the possibility of your heading it has been
mentioned to you, and kindly treated by you as a thing which
you would consider if it should come before you.' Elizabeth
had already talked the matter over with her father and he had
advised her to accept. Her beloved Aunt Lissy died on 20
November. A few days later, when Elizabeth and John met at
the funeral, she asked his opinion of the matter. 'Well,' came
the reply, 'If I thought your refusal would put an end to the
whole beastly thing I should say "don't go", but as I don't
suppose it would I think you had better accept it—go into it
with a good heart, and try to make it as little unpleasant as you
can.'

   The unknown person who first proposed Elizabeth for Lady
Principal, as she was officially to be called, did the new Hall
the greatest possible service. In 1878 very few women could
be found who were in any way fitted to take up such a position,
but even if the field had been a much larger one no more
admirable choice could have been made. As the daughter of a
bishop, grand-daughter of a Master of Trinity, and great-niece
of one of the greatest of English poets, she was immediately
acceptable both to Church people and to society at large. She
was already well-known and well-liked in Oxford itself, where
she had acquired a number of congenial and influential friends.

By character as well as by antecedents she was remarkably well suited to the post. She had the courage, energy, and determination necessary to anyone setting out on a new venture, and, as Tennyson wrote of the Duke of Wellington, she was 'rich in saving common-sense.' She liked and understood young people and she had a real gift for teaching. An absence of organizing ability and financial knowledge could be made good by utilizing the services of such devoted and competent women as Bertha Johnson and Charlotte Toynbee. Above all, as a devout and intelligent churchwoman, gifted with the rare power of 'putting religion across' to other people, she was the ideal choice for a Hall dedicated to Church principles. Her lack of formal education would have been a drawback but for the fact that it was a universal deficiency in days when educational facilities for women were practically non-existent. On this issue it might be relevant, though perhaps a little invidious, to inquire whether any of her more formally-educated successors were as generally well-informed as she was, or could rival her knowledge of Latin, Greek, Hebrew, French, German and Italian.

Edward Talbot must have been very certain of Elizabeth's acceptance since, without waiting to receive her reply to his letter, he allowed his committee to elect her unanimously as Lady Principal of the proposed Hall. On 21 November he wrote telling her of the committee's 'most cordial exchange of congratulations that our House should have the prospect of starting under one whose name, for her own sake, and for its older associations will do so much for success, and to whom we look as just the person to give it the tone we desire as at once an educational scheme of the most thorough and literal kind, and a work for the Church and its members.' In his original letter Edward Talbot had included a rough proof of a circula rsetting out the general aims of the new Hall, and asking for criticisms. Elizabeth made one objection, disapproving

of the clause 'with provision for the liberty of members of
other religious bodies' which would allow for the admission of
non-Anglican students. Talbot, who was himself of her opinion,
had to point out to her that it was impossible at this stage to
abandon a principle strongly supported by the majority of
committee members, and was able to assure her that as there
was also to be an undenominational Hall no nonconformists
were likely to apply. Though her view can only be judged
illiberal and narrow-minded, Elizabeth's ground of objection
is significant. She was more interested in the religious than in
the educational aspect of the work she had undertaken, and
she was always to regard L.M.H. as essentially a Church of
England institution. 'Personally, I should not have cared to go
near L.M.H. if it had not been for the *definite* Church basis,'
she remarked some forty years later.

In February 1879 Elizabeth visited Cambridge in search of
ideas that might help her in the running of the new Oxford Hall.
At Girton she was warned that she would find it impossible to
maintain any personal supervision or to exercise personal
influence over her students, a prophecy which she refused to
take very seriously. She was determined on maintaining a
closer and less formal relationship with her students than ever
existed at Girton. From the very first Emily Davies had insisted
that her 'College for Women' should be a real college, the two
'dons', for instance, dining at 'High Table' apart from the five
students. At Oxford the pattern was to be a much less formal
one. The prospectuses of both Oxford Halls put forward the
ideal of 'a common life with the way and tone of a Christian
family'; in the prospectus for the undenominational Hall the
word 'Christian' was changed to 'English'. Emily Davies
discouraged girls from taking any part in the social life of the
University. She had built Girton at a considerable distance
from Cambridge not because she wished to keep the girls
away from the undergraduates but because she wished to keep

them away from what she considered to be the time-wasting activities of the Cambridge ladies. Elizabeth, on the contrary, was to take her students with her to pay social calls, and expected them to help entertain the guests at her frequent tea-parties. She and the Hall of which she became Principal fitted easily and unobtrusively into Oxford society; for many years Girton was to remain figuratively as well as actually on the outskirts of Cambridge life.

Perhaps Newnham approximated more nearly than Girton to Elizabeth's pattern for a women's college. Anne Clough believed in the idea of family life, but though she did most admirable work during her forty years as Principal she did not stamp her personality upon her college. Young girls were not naturally attracted or impressed by her; students were frequently in revolt against her maternal government, which they regarded as fussy, over-precise, and interfering. Neither in their gifts nor in their limitations did Emily Davies or Anne Clough bear any resemblance to Elizabeth Wordsworth; it was clear that the Hall which she was to preside over would differ considerably from the two Cambridge colleges.

On 28 February Elizabeth was in Oxford attending a meeting of the Hall Committee for the first time. She then set out on a round of visits to friends, starting with the Bensons at Kenwyn, near Truro—her first recorded visit to their Cornish home. Her letter to Susan describing life at Lis Escop, the Bishop's house, is touched by a mordant humour very different from the blissful lyricism of earlier accounts of days spent with the Bensons at Wellington or Whitby:

> You know how the days go on here, early church, breakfast, prayers, bible-reading to which I don't get admitted, a hasty attempt on my part to get a few letters written more or less frustrated by circumstances, Minnie all over the place arguing with you at every turn and insinuating herself into

everything like the tooth-powder into the man's dressing-case compartments in *Somebody's Luggage* . . . E. W. Truro is in flourishing condition and we have great fun over his correcting my Latin prose, which I took to doing by John's advice and in an evil hour selected *The Pilgrim's Progress*. 'They asked him how he did and he answered worse and worse' is a long way off Cicero as you may imagine, but it is all the more fun. Of course he chaffs me whenever he gets an opening.

Though he was to take no active part himself Benson thorough-ly approved of the idea of a women's Hall at Oxford. 'Your plan is one to be rejoiced over,' he wrote to Edward Talbot. Not so Miss Yonge, with whom Elizabeth stayed after leaving Kenwyn. Ten years previously, when Emily Davies had asked for her support for the College for Women, Miss Yonge had replied with an unequivocal refusal, declaring that in her opinion 'superior women will always teach themselves and inferior women will never learn more than enough for home life.' More recently, in answer to a letter from Talbot outlining the Oxford proposal, she had expressed her disapproval of any women's college 'if it is to be merely a boarding-house run on good princi-ples where young ladies may be sent to prepare for examina-tions.' She added, however, 'If it were in any way possible to make it in some way an institution dedicated to Heavenly Wisdom, training the daughters of the Church to the more perfect cultivation of their talents whether as educators or as mothers of families, then I think there would be such salt of the earth in the College as to make it lasting and beloved and a real blessing in raising the whole ideal and standard of women.' In her long family chronicle *The Pillars of the House*, she puts the same sentiments into the mouth of Geraldine Underwood:

While woman works merely for the sake of self-cultivation, the clever grow conceited and emulous, the practical harsh and rigid, the light or dull, vain, frivolous deceitful, by way of escape, and it all gets absurd. But the being hand-maids of the Church brings all right; and the school of Saint Sophia develops even the intellect.

During Elizabeth's stay at Otterbourne, which was a more enjoyable occasion than her visit to Kenwyn, she had much talk with her hostess on the subject of the new Hall, and apparently succeeded in convincing her that it was indeed to be an institution dedicated to Holy Wisdom. A month or so later Miss Yonge was writing to her friend Julia Argles urging her to send her daughter there as one of the first students:

> I have great hopes of Elizabeth Wordsworth's College. I am very anxious about it by way of antidote and I have great confidence in her and her power of influencing, and I think it is a great plan to get a girl like your Edith, not very young and with formed, steadied principles, at the first start upon which everything really turns.

The Hall thus gained Edith Argles, who was to become one of its most devoted supporters and a great admirer of Elizabeth Wordsworth. It is noticeable that Miss Yonge, while praising Edith's principles, says nothing at all about her intellectual abilities, which were not inconsiderable.

From Otterbourne Elizabeth went on to London, where she had an interview with Baroness Angela Burdett-Coutts, the richest woman in England. Nor surprisingly, the Baroness's suggestions for the management of the new Hall were a little out of scale with the smallness of the initial enterprise. She urged Elizabeth to allow the girls to take up billiards and fencing, and insisted on the necessity for a paid housekeeper. In vain did Elizabeth protest that she could easily manage the house-keeping herself with the help of a few hints from her sister-in-law at Keble Terrace—'but you couldn't know about things as a servant would.' 'I thought of the probable *ménage* at Stratton Street,' Elizabeth wrote to her mother reporting this interview, 'as contrasted with the intimate terms Esther and her Mary are on with one another and with Mrs Hedges, and felt that on some points argument was useless.' In spite of the difference in outlook the two women took immediately to one another. 'She was so very kind and nice and squeezed my hand long and affectionately on parting; if she hadn't been a Baroness I should certainly have kissed her, but these are some of the disadvantages of rank.' It does not appear, however, that Angela Burdett-Coutts expressed any further interest in the Hall or made a contribution to its funds.

Back again in Oxford Elizabeth joined Lavinia Talbot in the business of house-hunting. One desirable house at the north-east corner of Crick Road they turned down because the key broke in the lock when they tried to open the front door. The committee finally decided on the white brick house at the end of Norham Gardens now known as Old Hall and des-cribed by Lavinia Talbot as 'a really pleasant habitable house with plenty of sun and air and a capital private garden.' She might have added that all the chimneys smoked, none of the windows fitted properly, and that the only access from kitchen to dining-room was through the drawing-room and up 'some mean little stairs in the greenhouse.' Now came the business of altering, decorating and furnishing the house, and the engaging of domestic staff. Because she was still living at Riseholme Elizabeth depended greatly in such matters on the little band of devoted Oxford ladies, and in particular on Bertha Johnson, who dealt firmly and with some efficiency with dom-estic detail. Her determined frugality would have scandalized

Baroness Burdett-Coutts. The cook was not to be allowed the
common perquisite of selling bones and dripping—'I *never*
buy any lard, and never allow cooking butter; any butter that
is wanted the cook has to contrive out of odds and ends.' Not
surprisingly, the standard of the resultant cookery was remarkably low and unfortunately remained so for many generations
to come. With the help of Miss Milman and Lavinia Talbot,
Bertha Johnson also set about the business of putting the
Norham Gardens house in order and furnishing it, a feat which
they accomplished for the sum of £454 6s. 5d. The shortage
of money made itself felt at all levels. In the 1870s a competent
governess earned a salary of £150 a year; the Lady Principal
was to be paid only £100.

Elizabeth's letters of this date show that she never thought to
let her new and absorbing Oxford interests crowd home and
family affairs out of her life; on the contrary, she sometimes
seems to treat the Hall almost as a side-show. A long and charming letter dated 19 May 1879 to her brother-in-law, James
Trebeck, is typical of all her correspondence. She writes to him
of books in general and of Law's *Serious Call* in particular—'I
know the feeling well when a book takes hold of you like that,
I have gone through it at different times with Pascal and
Thomas à Kempis'—then goes on to discuss a sermon which
John is planning to deliver on the Acts of the Apostles. She
tells him of the family doings, and of a London visit she hoped
to make: 'I can't much longer smother my desire to go to the
play. Do you ever have that feeling? They say *Pinafore* is very
good, a skit on W. H. Smith as First Lord.' In nine pages of
writing there are only two mentions of Oxford affairs, one in
joking reply to an invitation: 'Thank you for asking me to
Southwell. I hope I am not to gather from it that you never
intend me to come after next October because if so I don't see
that I have any alternative but to resign!' The other is in
reference to Shakespeare: 'I really think that if all the brains of

all the clever people of our own day had been put into one scale and Shakespeare's alone into the other his would have been far the heaviest, and am the more disgusted to find on looking over our Oxford "Association" prospectus that English is *not* among the pass subjects, only the honours subjects.'

Elizabeth Wordsworth was a remarkably strong and healthy person, but throughout 1879 the pressure on her was such that even she was forced to give way. In an undated letter, probably written in June, she refers to an illness or collapse brought about by overstrain—'I shall know now how to be sorry for poor, over-worked girls as long as I live.' It seems to have been no very serious matter because for the greater part of June she was back in Oxford keeping house for John and dealing with business connected with the new Hall. She met and made friends with Miss Shaw Lefevre who had been chosen as Principal of the undenominational Hall. 'It will require great efforts to make the halls chum together,' Bertha Johnson had written. 'I think you and Miss Lefevre will be the people to do it,' a prophecy which was most happily fulfilled. Elizabeth also took pains to contact Annie Rogers, whose success in the Oxford Locals had been the seed from which all these schemes had sprung. In this same year of 1879, at the age of twenty-two, Annie Rogers was elected on to the committee of the newly-formed A.E.W.; she was to become the power behind that institution and one of the most formidable and familiar of Oxford figures. Wisely Elizabeth determined to get on good terms with her from the start—'It will go hard if she and I do not make friends.' Because the A.E.W. was in charge of all educational arrangements, no tutorial staff would be required at the two new Halls. 'Miss Emma Laura Jones, who writes on wonderful notepaper with a wonderful monogram, has expressed a wish to come and assist in the duties of tuition,' Elizabeth informed her sister Dora; 'I have replied that a middle-aged housekeeper is the sort of person likely to be wanted.'

The undenominational Hall had already been christened Somerville after Mary Somerville, the woman scientist. Such uninspiring titles as Norham Hall and Cherwell Hall having been rejected, Edward Talbot's committee decided to accept Elizabeth's suggestion that they should call the Church Hall after a great benefactor of both Oxford and Cambridge, Lady Margaret Beaufort, Countess of Richmond, mother of King Henry VII. 'She was a gentlewoman, a scholar, and a saint, and after being married three times she took a vow of celibacy,' Elizabeth wrote of her; 'what more could be expected of any woman?'

Thus named, Lady Margaret Hall was all but ready to open its doors. One problem remained, and that a vital one; no students seemed to be forthcoming. 'Where are the girls?' Elizabeth wrote in some anxiety. 'I feel rather like a bald person carrying round a nearly useless brush and comb.' Even Edith Argles had not yet formally applied. At last a Mr Cobbe put down his daughter Winifred as a definite entrant. A trickle of entries followed, perhaps encouraged by the announcement of the award of an exhibition, the joint gift of Edward Talbot and Henry Scott-Holland. On 13 September Charles Merivale, Dean of Ely, wrote wishing Elizabeth success in her 'arduous undertaking', but declaring that he felt the greatest anxiety as to 'the possible ultimate effects of the present rage for stimulating young brains, and particularly young female brains.' 'This,' he added truthfully, 'is not giving you much encouragement, but I look very hopefully to your good sense to make the best of a difficult situation.' Other people beside Dean Merivale were looking to Elizabeth's good sense as the best, if not the only, guarantee for the success of the new venture. By Monday 13 October eight young women had arrived in Norham Gardens to begin their first term as students. (A ninth,

Edith Pearson, was very soon to join them.) Three days later
Bishop Mackarness held a short service and formally declared
the building open. Elizabeth Wordsworth was now the first
Lady Principal of Lady Margaret Hall.

Chapter 5

Early Days at Lady Margaret Hall

THE FIRST days of Lady Margaret Hall's existence were a chaotic period. Elizabeth Wordsworth found herself dealing with such varied problems as smoking chimneys, meat-hooks missing from the larder, badly-cooked food—in after years early students would recall almost with nostalgia the all-pervasive smell of burnt fat—unwritten letters and reports, quarrelsome committees, and, worst of all, the difficulty of getting both servants and students out of bed at a reasonably early hour in the morning.

Though she described this state of affairs as 'quite dreadful' she was nevertheless in control of the situation and enjoying herself greatly in spite of drawbacks and difficulties. At the age of thirty-nine she at last found herself in a position which gave full scope for the exercise of her special gifts and abilities. After the first confusion had subsided the running of a small establishment of three servants and nine students demanded little in the way of administration or organization. Where domestic affairs were concerned she had the very efficient help of Bertha Johnson. Financial matters were dealt with by the treasurer, Miss Bonamy Price, in conjunction with Sir William Herschel who was to be a very faithful friend to L.M.H. Miss Milman briefly succeeded Miss Bonamy Price, to be succeeded in turn by Charlotte Toynbee who remained for many years in charge of the day-to-day finances of the Hall. Her methods were effective if unorthodox. One term, when she lost all the students' fees in a box left behind on Paddington station, she remained completely unperturbed. 'I just told the students they must pay again,' she remarked, and apparently the students meekly did as they were told.

With the burden of financial and domestic affairs taken off her shoulders Elizabeth Wordsworth was free to deal not with an institution but with individuals. She could make personal friends of the girls, treating them as if she were their mother or perhaps a specially sympathetic elder sister. Later, when the numbers in the Hall increased, Elizabeth was to find herself less happily placed as its Principal. To an old student, come to congratulate her on her ninetieth birthday, she spoke wistfully of those early informal days:

Well, my dear, when I began at L.M.H. there were only eight students; I *was* able to get to know them. I wouldn't be head of L.M.H. now even if I could. You cannot know one hundred and fifty students.

Elizabeth Wordsworth always had to translate generalities into concrete fact. Students in the abstract did not exist for her; she was interested, and sometimes bored, by the individual girl. Her feeling of responsibility for those under her care was therefore slightly erratic; she could be deeply concerned about one and disconcertingly casual about another. One girl who complained of feeling ill would find herself tucked up on the Principal's sofa with *Cranford* for light reading and a poached egg for supper; another invalid, less articulate or perhaps less entertaining, would be left to suffer in silence. Edith Pearson, an early student who had little sympathy with her Principal's method, or lack of method, cited the case of a clever, but perhaps slightly unbalanced girl, a great favourite with Elizabeth Wordsworth, who remained completely unworried by this student's mental eccentricities, which included the hallucinatory notion that an errand-boy was a visitant from another world. The story is so odd that it is impossible to avoid a suspicion that the girl in question, obviously something of an original, was deliberately hoaxing the serious and rather unimaginative Edith. True or not true, however, the story aptly illustrates Elizabeth Wordsworth's rather haphazard concern for the students' well-being.

With obvious irritation Edith Pearson, herself an able and a logical woman, described Elizabeth as 'equally incapable of grasping a general principle or thinking it out to its logical conclusion.' Closely allied to this inability to think things out to a conclusion was her lack of interest in the future; she lived almost entirely in the past and the present. The ultimate shape and scope of women's education at Oxford interested her not at all, nor did the future development of L.M.H. as an institution; she was concerned with the education of individuals and the business of getting for these particular girls the best that Oxford had to offer at that particular moment. It cannot be denied that Elizabeth Wordsworth could not or would not see the wood for the trees; she did, however, take such good care of those trees that the wood she planted has grown into a flourishing forest.

Being an individualist she naturally set great store by the educational value of contact with notable people. Her views on this subject were only to grow stronger with the passage of time; as late as 1910, speaking to a conference of women workers, she stressed the importance of this personal touch:

All along the line at Oxford one big personality has been in the foreground and has dominated the thought and feeling of his day. What is the mere piling of information to this? If you want information you can get it from an encyclopaedia.

At lunch or dinner-parties, at her own 'At Home' days, even on casual strolls across the parks—'walking through Oxford with Miss Wordsworth meant meeting many interesting people'—she saw to it that her students met most of the famous University characters of the day. Maybe, however, she saw to nothing deliberately for that was not her usual method of action; maybe this desirable result came about simply because she herself had so many interesting and important friends and acquaintances. As Vera Brittain wrote, in Elizabeth Wordsworth's time L.M.H. students 'resembled daughters at home with a unique, original and much respected mother who knew everybody worth knowing.'

There were giants in the land in those days, or, as Eleanor Lodge put it, 'powers in a society so much smaller than the present Oxford society that each was felt in a way which is now almost inconceivable.' L.M.H. students would as a matter of course come in contact with such men as Benjamin Jowett, Mark Pattison, Edward Talbot, T. H. Green, Arnold Toynbee, C. L. Dodgson ('Lewis Carroll') or Minnie Benson's brother William Sidgwick with whom it was darkly rumoured that the Principal herself had once been in love though no shred of evidence remains in support of this intriguing theory. Many of these University notables were frequent visitors at the Hall. The students counted the days when Henry Scott-Holland came to tea as very special treats; they would sit round the table listening enthralled to the conversation between him and the Principal, sometimes bursting into incontrollable laughter at the flow of wit and repartee. John Ruskin's visit in December 1884 was a particularly memorable occasion. He went into the girls' rooms and admired their pretty belongings—'I should not like you to live like nuns'—he inspected chapel, gymnasium and library, he listened to Edward Benson's daughter Maggie 'looking very shy and engaging' as she recited a passage from *In Memoriam*, and praised a copy she had made of one of his own drawings. Surrounded by a group of attentive and admiring young women he was very much in his element—'How nice it is to be an old man of sixty-five and able to see all these delightful girls'—and as a memorial of this happy day he sent the Hall a gift of books, including a set of his own works.

These meetings with famous men were interesting and memorable occasions, but the most important contact which L.M.H. students made during their Oxford years was with their own Principal—'the greatest feature of our life at Oxford was our intercourse with Miss Wordsworth.' Yet though she lived so closely with her students, joining in their day-to-day occupations and sharing their thoughts and aspirations, Elizabeth Wordsworth never impinged upon their privacy of mind. Looking back on her time at L.M.H. one of the students wrote, 'she did not seem to influence us and she certainly had too much respect for human personality to set out to do so deliberately but she let us grow without any fussy interference.' Her natural reserve and good breeding made it impossible for her to pry into the recesses of another person's mind or soul, least of all where religious feeling was concerned. The students recognized that for her religion was all-important, but the astringent strain in her made her mistrustful of any outpouring of religious emotion. When an earnest but untidy and un-punctual student sought a special interview and confessed that she had lost her faith and therefore ought perhaps to leave the Hall immediately the Principal briskly replied, 'All right, my dear, stay on, of course, but *do* brush your hair and *don't* be late for breakfast.' What endeared her most of all to the students was her capacity for laughter; 'it was because she made us laugh that we delighted so in her,' wrote Gertrude Edwards, while A. E. Levett declared, 'she kept us constantly on the edge of laughter.'

Because of the sheer novelty of the situation and the lack of any guiding precedents the opening years at a women's college tended to be an anxious time full of occasions for friction or annoyance. Girton students resented Emily Davis's aloof attitude, complaining that 'her life seemed so much apart from ours and so solitary,' which was hardly a fair criticism of someone who was founder rather than head of the college. At Newnham Anne Clough's anxiety lest her students should do anything to prejudice opinion against them caused her to be so over-strict and fussy about small matters that Henry Sidgwick was not infrequently called in to soothe down irritation and incipient rebellion. Even the charming Miss Shaw Lefevre of Somerville seems to have had occasional difficulties with insubordinate students. 'Miss Lefevre has been sitting on the rug at Somerville hugging me for a whole afternoon,' Elizabeth wrote in an undated letter to her sister Susan. 'She is a great deal too gentle and humble-minded and we ought to change students as I think I could snub *hers* and mine do not need any snubbing.' Thanks in great part to the Principal's ready wit and to her ability to laugh herself out of a difficulty, L.M.H. suffered from no such troubles; the ugly white brick house in Norham Road was a happy place filled with 'an undercurrent of girls' laughing and talking'.

For the first four or five years of its existence L.M.H. had about it much the same atmosphere as Elizabeth Wordsworth's own home—religious, intellectual, upper-middle class and slightly old-fashioned. Like Anne Clough, and for the same reason, Elizabeth insisted on her students wearing gloves—'It makes a better impression on the University.' They were also obliged to observe an already outdated convention and put on a hat whenever they went into the garden. In all circumstances L.M.H. students were expected to behave like ladies and to cultivate the social arts demanded of a lady, one of the most important being the art of conversation. The Principal, who had all her meals at the same table as the students, would beckon to two chosen girls to sit one on each side of her; and woe betide them if they did not keep her properly entertained. In a letter of 1881 she described the students then in residence as painfully silent: 'They don't seem to have a notion of talking except Miss Lestrange whose remarks, though fluent, are rarely to the purpose, and Nellie Benson who (being her mother's daughter) has not much idea of conversation except by arguing, and Miss Luard, who would be the best talker in the house, only she won't condescend, or doesn't know how to condescend.' A probably apocryphal story has it that Elizabeth once seized a tongue-tied student by the arm, and, shaking her hard, exclaimed, 'Talk, can't you?'

Mornings were supposedly devoted to work. In order to save the cost of fires the students sat all together round the table of a room grandly described as the library. The name was a misnomer; when the Hall opened the shelves held exactly two books, one a copy of *The Newcomes*, the other an unintelligible treatise on sound and colour. Talk was almost continuous; if one of the more studiously-minded girls found the noise growing intolerable she would throw a dictionary at the chatterers. In the very earliest days the only available lectures were those given specially for women in a room above a bakery in Little Clarendon Street. However, following the pioneering example of Balliol, the men's colleges soon began to admit women to lectures. Attendance at college lectures entailed a chaperon, and because chaperons were not easy to find Elizabeth Wordsworth often undertook this duty herself. She had heard Lewis Nettleship's lecture on Greek philosophers five times before she finally struck, refusing to sit through a sixth hearing. If she was enjoying the lecture she would interrupt with questions and comments which the lecturer invariably treated with great respect even when she disagreed with him; if she was bored she would use the time for letter-writing. One letter headed 'Balliol Hall' begins, 'Can I keep my ideas sufficiently distinct from the Moral Philospohy of Plato which is going on over the way?'

Where private teaching was concerned the most notable women tutors were Clara Pater and Annie Rogers, both tutoring in classics. Elizabeth herself sometimes filled in a gap by giving a few informal tutorials, usually in Latin. Most students, however, had the privilege of being tutored by famous Oxford scholars, who gladly gave of their time and attention because of their interest in this new development in women's education. Attendance at such tutorials of course required the presence of a chaperon.

The only examinations open to the first students at L.M.H. were the special examinations for women organized by the Delegacy for Local Examinations. Neither teachers nor taught had any very clear idea as to the scope and standard of these examinations. The First Women's Examination or Preliminary proved to be such a stumbling block that the L.M.H. Committee, a body which kept a firm hand on all matters affecting the Hall, was moved to suggest that the less able students should be allowed to omit the examination altogether, an idea which Elizabeth Wordsworth opposed with the greatest determination. She knew very well that examinations were a much needed stimulus and spur for 'the class of young ladies of whom the Hall is mainly composed.' Coming from reasonably well-to-do families these girls would never be under the necessity to earn their own living. Few of them had been to school or learnt to work methodically. They would not understand the need for really hard and accurate study unless and until they had faced up to the ordeal of an examination. 'Nothing makes girls work so hard as being ploughed,' she remarked rather unkindly.

Afternoon was the time for recreation and exercise. Country walks were popular; and on wet days there would be skipping in the corridors. A makeshift tennis court, too short for proper play, had been marked out on the lawn; another cinder court, also too short, was not very popular since the players always ended their game begrimed in dust and ashes. Later in the afternoon, on the Principal's 'At Home' days, students would be expected to hand round tea and cakes and to help entertain the guests. This could be an alarming duty; on one occasion, Elizabeth Wordsworth, bored by some very dull ladies, retired to the back of the room with a book and left two shy students to carry on the conversation as best they could. Cocoa parties were the most popular form of entertainment among the girls themselves, although an unwritten law laid down that only tinned or powdered milk might be used and that if jam were provided there must be no cake. In the evening after supper everyone gathered in the drawing-room and while the Principal read aloud from some such classic as *Paradise Lost* the girls would tear paper into little strips to be used to stuff pillows for the poor. These evening sessions often ended in long discussions of 'things new and old which came to us as something of a revelation.'

By 1881 it had become clear that the experiment of a Church of England Hall for women was proving a real success, thanks in great part to the personality of its Principal. The first printed Report stated, 'the Committee would only say in the fewest words that they attribute it almost entirely to her that the Hall has been started in a way which bids fair to realize the hopes they entertained when they undertook its formation. The gentleman had reason on his side who, when introduced to a L.M.H. student, inquired whether she was at 'Wordsworth College'.

Success, however, brought its own problems; the Arcadian innocence of those first early days could not last. An increase in numbers inevitably meant a tightening of discipline; and, much as she disliked formal rules and regulations, as early as 1881 Elizabeth Wordsworth found it necessary to draw up a set of 'House Rules'. Students were to be present every day at morning and evening prayers and to attend Church at least once on Sundays; piano-playing was only permitted within certain hours; all students were to be in their own rooms by 10.30 p.m. Today the most interesting rule is the one dealing with social life and chaperonage:

> Students are allowed to lunch or dine with any lady member of the Committee, or with any friend mentioned by their parents in writing, but are not expected to visit in College rooms or to attend College chapels on Sunday except with some lady approved by the Lady Principal. Students are allowed to walk alone with their brothers. At other times it is preferred that they should go out two or three together, especially into the town.

These regulations accurately reflect the conventions of the day and age; in 1881 chaperonage was taken absolutely for granted and the daughters of Oxford residents never thought to walk in the streets alone. The niece of a Head of a House, coming to tea at L.M.H., brought a maid with her to accompany her home. When one student, 'such a proper, pretty, neat little girl', asked leave to go to tea in her brother's rooms to meet a young man who was a family friend, Elizabeth Wordsworth was quite understandably astounded and horrified—'What *are* the girls coming to?'

What indeed were the girls coming to? A twentieth-century member of L.M.H. might well repeat that question, though giving it a different emphasis. A noticeable characteristic of reminiscences and letters written by early students is the almost total absence of any reference to undergraduates, a term then applying only to men. To anyone familiar with Oxford not only in the 1970s but as far back as the twenties and thirties, this silence seems both surprising and unnatural. Elizabeth

Wordsworth was not faced with a difficulty which confronted Emily Davies and Anne Clough. Among the first students both at Newnham and at Emily Davies's Ladies' College at Hitchin were two or three real beauties certain to attract the attention of any young male. Judging from photographs none of the little group at L.M.H. were more than passably good-looking; they were, none the less, girls of an age when falling in love is the most obvious and the most popular of occupations. And unlike Girton and Newnham students they were not encouraged to look on themselves as women dedicated to a career. Elizabeth Wordsworth once disconcerted the parent of a would-be student by remarking, 'I think I ought to tell you that few of our girls marry really well.' But, well or not so well, she was all in favour of them marrying. 'I know you will be glad to hear that I am engaged to be married,' one old student wrote, 'for you always did approve of that course of action.' As might be expected, her comments on marriage were shrewd and to the point. 'She told us,' Winifred Peck recorded, 'that in her experience plain girls married most suitably because they had the sense to accept their first offers, whereas pretty girls hesitated between their choices until it was too late.' Some girls were of course destined to remain old maids, but all of them hoped to marry. Why then were they so slow to use the opportunities that could be expected to arise, in spite of chaperons, in a society where women were few and men were many?

This apparent lack of interest in young men was in part due to the conventions of class and period. 'Some of the girls are really awful in some respects,' Barbara Bradby informed her mother. 'The one I was out with today said with a giggle, "I don't suppose one ought to look at the men".' Barbara was right; the really awful young woman's remark was most un-ladylike. However, to judge from contemporary novels, the best brought-up young ladies took a considerable if discreet interest in men, discussed them with their girl friends, and frequently fell in love with them. Why then were the women students oblivious of the undergraduates?

The answer would seem to be that the undergraduates were oblivious of the women students. If they thought about them at all it was as blue-stockings,[1] strange and for the most part plain creatures, not as other girls to be flirted with, kissed, and perhaps one day married. On their side the women knew that they must be particularly circumspect in their behaviour since they were still on probation at Oxford and any misdemeanour might prove fatal to their hopes of acceptance by the University. The women were too timid, and the men felt no desire to cross the barriers erected between the sexes. As Mr Harold Macmillan makes clear in his memoirs, this attitude persisted right up to the First World War; vestigial traces remained even in the care-free unchaperoned twenties.

By the end of the first year of its existence the Hall was full to capacity and would-be students were being turned away for want of room. As early as the winter of 1879–80 there was talk of building on to the original house and plans were drawn up for an extension. Various difficulties, however, delayed the completion of the red-brick addition to Old Hall until 1884; and meanwhile a house in Norham Gardens was taken to accommodate the overflow. Miss Yonge's protégée, Edith Argles, who was one of the most successful and popular of the first batch of students, now returned to L.M.H. to take charge of this temporary hostel. Elizabeth had a special affection for Edith Argles; 'I shall break my heart when she goes,' she had written to Edith's mother, 'it gives little ominous cracks, like ice, whenever I even think of it.' Like many people who do not suffer fools gladly she had her definite favourites, of whom

1. When the red-brick addition was built on to the white-brick Old Hall L.M.H. was christened 'the red, white and blue'.

Edith was one. There was nothing even faintly lesbian about these attachments nor do they appear to have been resented by the other students, although it was well known that she opened her mind very freely to the chosen few and discussed L.M.H. problems and personalities with them. 'She could be blazingly indiscreet, not without intention,' wrote Dame Kathleen Courtney, 'and the hints she gave to her *confidantes* anent the character and potentialities of other students were at once a delight and a warning.'

A year or so later another old student, Edith Pearson, also returned to help with the running of the Hall. Though Elizabeth Wordsworth never had quite the same feeling for her as she had for the other Edith, in her Report to the Committee she was quick 'to acknowledge with much gratitude her efficient services,' while in a letter she wrote less formally that 'if it weren't for Edith Pearson I don't know how we should get along.' Meanwhile Bertha Johnson was almost daily at the Hall, acting both as secretary and as what would now be called domestic bursar. Charlotte Toynbee too was a constant help and standby, and after her husband's untimely death in 1883 she devoted yet more of her time and attention to the affairs of L.M.H. Elizabeth loved and appreciated these two friends to the full, while firmly refusing to be bullied by them. During one of her rare temporary absences from the Hall, her sister-in-law Esther reported that Edith Argles was doing well as Vice-Principal but that 'Mrs A.J. was sitting on her and bullying her in a way she daren't do to Elizabeth.'

In 1884 the new building was completed except for the chapel which, to the Principal's great disappointment, was not ready for use until February 1886. It was now possible to accommodate about twenty-five to thirty students. If Elizabeth Wordsworth could have had matters her own way the numbers at the Hall would never have exceeded this modest level. 'Somerville is going to grow as large as it can be,' Barbara

Bradby's sister Dorothy informed her mother. 'We are never
to be more than thirty; there is more demand that they set up
another Hall.' This would have been Elizabeth Wordsworth's
own solution; as yet, however, she had neither the means nor
the opportunity to put it into practice.

With a gymnasium in the new building, and with numbers
sufficient for a game of hockey, the students now had better
opportunities for physical exercise. Elizabeth was always a
great advocate of outdoor games for girls, an attitude which
she herself attributed to her year's experience as a pupil in a
Brighton boarding-school where none had been provided:

> There was a good deal of silly nonsense about dress, flirt-
> ations and the like, which centred round an Italian singing
> master, who was the idol of a certain set of girls. I often
> think that if some of this enthusiasm could have been
> expended on a tennis or hockey match it would have been
> better for both mind and body; and a great deal of my readi-
> ness to encourage games in later years at Lady Margaret Hall
> is traceable to my Brighton experiences.

She was therefore extremely annoyed when in 1885 the Committee banned the playing of hockey, believing that the poor
showing which the Hall had made in the previous year's
examinations could be attributed to the undue amount of time
and attention given to games. This same failure provided an
excuse to renew the old argument that it might be as well to
allow the less able students to opt out of examinations altogether.
Elizabeth Wordsworth, who was determined not to give way
on this issue, expressed her objections with force and lucidity:

> '*Il nous manque, Monsieur, qu'un peu de nécessité,*' was
> Poussin's reply to an amateur who asked his opinion of his
> work; and the same may be said of many of the L.M.H.

students as compared with those at other Halls. There is therefore all the more reason to make examinations supply the stimulus which having to work for their living does not in their case afford . . . Many more L.M.H. girls go back to their homes than is the case with Somerville.

Bowing to the force of this argument the Committee adopted the opposite plan of excluding less able girls altogether by tightening up the conditions of entry to L.M.H. and insisting that any student who failed to pass the Preliminary examination within her first year should be sent down permanently.

The 1884 results were the more disappointing because in that year a great step had been taken towards the recognition of women by the University. At the end of 1883 the A.E.W. put before the Hebdomadal Council a petition, signed by a majority among the resident senior members of the University, requesting Council 'to lay before the University some scheme by which women may be admitted to some at least of men's Honour Examinations.' (There was, of course, no mention of the granting of degrees.) In reply to this petition a statute was promulgated admitting women to Honour Moderations and to the Final Schools of Mathematics, Natural Science and Modern History. This statute was to be submitted to Convocation in April 1884.

The more moderate supporters of women's education were not altogether pleased with this move, feeling that the time was not yet ripe for a measure which might provoke unexpectedly fierce and powerful opposition. Edward Talbot in particular seems to have suffered a surprising failure of nerve at 'this anxious and straining moment'. He worried lest Elizabeth Wordsworth, who was already preoccupied by the serious illness of both her parents, might find the strain of controversy too much for her: 'Dear Miss Wordsworth, I know a struggle or a fight is altogether distasteful to you; I am glad you do not come too much into it.' He had, however, totally misread her reaction. A letter dated 25 April throws an amusing light on the difference between Talbot's tormenting anxiety and her own more casual attitude. In 1883 Edward Benson had been appointed Archbishop of Canterbury. Both the Benson daughters went as students to L.M.H. Nellie left prematurely in order to help her mother with the social duties required of the wife of an Archbishop, but she nevertheless succeeded in gaining a second class in Modern Languages. Her place at the Hall was taken by her brilliant younger sister Maggie, shy, attractive, and fatally unstable. Now, at the very height of the examination controversy, the Archbishop and Minnie chanced to come on a visit to Oxford. Elizabeth describes their reactions towards the great question of the hour:

> He was delightfully sound on the new statute as he says what is wanted is for the Church to reach the teachers and how is she to do this if they are all to go the Cambridge?[1] Minnie was in a red-hot rage with the Warden of Keble because he has been so bullied by Liddon and Co that he won't let the Archbishop say a single word at the Keble dinner on Women's Education which was *the* thing he wanted to talk about apparently. The poor old Warden[2] is in a miserable frame of mind between them all; he is afraid, he says, that he may be introducing a cancer into the University. I said to Minnie Cancer is no very great way off Virgo, but we must hope Libra will also have its proper place in the deliberations.

1. Certain Cambridge examinations were already open to women. It was feared that if the same plan were not adopted at Oxford, an Oxford qualification would be regarded as inferior to a Cambridge one, and that therefore women who wished to enter the teaching profession would go to Cambridge rather than Oxford.
2. Edward Talbot was four years younger than E.W. who habitually used 'old' as a familiar term of endearment.

Although Elizabeth Wordsworth appeared to be taking the affair in a calm, not to say light-hearted, spirit, she very well knew that the examination issue was an all-important one. On 29 April, returning from a country walk with her hands full of fritillaries, those flowers so closely associated with the Oxford spring, she met a Mr Prickard of New College coming to tell her that Convocation had passed the vital statute by a majority of 143 votes. For the rest of her life the sight of a fritillary was always to remind her of what she described as 'this turning-point in our history'.

Chapter 6

Author and Lady Principal

APART FROM her official position as Principal of L.M.H. Elizabeth Wordsworth's life revolved round her writing, her social life at Oxford, and, most important of all, her family. In 1881 she published *Indoors and Out*, a small volume of poems which won praise from friendly critics, *The Guardian*[1] going so far as to declare that although the poems were unequal in merit 'not one of them fails to show the spark of divine fire which shines with so brilliant a light in the immortal works of William Wordsworth.'

Indoors and Out is indeed of a higher quality than any other published collection of Elizabeth Wordsworth's poems. Some of the verses have the simplicity of 'Lucy Gray'; one or two, in particular a poem to an unidentified song bird—'Is it a nightingale or a thrush?'—show a command of metrical variation and rhyme most unusual in her writing:

> The oft-repeated, delicious thrill,
> The sob, sob, sob of a heart half breaking;
> The pauses where delight is dwelling,
> Breathless, expectant.
> What matter the name that we give to her?
> No bird is she, but our own hearts singing,
> Back to the summer.

1. In any mention of *The Guardian* the reference is to a now defunct Church weekly, not to the daily paper then known as *The Manchester Guardian*.

Many of the poems were written eleven years previously, during or shortly after that memorable holiday at Whitby with Edward Benson and his family. Knowing the circumstances it is all too easy to read into them a significance which is not in fact there; they seem however to have an immediacy which is lacking in the rest of Elizabeth's poetry. In a word, they are alive. Their quality is best explained by quoting one rather long poem in full. No one could claim that 'The Railway Platform' is great, or even good, poetry; equally, no one who has ever experienced a parting similar to the one it describes could fail to recognize it as a genuine cry of emotion:

Yes, we have said farewell, ere yet
    The long tight pressure from my hand
Fades, where your clasping fingers met;
    And in the crowd alone I stand

Like one just struggling with a dream;
    And listen to the harsh-voiced wheels,
And watch the melting flakes of steam,
    And hear the arches' echoing peals,

And fancy I behold your face,
    And think how others see it now,
Indifferent, and untaught to trace
    The thoughts that dwell beneath your brow

Or flash and twinkle in your eye;
    Who read you as a tongue unknown,
Nor deem this word is passion's cry,
    And that, the image of a groan.

Who con, in one unvaried key
    (As children spell their school-room task)
The signs of sorrow, hope, or glee,
    And never care to lift the mask.

And all that full, rich world of *you*
    Is wasted on them, aye, unguessed;
And e'en your outward form they view
    Blindly—and deem you like the rest.

They never saw the tears that swell
    So quickly in those earnest eyes;
That voice, they never heard it tell
    Its love, its mirth, without disguise.

Must you be dumb, since they are deaf?
    Oh no, dear friend, that cannot be;
For now from blade, and stone, and leaf,
    There comes a voice of yours to me.

What your own presence could not do
    To hearts that never learned your power,
In absence, even the thought of you
    Still brings to love, from hour to hour.

As on a sun-deserted peak
    Men picture how the sunshine shone,
We see you smile, and hear you speak—
    And can we call ourselves alone?

Ebb and Flow, the novel which Elizabeth had written as long ago as 1878, appeared in 1883 under her previous pseudonym of Grant Lloyd. In the published version the model who had incurred Miss Yonge's displeasure at the 'less than lightly clad Andromeda' poses instead as the murderous Medea. Although *Ebb and Flow* is inevitably reminiscent of Miss Yonge's own books it has a definite charm of its own. The story follows the contrasting fortunes of two young artists (both Charlotte Yonge and Elizabeth Wordsworth chose to write about artists though neither of them had any personal knowledge of the art

Elizabeth Wordsworth surrounded by the cast of one of her plays performed by L.M.H. students

L.M.H. hockey team 1895–6

world), the one, charming, gifted, successful, but facile and lacking in 'soul', the other a failure and a genius. The shallow but kind-hearted Frank befriends the brilliant Lewis or Luigi, a runaway Italian monk who has lived in South America and lost his faith because of the scandalous state of religion in that continent. Knowing himself to be the more gifted artist of the two, Lewis is embittered by Frank's undeserved success and in a fit of temper slams a door and causes an accident which costs Frank his right hand. This catastrophe has the desirable effect of deepening Frank's character; he behaves with the utmost magnanimity towards Luigi (here the Miss Yonge addict catches echoes from *The Heir of Redclyffe*) who bitterly repents his action, recovers his faith, and dies painfully but in the odour of sanctity. With the exception of the model Emma Barker (had Elizabeth ever as much as seen an artist's model?) the young men and girls—Frank and his two sisters Eva and Pauline, Gervase Attiwell and his sister Millicent with whom Frank falls in love, and even the melodramatic Lewis—are lively, entertaining characters, acutely observed and sketched in with a light touch and considerable humour. The first volume ripples along happily enough, but in the second, which opens with the fateful accident, the story falls to pieces. The brisk narrative loses itself in long and dull descriptions of Rome, Siena and Ravenna, complete with Elizabeth Wordsworth's reflections on the various works of art to be found in those places; the pleasant young people, with all their amusing human imperfections, turn into a row of plaster saints. Elizabeth Wordsworth lacked Charlotte Yonge's rare gift of making goodness attractive.

Elizabeth remained on very friendly terms with Miss Yonge, sending her information needed for the writing of *Unknown to History*, and in June 1885 visiting her at Otterbourne. Predictably, the entertainment provided consisted of 'quite an ideal missionary meeting'. Elizabeth sincerely appreciated the

D

peace of Otterbourne and its atmosphere of reticent, old-fashioned piety reminiscent of her own childhood:

> The three days here have been a great treat and refreshment, so like Stanford, the quiet Church service, catechizing, etc., and the real work going on without any fuss, with a loveliness of country which Stanford did not possess.

In 1885 Elizabeth Wordsworth was writing about another and very different contemporary woman novelist whom she describes as 'the marvellous woman whose genius is the crowning glory of the literature of this age, as her personal history is one of its most painful episodes.' The article which appeared in *The Guardian* on 4 March under the title 'The Watershed in George Eliot's Life' is one of the most interesting Elizabeth ever wrote, not only for its own sake but also as an illustration of the extraordinary difference in outlook between her generation and our own. Not even in the most conservative of Church journals would any modern critic think to approach the life and work of a famous writer, who had only been dead five years, from such a determinedly religious and moralistic angle. Elizabeth Wordsworth, however, specifically states her conviction that for readers of *The Guardian* the most interesting part of any biography of George Eliot must be 'the description of the religious crisis of her life.' Granted this premise, her article is, as might be expected, an able and interesting piece of writing.

She describes the narrow Evangelicalism in which George Eliot was brought up as a form of religion particularly unattractive to a person of literary talent. 'This pietism is often combined with crude and materialistic ideas about a future state, and a narrow and injudicious standard of life in this, which could not fail to offend a man or woman who possessed (what many people do *not* possess) the power of vividly realizing the meaning of the words they use.' With admirable impartiality she points out that George Eliot was equally repelled by the arid teaching of the High Church Oxford Movement—'when a mind is looking about for first principles it will hardly be satisfied by appeals to St Irenaeus or St Chrysostom.'

In Elizabeth's opinion a lapse in faith is almost inevitably followed by a lapse in morals:

> The next step does not surprise us. After religion goes what at least in ordinary cases would be called morality. It is most painful to have to say so, but having turned the subject over in all possible lights, we fail to see how conduct which we should deem reprehensible in any poor labouring woman living in the 'East End' can be called by a different name merely because it is practised by a lady of genius.

After reading this condemnation it is a relief to discover that she admits there are degrees of immorality and that other writers had sinned worse than George Eliot—'When we think of the life of her great French rival, Georges Sand, we feel how the advantage is with the English woman.'

Taking George Eliot as an example, Elizabeth goes on to ask the pertinent question, 'How is the Church to keep or gain a hold on men and women of genius?' Such people will not be attracted by any narrow or inadequate presentation of religious truth:

> There is the sense of the largeness of life, whether from the historical or scientific standpoint, to which popular religion is often painfully out of proportion in its childish and limited view of truth; there is the need of an intellectual as well as of an emotional basis for our faith or opinion, the disgust at petty and illogical narrowness; and no presentation of

religion will ever satisfy the highest minds which is not at once philosophical, historical, and practical.

To put forward a view of religion adequate to meet these demands the Church requires 'an enlightened, a scholarly, a thinking clergy'. This is the more important in an age which has seen such great advances in the education of women, always the traditional prop and support of the clergy:

> The present century has been marked in a signal degree by the advances made in women's education. Unless the Church and the clergy keep pace with this we shall soon have to lament that religion has lost its hold on a most important class which has hitherto in this country been one of the strongholds of faith, while that class will on its side have lost all the hallowing, endearing, and refining influences which 'show us how divine a thing a woman may be made.' In the case of George Eliot her poetic instincts and her delicate natural sympathies kept the womanly nature alive. But there are many natures less happily balanced to whom intellectual culture apart from religion would be absolutely fatal in this respect.

For several years Elizabeth Wordsworth's father had been engaged in a running fight with a famous woman rebel against religion and morals who certainly did not appear to be 'happily balanced' or to possess the 'poetic instincts and delicate natural sympathies' of George Eliot. Annie Besant, socialist, free-thinker, advocate of birth-control, and later to become high priestess of Theosophy, had married a parson in the Lincoln diocese. She ran away from him, maybe with good reason, and became involved in a long and bitter struggle over the custody of her little daughter. As might have been expected Bishop Wordsworth had taken sides with Frank Besant, holding that

an atheist and a supporter of so immoral a practice as birth-
control was an unfit guardian for any child. Annie Besant, who
was no mean hater, attacked him furiously in the pages of *The
New Reformer* and in speeches at meetings up and down the
country. Though for years she continued to torment him her
darts probably had less effect than she supposed; the Bishop
was unlikely in the extreme to read a free-thinking paper and
he certainly never attended any of Mrs Besant's meetings.

Throughout her life Elizabeth was to be a frequent contributor to *The Guardian*. At this period she was also writing for
Aunt Judy's Magazine, a magazine for children edited by Mrs
Gatty and her daughter Juliana Horatia Ewing, and, of course,
for Miss Yonge's magazine for girls, *The Monthly Packet*. One
of the most interesting and amusing of her *Monthly Packet*
articles was later reprinted in a book entitled *Ladies at Work*
appropriately edited by a Lady Lejeune. The emphasis is on
the word 'lady'; Elizabeth's remarks on the subject of incomes
imply that of necessity most 'women' would be workers. The
article deals with Colleges for Women, which were, of course,
attended exclusively by ladies. The first paragraph must be
quoted in full:

> In my younger days, if I had been told at a party that a
> young lady belonged to a Ladies' College I should have
> preferred occupying the stiffest of upright chairs, in a
> thorough draught, to sitting by her on the most comfortable
> of sofas. And, even now, I heartily wish that we were in a
> state of society where no such things were needed. My ideal
> woman is always graceful and beautiful, better with her
> hands than with her head, and best of all with her heart. She
> has many admirers but is constant to one whom she marries
> at five-and-twenty. She has at least five children, all healthy
> and good like herself. She can cook and sew and dance and
> sing—she is very likely accomplished and well-informed.

She is not a bore because she has never overworked her brain and is really interested in all she knows. She has an income, if a lady, of from £500 to £1,000 a year; if a poor woman, from 20s. to 30s. a week. She is a grandmother at sixty and sings 'John Anderson my Jo' at seventy-five. I need hardly say that she is religious, but not at all controversial. She cannot argue but she *lives*.

So much for the ideal—'but what are the facts?' Many women reach twenty-five, or even thirty, without receiving a single proposal of marriage; and even those with better matrimonial prospects are harder to please than their great-grandmothers were—'people still marry for love at least as much if not more than they did, but it may be doubted if love is quite as blind as he used to be.' Ladies' Colleges, however, do not exist merely to meet the needs of unmarried women and to find occupation for them; they also afford excellent training for future wives and mothers. 'Why should stupidity and ignorance be taken as a qualification for married life?' Men may actually prefer educated women as wives:

> Even Thackeray evidently felt, when writing the last pages of *Vanity Fair*, that William Dobbin would be considerably bored by Amelia; and, speaking for myself, I should *like* to have had Becky Sharp for a student. Very likely something might have been made of her if she had been taken in time, and her future husband might have reaped the advantage.

Later in the article she returns to this point, quoting an actual remark made apropos L.M.H. students, 'They'll none of them ever be able to talk to a Guardsman!' Her comment is pungent and to the point:

> If they can't, we may reply, there are plenty of other girls

who will be delighted to do so. But I think some Guardsmen might like for a change to have a young lady of this type next them at a dinner-party. They might never discover how she has been spending her time, and yet they might find her very good company.

Some of the most entertaining and perceptive passages are obviously sketches of life and characters at L.M.H. Take this picture of 'the clever girl of the family':

By the end of her first term she is thoroughly disliked; in her second she is miserable; in her third some of the nicer girls are sorry for her and make friends; in her fourth people begin to like her; in her fifth she *really* distinguishes herself, after which time a reaction sets in and the rest of her career, culminating in a First Class, is all that could be wished; but she never is *quite* so conceited again.

A description of 'silly seventeen' explains Elizabeth's declared preference for slightly older girls as college entrants:

It is generally very silly. It sits in wet boots, has an insane passion for draughts, thinks it interesting and refined to give up animal food or indulges in the strongest tea (if procurable) at the most unseasonable hours, glories in working till two a.m. and in fact in doing everything that mothers, maiden aunts, and governesses have hitherto been able to prevent.

In another passage she declares her profound belief in the educational value of good conversation:

In old days a real lady was educated by the atmosphere she habitually breathed. Many women go through the world

without ever hearing as much good conversation as might
be picked up at the breakfast table on a week's visit at some
privileged house. A Hall or College offers indeed a very poor
substitute for the best home-made article, but I have heard ...
really very respectable talk among women and girls and can
imagine it would have been better still in my absence.

The article ends with what Elizabeth calls 'Syllogisms' though
the singular form would strictly be more accurate:

There are a good many women in England with spare time
and faculties.

God must have meant them for something.

How are we to find out what He meant them for? Clearly
by (a) educating them and thus giving them a chance to
develop their natural gifts whether in the home or elsewhere;
(b) by training them to work in concert with others especially perhaps with a view to some of the great charitable
movements of the day.

The social life of Oxford was something very much to Elizabeth Wordsworth's taste. As the daughter of a bishop and the
Principal of an Anglican Hall she might have been expected to
choose her acquaintances from among the conservative
churchmen of Christ Church and Keble, but, little as she
approved of their opinions, she found the liberal thinkers of
the Balliol group much better company. Among her friends
of an older generation was that formidable agnostic, Mark
Pattison of Lincoln College. She was extremely annoyed if, as
frequently happened, Pattison was identified as the original of
the unattractive Casaubon in *Middlemarch* and of Professor
Forth in *Belinda*, a now-forgotten novel by Rhoda Broughton.
'I was glad to see that notice of Mark in *The Academy*', she

wrote in August 1884, a month after Pattison's death. 'It is too bad to have him handed down as Professor Forth, and no one who knew him would think him any more like Casaubon than Mrs Pattison was like Dorothea.' It may be noticed that she refers to Mark Pattison simply by his Christian name, thus implying a considerable degree of intimacy.

Among her Balliol friends were the famous philosopher T. H. Green, who she herself describes as 'not a Churchman in the strict sense of the word', the classical scholar Strachan-Davidson, Jowett's future biographer Evelyn Abbott, and of course 'the Master', Benjamin Jowett himself. Most people found Jowett formidable; but not so Elizabeth Wordsworth. She described an encounter with him at an Oxford dinner-party:

> I chaffed him ruthlessly, or rather, we chaffed one another. He is not a man I *can* feel afraid of, because he always looks so desperately tired. I suppose one has the instinct of trying to make life as easy to him as one can.

Life had in fact been anything but easy to Benjamin Jowett. Of lower middle-class origin, and lacking both money and social position, he had come up the ladder the hard way. Regarded by the members of the Balliol Senior Common Room as a difficult, opinionated character, and rightly suspected of unorthodox religious views, in 1854 he failed to win election to the vacant Mastership, the final vote going to an admittedly inferior candidate. That same year he was appointed Regius Professor of Greek; but the University authorities, disapproving of his religious views, refused him an expected increment to the tiny professorial salary of forty pounds a year. In 1860 the appearance of *Essays and Reviews* confirmed Jowett's reputation as a dangerous heretic. The book was a collection of essays on religious subjects by various writers, the last and best essay being by Jowett himself. Today the views expressed in *Essays and Reviews* would not cause the faintest stir; as Geoffrey Faber wrote, 'Jowett's only mistake was to be a little in advance of his time.' On its first appearance, however, the book aroused a storm of protest, two of the essayists actually finding themselves facing charges of heresy in the ecclesiastical courts. By 1870, the year when Jowett at last achieved his ambition and became Master of Balliol, the uproar had had time to die down, though it was not entirely stilled.

During the *Essays and Reviews* controversy Bishop Wordsworth had attacked Jowett in print with considerable ferocity. Elizabeth much admired the generosity of spirit which could show her so much real kindness in spite of this behaviour on her father's part. Jowett for his part very much enjoyed the company of clever women; Florence Nightingale, who counted him one of her dearest friends, described him as having a genius for friendship. Elizabeth Wordsworth was never on such intimate terms with him, but she understood his complex character very well, recognizing the shyness and uncertainty hidden behind his wit and satire. 'He was kind, shrewd, generous, infinitely painstaking, and yet somehow I should say he was timid.'

To Elizabeth Wordsworth, whom he admired and appreciated, Jowett showed himself as 'always most friendly to women's education'. In point of fact his attitude towards the question was an ambivalent one. Though he was one of the guarantors of the funds raised for the women's colleges, and though he twice lectured for the benefit of the A.E.W., at heart he was never convinced of the desirability of allowing women to attend universities or to enter into competitive examinations side by side with men. His biographer, Evelyn Abbott, writes of him that 'in all that concerned the relationship of the sexes he was most unwilling to change the ordinary rules though he was far from regarding them as perfect,' sentiments with which Elizabeth Wordsworth would certainly not have disagreed.

Much as she enjoyed and appreciated her Oxford friends Elizabeth did not as yet think to make her permanent home there; as soon as possible at the beginning of every vacation she would be off to her family at Riseholme. In 1880 Dora had married Edward Leeke, Benson's successor as Chancellor at Lincoln, leaving Susan as the daughter at home and therefore the most readily available companion for Elizabeth on trips abroad. In the summer of 1881 the two sisters joined the Benson family on holiday in Switzerland. They spent their time in walking, talking, sketching and admiring the scenery, and on wet days playing paper-games with the Benson children and suffering the indignity of being beaten at chess by the nine-year-old Robert Hugh. Elizabeth's letters home say little or nothing about Edward Benson but they contain a few slightly acid comments on the intensity of Minnie Benson's feelings and her habit of interfering in other people's affairs:

> Minnie has lost her heart to a German lady and they have been bothering an unfortunate magistrate about a cruel step-mother who beats her husband's children and who I believe will beat them all the more when their visitors are gone.

A year later Elizabeth broke new ground and travelled to Spain with John and Esther, her young cousin Gordon Wordsworth, and Esther's brother, Hilgrove Coxe. Spain appealed profoundly both to her artistic feelings and her historical sense—'I feel in such a dream I don't believe I *can* write; it is really the most wonderful place I ever was in,' and again, 'The place makes one feel almost tipsy with its beauty and suggestiveness, its light and colour and the sort of epic dignity of its people.' She much preferred the dignified

Spaniards to 'those monkeys of men one sees in Paris.' At
Burgos she was much struck by the devout behaviour of the
congregation in the cathedral, 'every face full of gravity,
devotion, and a kind of dignity.' From Burgos the party
travelled to Avila, arriving at five o'clock in the morning 'with
Saint Teresa's stars looking down on us.' 'The whole place is
like a bit of the Middle Ages,' she wrote to Susan, 'a wonderful
walled town with towers at intervals just like an old picture,
stern brown flowerless landscape with blue hills, not without
traces here and there of snow in the distance.' Madrid was much
less enjoyable, 'so dusty and east-windy and modern.' Only
the pictures in the Prado provided consolation for the necessity
of remaining there long enough to allow John to examine a
manuscript of the Vulgate which was the ostensible object of
their journey. Toledo, however, enchanted her with its
churches and mosques and its 'inconceivably lovely sunsets'.
Easter was spent at Valencia before setting out on the homeward journey by way of Tarragona, Narbonne, and Nîmes.
Even the return to Oxford was not without adventure:

> I must have been the only woman on Oxford platform at
> 11 p.m. *Swarms* of undergrads, portmanteaux and cricketing
> things, strings of cabs (all engaged). But the cup of my despair
> was not full yet. After driving me at a frantic pace round
> corners and past other vehicles in the very shakiest old
> phaeton you can imagine my man put me down at L.M.H.
> with my goods on the doorstep and left me *à la belle étoile* in
> the silence of midnight. I rang and rang again without
> producing any effect whatsoever. After wandering about I
> discovered the kitchen window warm and glowing and only
> protected by a bolt. On the whole I thought it best to run up
> a glazier's bill rather than stop there bag and baggage all
> night so I ran my parasol through the upper pane, carefully
> pulled out the glass, turned the bolt, and found myself in the

kitchen . . . Most luckily the maids had not locked the door so I groped my way upstairs shouting for Freeman. I seemed to hear a distinct wailing as of someone in hysterics. This was the maids crying 'Murder, murder', as they fully believed, having heard the window crash (though not the bell), that I was a house-breaker, and it was some time before I could get them to come and help me get in my baggage which was lying at the mercy of any passer-by.

This Spanish holiday, which had in fact proved so pleasurable, might well have been a complete failure. John Wordsworth was suffering from the after-effects of a severe riding accident that had left him nervous, irritable, and in no state to face the difficulties and discomforts of Spanish roads, railways and hotels. Elizabeth, however, determined from the very start that they could and would enjoy themselves. Writing in 1936 Gordon Wordsworth recalled 'her imperturbable good temper under the mischances of travel in the almost medieval Spain of fifty years ago, the amount of time she devoted to her sketching, chiefly, if I remember right, of architectural subjects both Christian and Moslem, and the undaunted conversations she carried on in voluble and, I fancy, execrable Spanish at every opportunity possible and impossible.' Sketching was always her favourite holiday occupation though her artistic talents did not equal her enthusiasm.

No very long or distant holiday was possible in 1883. In the spring of that year Bishop Wordsworth, now a man in his seventies, appeared more than usually ailing and over-tired. It was not he, however, but his wife who collapsed, so seriously ill that she had to leave Riseholme and take a complete rest at the Yorkshire home of Priscilla and her doctor husband, Percy Steedman. Neither Mrs Wordsworth nor the Bishop were well enough to attend Edward Benson's enthronement as Archbishop of Canterbury, which took place in April; and though

Mrs Wordsworth recovered sufficiently to return home for the summer, from now onwards a cloud of anxiety hung over the family. In August, however, Elizabeth and Susan felt that they might safely take a short holiday in Belgium with their friend Alicia Blakisley, daughter of the Dean of Lincoln. Ghent in particular pleased Elizabeth—'It is not often one sees so much antiquity combined with so much actual prosperity, not like Venice, where history seems to have stood still.' She was interested and amused by a visit to that peculiarly Belgian institution, a *béguinage*—'In England *béguinages* could never thrive, you could never get five hundred women to live peaceably together with no greater excitement than making lace or knitting stockings, with intervals of church-going with a white napkin over your head.'

Throughout the next winter and spring Bishop Wordsworth carried on his episcopal duties, but in July 1884 he fell so critically ill that for weeks his life was despaired of. Not till 15 August could Elizabeth tell her sister-in-law Esther that he had at last been allowed to come downstairs and that he appeared to be looking forward to 'something like recovery'. That same letter contains a description of a harvest scene which deserves quotation:

Edward [Leeke] and I had a lovely walk in that big cornfield on your right hand at the top of Nettleham Hill. The reapers, men, women, children and horses drawing those picturesque machines, all looked as though they were beautifully painted on a gold background, and the bluish purple sky, and the pigeon-house, and the grey hazy cathedral [*sic*]. Two unfortunate little leverets were startled from among the corn. One got away, the other, after doubling gallantly among the sheaves with a black sheep-dog after it was caught and killed, poor little thing. I felt quite sorry it should be sent out of that lovely summer evening into blank non-existence, all in the space of five minutes. It is odd we should have but one word to express a hare or a rabbit being knocked on the head by a ploughboy and the *Nunc Dimittis* of the greatest and best of mankind.

As soon as the Bishop was well enough to travel he and his wife returned to the Steedmans' house at Harewood, where Susannah Wordsworth fell seriously ill again. For the sake of her health it was decided that she should be moved to Harrogate, although both she and her family realized that there could be no hope of permanent recovery. Back at Oxford and preoccupied with the work and organization entailed by the opening of the new extension to L.M.H. Elizabeth Wordsworth found herself in an unhappy predicament, longing to be with her parents but knowing that duty demanded she should stay in Oxford. She rejoiced to remember that three years earlier, in the summer of 1881, both her parents had visited L.M.H. and had, as it were, given the place their blessing. They would realize how important it was that she should be there at this critical moment and would understand why she must not come to them. On 16 October she wrote her mother a loving letter describing the new building and explaining her own feelings:

It seems very strange to be going on with all this when one's thoughts are so much elsewhere, but it is I am sure a duty that ought to be done, and I cannot but feel that the real being together is in trying to do God's will which is a thing which is eternal, and not merely in having the bodily presence of those one loves; though I do hope to get back before very long, and it is the greatest comfort to know that you and my dear Father are giving us the benefit of your prayers. Any good that is done here will mainly be your work and his.

Susannah Wordsworth died at Harrogate on 28 October. The
funeral took place at Riseholme; Elizabeth was touched and
delighted that the L.M.H. students should have thought to
send a wreath. As always, she fought shy of any expression of
emotion. 'You will understand how hard it is to write about
what is uppermost in one's thoughts,' she told Alicia Blakisley.
'I wonder if you have as I have a kind of dread of losing the
reality of it all by talking about it. Things seem to evaporate
when put into words.' She found relaxation in watching the
antics of her small nephews and nieces—'The children are
playing at trains all over the drawing-room floor; it is such a
refreshment after the state of tension we have all been living
in.' Elizabeth was writing on a Sunday, a day when such games
would have been forbidden in many Victorian homes, but
strict as they were as to religious observance, the Wordsworths
were not severe sabbatarians.

Bishop Wordsworth never recovered from the shock of his
wife's death. Immediately after her funeral he returned to
Harewood, and realizing that he would never again be fit to
undertake diocesan work, he resigned his see. His successor as
Bishop of Lincoln was John's Oxford friend, Edward King, an
appointment which Elizabeth described as 'the greatest comfort and blessing to ourselves as well as to the diocese.'

The last months of Christopher Wordsworth's life were
overshadowed by appalling depression and melancholy.
Physically he was well enough to take short walks and to
attend an occasional church service; mentally he was sufficiently alert to be able to read and enjoy Elizabeth's article on
George Eliot and to write her a charming letter of congratulation. His struggle was a spiritual one. As sometimes happens
with saintly characters the approach of death was not a peaceful
ending to a holy life but a battle against what a more simple-
minded, or perhaps a more believing generation, would have
described as a final assault by the powers of evil. His sons and

daughters looked on helplessly, deeply distressed but unable to bring him any comfort. At the very end, however, he fell into a calm sleep and died quietly at midnight on 20 March 1885.

Elizabeth was not given to much lamentation; as might have been expected, her attitude towards death was a compound of Christianity and common sense. To draw pictures of the dead was a common Victorian practice; there was nothing specially morbid about her wish 'to get a sketch of the dear figure in the little room where it lies strewn with flowers and dressed in the clean white lawn robes and scarf.' The day on which she made that drawing of her dead father Elizabeth's thoughts were all of 'brightness and glory, the Psalms, the Resurrection Lessons and Gospel, the hints of spring in the shrubbery where we walked so often.'

After the funeral Elizabeth remained on at Riseholme to help with the business of sorting and packing up. Her sister Dora was inclined to be lachrymose over this break-up of the family home, but Elizabeth's reaction was a purely practical and businesslike one. She must now find some place which she could make her headquarters during vacations, and she decided that she would share a house in Lincoln with her sister Susan. A suitable house was found in Pottergate near the cathedral, and here the two sisters made their home with their old nurse, Janet McCraw, who lived until 1899. Elizabeth took infinite pains to be kind to this old woman whom she dearly loved. On one occasion she appeared in a bonnet so ugly that it aroused considerable comment from her friends and relations. Janet, it seemed, had heard her remark that she must make some effort to economize, and had therefore concocted this bonnet out of old bits and pieces. In spite of protests Elizabeth persisted in wearing it rather than risk hurting Janet's feelings.

In the year of her father's death, Elizabeth was bereft also of John and Esther's company at Oxford. In 1883 John had been appointed to a canonry at Rochester which he could hold simultaneously with his Oxford appointments since he was only required to live at Rochester during his period as canon in residence. This arrangement, however, only lasted for two years; in 1885 he left Oxford for good on his appointment to the see of Salisbury. John Wordsworth was a curious choice as bishop of a predominantly rural diocese. A learned scholar, lacking any experience of pastoral work, he found great difficulty in making himself understood by the inhabitants of a country parish. Not only did he preach sermons which were well above their heads—'My friends,' he remarked to one country congregation, 'I know that you can quote Irenaeus against me'—but he could not resist the temptation to preach on whatever topic chanced to interest him at that moment, no matter how irrelevant or how unsuited to the needs of his hearers. On one occasion, after speaking in the House of Lords against the Marriage with Deceased Wife's Sister's Bill, he went down to Marlborough to take a confirmation in the school chapel, and in his address solemnly adjured the boys not to marry their future sisters-in-law. Maybe he would have served the Church better had he remained a learned and pious Professor. Elizabeth rejoiced to see him elevated to the episcopate, but she sadly missed him and his charming Esther, whose near neighbourhood had been one of the great pleasures of her Oxford life.

Chapter 7

Foundation of St Hugh's College

BISHOP WORDSWORTH had not been dead a year before it was decided to start work on his biography. He himself had expressed a wish that if such a book were ever to be written it should be by his daughter. Feeling that she could not undertake the work single-handed Elizabeth enlisted the help of Canon John Henry Overton of Lincoln. She discussed the shape of the book with Archbishop Benson but decided not to adopt his suggestion of a two-volume biography, the first volume of which would be a personal memoir, the second an account of the Bishop's public life. The book which appeared in 1888 was a single-volume biography of the usual Victorian type, neither better nor worse than others of its kind. Though it is difficult to disentangle Elizabeth's share from Canon Overton's, it would seem likely that she supplied much of the material while he did most of the writing.

Two years after the appearance of this biography she published *Saint Christopher and Other Poems*. The printed version describes *Saint Christopher* as a cantata; the manuscript calls it 'a libretto for an oratorio'. Though it is reminiscent of *The Shadow of the Sphinx* it is a more finished and workmanlike piece of writing than that strange production. Many of the other poems in the book were written during a visit to Italy in the Easter vacation of 1889; it would be fair to describe them as competent though not particularly distinguished. The last item in the volume is a 'chronicle play' dealing with the Dauphin who was son to Louis XIV and father to Louis XV.

A year later in 1891 Elizabeth Wordsworth published a biographical and critical study of her great-uncle William. Elizabeth's tie of kinship with 'the poet', as the family invariably called him, might have given her unique insight; his poetry could have been to her something 'felt in the blood and felt along the heart.' Anyone opening *William Wordsworth* with these high hopes is bound to be disappointed; it is as if her father's ponderous biography of the poet had risen up to obscure Elizabeth's personal view. She has an unusually good knowledge of the poems, and occasionally she makes a particularly perceptive remark, as when, for instance, after writing of 'the insight of a philosopher and the foresight of a prophet' she coins a happy word and credits him also with 'the outsight of an artist'. In describing his Cambridge days she shows special understanding of his state of mind, 'a strange, perhaps an almost unexampled fermentation not of the passions but of the intellect.' On the whole, however, her relationship to Wordsworth is only apparent when she records some little-known saying or anecdote, such as his touching encounter with a little blind girl:

> One day she was in the room alone when he entered. For a moment he stood silent before the blind child . . . then he gravely said, 'Madam, I hope I do not disturb you.' She never forgot that 'Madam', grave, solemn, almost reverential.

On one point Elizabeth is determinedly blind, recognizing no difference in outlook between the young Wordsworth and the old, and attributing to the twenty-year-old enthusiast for the French Revolution the respectable Anglican views held by the sage of Rydal Mount.

One more publication of this period deserves special notice. Plays written by the Principal and performed by the students were a notable feature of L.M.H. life. The first one of these plays to be printed was *The Apple of Discord*, a short comic opera in the manner of Gilbert and Sullivan on the theme of Paris's award of the golden apple, which here represents not only the prize of beauty but also

> The golden fruit of learning which till now
> No woman's hand has plucked from mystic bough.

The tree which bears the golden apple is guarded by a 'chorus of conservative dons' who march round it singing a song whose theme is summed up in the fourth verse:

> What is right is always right,
>   What is true is ever true;
> Who are we to boast of light
>   More than our forefathers knew?
> We are wise to tread, tread, tread
>   Just the path where erst they led!

Overcome by 'sipping sound port wine after Hall at five-fifteen', these guardians fall asleep. Enter three goddesses, Juno, Pallas Athene, and Venus (the confusion of Greek and Latin names is Elizabeth Wordsworth's own) who steal the golden apple, only to be caught by many-eyed Argus in the guise of a proctor, who lets them off with a caution:

> Begone, begone! for if you linger here
> You'll have to see the Dean at half-past nine,
> And pay the Varsity chest a thumping fine.

The play continues on its witty way, with Paris appearing as a

History tutor and a chorus of nymphs complaining that they are kept 'Slave to worn-out superstition, Bounded by a wedding-ring.' The conservative dons sing a rousing chorus to the tune of 'The Vicar of Bray':

> But I'll maintain it, for 'tis true,
>   Until my dying day, Sir,
> That Learning's for the favoured few
>   Whate'er the many say, Sir.

Venus throws away the apple which is retrieved by two Extension students, one of them an American visiting Oxford for the first time:

> I guess it's lovely in this calm retreat;
> Indeed, the whole location's very sweet.
> I calculate the alumnae of this college
> Have every spur to the pursuit of knowledge.
> It's fixed up very smart s'fur's I can see,
> But pity they won't give them a degree.

All entanglements are, of course, finally sorted out; and the play ends with each nymph selecting a conservative don for partner. They dance and sing in chorus:

NYMPHS Now, at last, we're all delighted,
          All is smooth as smooth can be;
          Woman's wrongs at length are righted,
          See how nicely we agree.
DONS   Now our labours are requited,
          And from cares and troubles free,
          We shall live, with them united,
          In this University.

NYMPHS Now we'll learn, with you our teachers,
     Twice as fast as e'er before;
    Taught to mark the leading features
     Found in every branch of lore.
DONS While your instincts, lovely creatures,
     Penetrate Truth's inmost core,
    One and all unconscious preachers;
     Woman's *never* found a bore!

NYMPHS Let the fruit of learning never
     Henceforth bear foul Discord's name.
    What's the good of being clever
     If you grudge another's fame?
DONS Nay, but let us all endeavour
     Each to help his fellows' aim;
    So shall truest wisdom ever
     Light us with undying flame.

Even today, when the jokes have lost their topical flavour, *The Apple of Discord* amuses and entertains; when it was first produced it must have brought down the house.

Elizabeth Wordsworth's chief academic concern at this time was the founding of a new Hall for women students. She is sometimes accused of interesting herself only in the education of well-connected, tolerably well-to-do ladies. Nothing could be farther from the truth. In early life, first at Stanford and then at Lincoln, she had given of her very best to the work of teaching poor girls. It would be ridiculous to blame her because the education she worked so hard to give them today seems old-fashioned and inadequate. At a time when the higher education of women was in its very earliest infancy no one imagined that working-class girls ever could or would become University students. There was, however, an intermediate group, daughters of professional people such as doctors, parsons, or service officers, often as well-born, but not as well-off, as the L.M.H. ladies. It was for these girls that Elizabeth felt special concern. She wished to give them a chance of coming up to Oxford not merely because a University education would qualify them to earn a better salary as school-teachers or governesses, but because the time they spent there would be a bright spot in their rather drab lives. Years later when addressing a Women Workers' Conference she described the effect that Oxford might have on such a girl:

> I can think of a girl who comes to Oxford from some school where she has been crammed for examination after examination. I can see her head-achy face now. After she goes down she perhaps has to go to some other school as a teacher, where another dull round and more cramming (this time of other people) awaits her. Those three years at Oxford have been her one bit of real sunshine in a life too full of grey tints. For once she has felt what it is to be alive, to be eager and young. All her life will be different just because of this; she has made friends, she has had her horizon enlarged, she has been lifted up a step or two on the ladder of existence.

When L.M.H. first opened the fees had been fixed at £75 a year, and they were to remain at this figure for the next thirty years or so. Though the sum was not a large one it was beyond the means of many professional people, especially those with large families to educate. At the men's colleges, with the exception of Keble, a scale of varying payments for varying standards of accommodation, and the system of 'battels' rather than a fixed payment for meals, provided a realistic and, up to a point, helpful recognition of the fact that some undergraduates had less money than others. A similar arrangement had

been considered at L.M.H. but had been rejected on the ground
that it would lead to invidious distinctions between rich and
poor. In practice Elizabeth Wordsworth had adopted the
opposite course. A needy girl who had been granted a reduc-
tion of fees would be given one of the best rooms so that she
could have no reason to feel herself slighted because of her
poverty, while the worst room would go to some rich student
blessed with sufficient sense of humour to make a joke of
living in unaccustomed discomfort. Lack of funds, however,
made it impossible for the Hall authorities to take more than a
very few students at reduced rates; and meanwhile the problem
of 'the girls of slender means' remained unsolved.

In 1886 an unexpected financial windfall gave Elizabeth
Wordsworth the chance to tackle this difficulty. When the
diocese of Lincoln had been divided into two in 1884 Bishop
Wordsworth had given a personal guarantee of some thousands
of pounds for the foundation of the new diocese of Southwell.
This money had remained unused and now reverted to the
Bishop's children, £600 being Elizabeth's share. Though the
amount was ludicrously inadequate for the scheme she had in
mind she was not to be daunted. With this money which had
come to her from her father she determined to found a Hall in
his memory, to be named after St Hugh, patron saint of the
diocese of Lincoln. In a letter written to her sister Dora Leeke
and dated 18 May she described her plan:

> You will see in next week's *Guardian* I hope a letter about a
> house in which I *hope* to install Annie Moberly and half-a-
> dozen really *poor* students next October. This is a venture of
> my own, a risk of about £500, though with the consent of
> the Committee, and John's and the Warden's approval. I
> do hope it will succeed, please God, for I do not feel we are
> doing enough for the class that really needs our help the
> most.

It was typical of Elizabeth that she should buy the house before securing possession of her very small capital; the last instalment of the £600 was not in fact paid her until August 1889. The financial side of the founding of St Hugh's is wrapped in mystery. No appeal for funds appears to have been issued, the letter to *The Guardian* being merely a statement of her intention to open a new Hall for the benefit of those who could not afford the charges at L.M.H. When a larger house was bought in 1888 she specifically states that this was made possible 'through the kind help of friends who lent us money on very advantageous terms,' but she never mentions the existence of any such kind friends two years earlier. Her own £600 was just sufficient to pay for furnishings and equipment. Possibly she borrowed the necessary money herself; if so, her personal liability must have considerably exceeded the 'risk of about £500' which she mentioned in her letter to Dora.

Certainly no help was forthcoming from the funds allotted to L.M.H. From the very first it was made clear that there was to be no connection between the two Halls. The Report of the L.M.H. Committee for 1886 states the position precisely:

> The Lady Principal informed the Committee of her wish to open at her own risk a small house for the reception of students of narrower means at lower fees, and with a different scale of living and accommodation. The Committee saw no reason in the interests of L.M.H. to object to such a scheme, while they welcomed a fresh extension of women's education at Oxford. The House has since been opened under the name of St Hugh's Hall and with Miss C. A. E. Moberly as its head. The Church principles are the same as L.M.H. but it is in no way connected with the Hall or with the Committee.

To Elizabeth's mind this freedom from committees was one of

the most attractive features of the new scheme. 'I am very glad to have had the experience of working with a committee,' she told Dora, 'yet this arrangement will be an immense saving in time and trouble.' By the beginning of October a small, semi-detached house in Norham Road was ready to receive the four students of the new Hall and its Principal, Annie Moberly, who was one of the fourteen children of George Moberly, John Wordsworth's predecessor in the see of Salisbury. 'All I hope is that she will prove an economical housekeeper,' Elizabeth wrote, 'but episcopal training, as I have found to my cost, is not the best thing in the world for temporal, whatever it may be for spiritual, oversight.'

Annie Moberly belied her fragile appearance—'a piece of Dresden china'—by proving a tough and efficient adminis-trator. 'Annie Moberly is coming out as a capital housekeeper,' was Elizabeth's delighted comment, 'though I hope she does not restrict them exactly to Cistercian[1] fare.' Little beyond 'Cistercian fare' was to be expected in a Hall where the fees were as low as £45 a year. Life at L.M.H. was far from luxuri-ous; food was of the custard and prunes variety, baths were scarce, and beds reputed to be the hardest in the world. St Hugh's was even more austere. Little or no money could be spent on decoration; at one time the wallpaper on the main staircase was peeling off in strips. In winter the cold was intense, the chapel being so peculiarly icy that the congregation was popularly supposed to be in danger of frost-bite.

Yet from the very first St Hugh's was a success. Numbers increased so rapidly that in 1887 Elizabeth Wordsworth took the next-door house to accommodate the overflow and in the following year moved the whole Hall to more spacious quarters at 17 Norham Gardens. In 1891 it was found necessary to enlarge this house, other neighbouring houses being acquired

1. This appears to be a reference to the religious Order to which St Hugh belonged. If so, E.W. is wrong; St Hugh was a Carthusian.

in 1901 and 1909. Finally, in 1916 St Hugh's College, as it had now become, moved to its present spacious site between Banbury Road and Woodstock Road. This rapid progress was the more remarkable because at the beginning St Hugh's was entirely a 'one-woman' venture, that woman being Elizabeth Wordsworth. For the first four years of St Hugh's existence she and Annie Moberly dealt with all financial matters themselves without any outside help, until in 1890 she decided that the time had come to set up a Council under the chairmanship of Sir John Hawkins. From that moment Elizabeth Wordsworth relinquished all control over St Hugh's. She became, of course, a member of Council but she took no great part in its deliberations, and she never interfered with Annie Moberly's management, leaving her a completely free hand.

Annie Moberly's father had been for thirty years headmaster of Winchester where he was reckoned a reformer of the calibre of Arnold of Rugby or Thring of Uppingham. When he retired he took a country living which he combined with a canonry at Chester before being appointed Bishop of Salisbury. Annie Moberly therefore shared Elizabeth's background of headmaster's house, country parsonage, canonical residence and bishop's palace. She also shared Elizabeth's devotion to a Tractarian type of Anglicanism (the Moberlys' best friends at Winchester had been John Keble and Charlotte Yonge) and her interest in classical studies. In character, however, the two women were poles apart. 'I've gone dancing through life,' Elizabeth declared in old age; but not so Annie Moberly. Introverted, shy, intense—'remoteness' was the word which a St Hugh's tutor was to apply to her—in her home circle she had felt herself overshadowed by her more obviously brilliant brothers and sisters. Now her chance had come; and her manner of seizing that chance was totally unlike Elizabeth's matter-of-fact, almost casual reaction to the same opportunity when it had come her way. Elizabeth went down to Salisbury to offer

Annie the headship of the new Hall. The writer of Annie Moberly's obituary in the *Oxford Magazine* tells how she went out on a solitary walk, 'idly picking up and dropping beech-nuts while debating within herself the enterprise offered to her untried powers. A voice uttered itself in her spiritual ear, bidding her "go on". She made her resolve; the nuts on which her hand had closed at that moment she found still in it on her return home, and she kept them as a memento till the day of her death.'

In public, relations between L.M.H. and St Hugh's were perfectly amicable, if slightly distant; in private, Annie Moberly resented what she believed to be the difference in status between St Hugh's and the more expensive and select establishment on the other side of Norham Gardens. St Hugh's, she felt, was regarded as the Cinderella of the women's colleges; under her breath she was heard to murmur that 'Miss Words-worth had founded St Hugh's to be a rubbish-dump for L.M.H.' She would have been hardly human if she had not felt slightly aggrieved to see the head of L.M.H. sought after and invited everywhere, dining one week with a future archbishop, Ran-dall Davidson, and with the Chancellor of the Exchequer, Lord Goschen, the next a fellow-guest with James Russell Lowell, Max Muller and Francis Palgrave, while the head of St Hugh's was invited nowhere and saw nobody. The situation was the more difficult for her because she could not understand the reasons for Elizabeth Wordsworth's social success. A person of delicate perceptions and naturally critical, she was irritated by what most other people found amusing: as a St Hugh's tutor wrote, 'she had no smile for Miss Wordsworth's idiosyncrasies.'

Annie Moberly, however, was a thoroughly good woman, too loyal and well-bred to give expression to these bitter feelings, which were known only to those in closest contact with her. As for Elizabeth Wordsworth, she either did not know that her friend and fellow Principal harboured any resentment against her or she put the knowledge clean out of her mind and behaved as if their relationship were a perfectly harmonious one.

Where the students of the two Halls were concerned the feeling seems to have been one not of inferiority but of difference. Just as it was taken for granted that Balliol, Lincoln and Brasenose, to name three very different colleges, would not attract the same type of undergraduate as Christ Church and Magdalen, so it seemed right and natural that the students at each of the women's colleges should exhibit slightly different characteristics. Only of recent years, when competition has become so fierce that a candidate cannot be sure of entering the college of his or her choice but must accept a place wherever one is offered have the old distinctions blurred into a featureless uniformity.

At L.M.H. the late eighties and early nineties were a period notable less for important events than for a succession of brilliant students. It is astonishing that a Hall whose numbers at this period never exceeded forty could have produced such a crop of remarkable characters. First among them was a trio of friends who took Finals in 1887 or 1888, two of them achieving Firsts. Since Greats was not opened to women till 1890 Janet Hogarth had to be content with a First in the Final Examination in Philosophy. On leaving Oxford she worked for the Royal Commission on Labour, then took a post at the Bank of England which she held until 1900 when she became Head Librarian of the Times Book Club. In 1911 she married W. L. Courtney, brother to another L.M.H. student Kathleen Courtney, and editor of *The Saturday Review*. Janet was subeditor of that paper until the First World War, when she did important work at the Ministry of Munitions. Judging by her three books, *Women of my Time*, *An Oxford Portrait Gallery*, and *Recollected in Tranquillity*, she must have been a vital and entertaining personality with an observant eye and a gift for lively description.

But even the clever, vivacious Janet pales into comparative insignificance when set beside the vivid personality of her friend Gertrude Bell. Daughter of a well-known north country family of wealthy iron-masters, Gertrude came from a smarter and more sophisticated background than the average L.M.H. student, and she had been brought up in an atmosphere of Liberalism and free thought very different from the Anglican tradition prevalent at the Hall. Since university education for girls was still regarded as a strange and rather advanced notion, few parents thought to send their daughter to Oxford unless and until that daughter was old enough to choose for herself; twenty was therefore the average age of a first-year student. Gertrude Bell came up at seventeen, intent on fitting in two years at Oxford before she was launched on London society. Again defying convention, she arrived in the third, and not the first, term of the academic year, young but self-confident, displaying 'a most confiding assurance of being welcome in our society.' That assurance was not misplaced; 'from the first,' writes Janet Courtney, 'we took her to our hearts.' Green-eyed and auburn-haired, with a long pointed nose, she was not technically pretty, but she had an attraction all of her own. Blessed with an excellent dress sense and the means to indulge it, she delighted in clothes, but with such childlike enjoyment that no one could think to be jealous—'I've got a hat, Janet, but a hat! Come and see it!'—and her outfit for 'Commem' was one of the talking-points of the summer term.

Gertrude, however, was not merely a social butterfly. She swam, she rowed—in 1885 L.M.H. had acquired its first boat on the Cherwell—she fenced, she played tennis, and she worked for seven hours a day, cramming three years' reading into seven terms. When she took History Finals in the summer of

1888 the examiners were staggered by what Janet Hogarth describes as 'the unusual sight in the Schools of a girl intensely vital, perfectly dressed'—these were the days before women were required to wear subfusc for Schools—'and entirely self-possessed.' At her viva the first man to question her was S. R. Gardiner, the great authority on the Civil War. 'I'm afraid I don't quite agree with your view of Charles the First,' Gertrude remarked with a disarming smile, whereupon he made haste to hand her over to a colleague who in the course of his questioning chanced to describe a certain German town as being on the left bank of the Rhine. At once Gertrude queried his statement. Ill-advisedly, he stuck to his guns, only to give her the chance to correct him in a high, clear voice which carried all over the room, 'I'm so sorry, but it really *is* on the right bank; you see, I've been there.' All the same, they gave her a First.

Gertrude Bell regarded her Principal with a slightly critical eye. 'Really Miss Wordsworth is too astonishing for anything,' she wrote home on 30 May 1887. 'She propounds the most extraordinary theories one after the other in no sort of sequence and quite naturally as if she were talking platitudes. However, she gives one enough to talk about! She gets more and more absent-minded—it takes the form of asking you torrents of questions about whatever you are doing without listening to your answers in the very least or thinking about what she is asking. She will talk to me the whole of lunch-time about Mr Johnson's lectures and ask me at tea whether I ever heard of the Arthur Johnsons! That is really no exaggeration. Much as I like her, I think she is a little mad.'

This critical attitude was reciprocated. As traveller, archaeologist, author, diplomatist, and a world-authority on Persia, Gertrude Bell became one of the best-known women of her generation and a bright peculiar star of L.M.H. Yet Elizabeth Wordsworth never really liked or approved of her, though

Janet Courtney (née Hogarth)
L.M.H. 1885–8, Civil Servant,
journalist and author

Gertrude Bell, C.B.E.
L.M.H. 1886–8, explorer,
archaeologist, author and
diplomat

Eglantyne Jebb, L.M.H. 1895–8,
Founder of the
Save the Children Fund

Lavinia Talbot, wife of
Bishop Edward Talbot and
with him co-founder of L.M.H.

she came in time to recognize her mistake and to admit that she had never given Gertrude her rightful due, justifying herself with the query, 'Would she be the sort of person to have in one's bedroom if one were ill?' The question was all the more damning because Elizabeth's standard of sick-room attendance was not a high one. On one occasion when she was lying ill with influenza Eleanor Lodge, after attempting to make her tidy and comfortable, emerged from the bedroom exclaiming, 'I believe she *enjoys* discomfort.' Elizabeth described the ideal bedroom as 'one where you could stand in the middle and reach for all you wanted.' She would deliberately allow a cup of tea to grow cold and heat it up again later for a bedtime drink. As Evelyn Jamison commented, echoing Eleanor Lodge's remark, she had 'a genius for discomfort.'

The third member of this trio of student friends was Mary Talbot, niece of the Warden of Keble. Six years older than Gertrude Bell, she supplied the judgement and balance necessary to counteract Gertrude's impetuosity and self-assurance—'cockiness' would not be an unfair word. Quiet, unobtrusive, and not as clever as either Janet or Gertrude, Mary Talbot did not appear to be either remarkable or outstanding, but when she died in childbirth after a year of happy marriage all those who had known her felt that they had suffered an irreparable loss.

Living in a room between Gertrude Bell and Janet Hogarth was Edith Langridge, a girl who might be taken as the fulfilment of Elizabeth Wordsworth's pattern for the ideal woman, 'better with the hands than with the head and best of all with the heart.' Edith was so kindhearted and so skilled with her hands that both Janet and Gertrude would instinctively turn to her in any practical difficulty. Not that there was anything wrong with Edith's head; at school she had done very well at mathematics and came up to L.M.H. intending to read that subject. Elizabeth Wordsworth, however, thought otherwise: 'You

E

simply can't come to Oxford and do mathematics. They say
your Greek is very good; what about your Latin?' Edith had
to confess that she knew no Latin. 'Don't know Latin! Why,
your education cannot be complete without Latin. There is
a Responsions Examination in two months' time; the set book
is *De Senectute*, quite simple—then you can read for Honour
Mods.' Obediently Edith applied herself to Cicero and the
art of writing Latin prose to such effect that she passed
Responsions and astonished the examiners by using correctly
not one but two words each known to occur only once in
classical Latin.

C. L. Dodgson ('Lewis Carroll') was among the more
frequent visitors to L.M.H. Himself a mathematician, he was
fond of inventing complicated games and puzzles which he
tried out on the students, the most baffling being a series of
word-problems which he called 'Syzgies'. He was considerably
disconcerted when Edith ruined the game by discovering a
method of increasing one's score without contravening the
rules. Edith took a Second in Honour Mods (would she have
won her First had she been allowed to follow her real bent and
take Mathematical Mods instead?) and followed this not with a
Final Honours School but with a course of study abroad.
When the L.M.H. Settlement was founded, she was appointed
its first Warden. Later she joined an Anglican sisterhood,
becoming Mother Superior of the Sisters working with the
Oxford Mission to Calcutta. Clearly Edith Langridge was a
character after Elizabeth Wordsworth's own heart.

In these early days history was by far the most popular
subject with women students, so that it is not surprising that
the two most notable L.M.H. students of the nineties should
have been historians. Eleanor Lodge came up in 1890, 'a tall,
slender, grey-eyed girl, fresh and vivid as a spring day.' A
natural leader, she excelled at tennis, skating, rowing, hockey,
and all forms of sport. Long walks were her delight; the

Brown Book credits her with covering forty miles in a day. Though she only succeeded in gaining a Second, she was to become something of an authority on the history of medieval France, and of Gascony in particular, winning the gold medal of the Institut Historique de France, and being the first woman to receive the Oxford degree of D.Litt.

In the summer vacation after her Finals Eleanor Lodge went on holiday to Switzerland with Elizabeth Wordsworth. She found her ex-Principal 'a most entertaining though occasionally embarrassing companion' with an almost uncanny aptitude for choosing extremely uncomfortable inns or hotels. As a walker Elizabeth was no match for Eleanor, her idea of walking being to run uphill as far and as fast as her legs would carry her, then to rest exhausted until she felt sufficiently recovered to attempt another spurt. Of an evening she enjoyed a game of whist or a chat with an interesting fellow guest, if she could find such a person. Eleanor described one encounter:

At one place an American man pleased Miss Wordsworth very much, and after a long talk with him till quite late she came and sat on my bed and remarked gravely, 'Nellie, I have met my fate.' Unfortunately her 'Fate' had departed before we went down to breakfast, so that we had a good laugh together over her blighted affections.

In 1895 Eleanor returned to L.M.H. and stayed there till 1921, first as librarian, then History Tutor, and finally Vice-Principal. She is fittingly commemorated by the building which bears her name on the south side of the present quadrangle. Eleanor Lodge was essentially a university woman, and her historical work, valuable though it may be, is unknown outside university and specialist circles. Barbara Bradby, better known as Barbara Hammond, was a historian of a different type. In partnership with her husband, J. L. Hammond, she produced a series of books on economic history, at once scholarly and popular, which are still in print and widely read both by the student of history and the general public.

Coming up in 1892 Barbara Bradby made her mark at Oxford in more ways than one. She did not read History but Honour Mods followed by Greats, becoming the first woman to achieve the distinction of a double First. This was the more remarkable because she did not avail herself of the latitude permitted to women in the matter of residence but stayed up only for the statutory four years. She was the heroine of a famous limerick:

> In spite of long hours with a crammer
> I never get more than a Gamma,
>   But the girl over there
>   With the flaming red hair
> Gets Alpha Plus every time, damn her!

Barbara has one more claim to be remembered in Oxford; she was the first woman to ride to lectures on a bicycle.

These students of a later generation led very much the same life as their pioneering predecessors, though now that the Hall had increased in numbers the division into years became more apparent. Third year students sat together at meals and kept somewhat apart from the rest of the community, an attitude which did not please those of their juniors who happened to be senior to them in years (it was not uncommon for a girl to come up in her mid-twenties). Both second and third years joined in regarding the first-year students as frivolous children intent only on enjoying their freedom from the restrictions of home or school. This passion for liberty took very innocuous, not to say childish, forms. 'Miss Wordsworth is out,' said one 1886 first-year to another; 'let's toboggan down the front staircase in our baths'—a reference to the tin hip-baths to be found in every student's bedroom. In her bible class that term the Principal was reported to have 'spoken solemnly of our childishness and frivolity of conversation'; it would seem that she had good reason for her remarks.

A combined Somerville-L.M.H. debating society flourished, and so, to a lesser degree, did a Shakespeare reading society and a 'Sharp Practice' group, whose members were required to speak extempore for five minutes on any subject put before them. Curiously enough, students were allowed to attend political meetings, though of course with a chaperon. Elizabeth Lea (afterwards Mrs Joseph Wright) remembered listening to Home Rule speeches in the Town Hall when 'Lord Ripon uttered much butter', and attending a 'strike meeting' at the Clarendon Rooms, where Ben Tillett was the chief speaker. She also mentions 'the Russian Nihilist meeting to which nearly everybody went,' but, tantalizingly, records no details. The ban on hockey was soon lifted, much to Elizabeth Wordsworth's satisfaction, who believed that this prohibition had been injurious to the general health of the students. The game was taken up again with great enthusiasm; according to Barbara Bradby, herself a keen player and a member of the L.M.H. team, 'hockey loomed large in our lives and conversation.'

The barrier between men and women remained all but insuperable. At her first interview with her daughter's Principal, Elizabeth Lea's mother chanced to mention that her two sons had been up at Oxford but had now gone down. 'What a blessing!' was the comment, uttered with unmistakable relief. Janet Hogarth's brother had offered to coach her if she could come to him in his rooms at Magdalen:

He was prepared to take me alone, but how about getting me in and out of College? It was finally decided that, as a great exception, not on any account to create a precedent, I might go, provided I approached the College by way of Mesopotamia, and was met by him at the private Fellows' Gate, and let out again the same way.

It is pleasant to know that a particularly lucky or determined young woman occasionally succeeded in surmounting these barriers. Elizabeth Lea was escorted back from a dinner-party by a young Captain Burrows, 'all moustaches and eyes', on the plea that he had to fetch his sister home from the Hall. Two of her friends actually succeeded in getting engaged, one of them being proposed to on the roof of the Radcliffe Camera, the other in Holywell churchyard.

On the whole, however, the students behaved with remarkable discretion. 'I came back to the usual household of girls,' Elizabeth Wordsworth wrote on 7 February 1892. 'They strike me when I see them again as very pretty, taking one with another, but it is a comfort they are not up to as much mischief as they might be.' She herself was never one to enforce the strict letter of the law. A set of House Rules drawn up in 1891 explicitly states, 'It is not considered desirable for students to go to dances; and to this rule there is absolutely no exception.' ('Commem' did not fall under this ban since it occurred out of term-time.) In fact, exceptions were frequent, the Principal's incurably romantic nature making it impossible for her to meet an eager request with a hard-hearted refusal—'She was *so* anxious to go and I was not sure that it might not be *the* dance.' No one was more pleased than Elizabeth if an engagement followed one of these officially illegal outings.

Girls going to dinner-parties usually hired a bath-chair which cost less than a cab and obviated the necessity to take a chaperon, presumably because two could return from dinner in a cab but only one in a bath-chair. Even if a determined young man walked beside the chair the aged chairman would make a third and lend an air of respectability. With misplaced kindness Bertha Johnson made a point of giving 'student dinners' at which Somerville and L.M.H. girls could meet one another. These entertainments were voted a horrid bore; no one wanted to go out to dinner simply to meet other women students. On Sunday evenings no outside visiting was allowed and even late church-going was forbidden. Everyone had to be present at the evening meal which on that day only was dinner and not supper, complete with such luxuries as chicken and coffee. Chapel followed with an address by Elizabeth who would afterwards invite a few girls to her room for conversation and reading aloud. To the students any contact with their Principal was both a stimulus and a delight. 'Miss Wordsworth herself was most truly the centre of life in the Hall,' said Edith Langridge; 'I don't think there can ever have been anyone of whom it was more true that to know her was a liberal education, not only intellectually but for all living.' As another student from those early days was to write years later, expressing herself with the simplicity of old age, 'Miss Wordsworth inspired us both mentally and spiritually, and we were very happy.'

Chapter 8

Degrees and Development

Two issues occupied Elizabeth Wordsworth's time and attention during the early days of the 1890s; the first was the granting of the B.A. degree to women, and the second was the future development of L.M.H. Her attitude towards these questions might be described as temporizing and inconsistent, or, more kindly, as an example of her willingness to bow to the logic of events.

The degree question was complicated by the fact that on this issue the supporters of the women's cause at Oxford were hopelessly divided among themselves. The large majority, who favoured a request to the University for the granting of the B.A. degree, were opposed by a small but powerful and very vocal minority who maintained that the time had not come for such a request. Degrees were not as yet given in Modern Languages or English, two subjects particularly popular with women students. The most serious stumbling-block, however, was the examination in Latin and Greek which formed an essential part of the full B.A. course. The existing system of girls' education made no adequate provision for the teaching of classical languages; if faced with compulsory Latin and Greek women would find themselves at a great disadvantage. Their needs and abilities, it was argued, were better met by the more flexible system already in existence which allowed women to proceed to Finals without taking an intermediate examination in Latin and Greek, or, if an intermediate examination were in fact taken, to offer modern languages as an alternative. The chief supporters of this point of view were Bertha Johnson and her husband. As well as acting as secretary to the L.M.H. Committee Bertha Johnson had been for years secretary to the A.E.W. In 1894, on her appointment as Head of the Home Students, she relinquished the post of secretary in favour of Annie Rogers, a keen advocate of the move for degrees, but she remained a member of the A.E.W. Council and a power to be reckoned with on that body.

Joining with the Johnsons in opposition to the request for the B.A. degree was a new friend of Elizabeth Wordsworth, Miss Soulsby, headmistress of Oxford High School and from 1888 a member of the L.M.H. Council. Lucy Soulsby was a remarkable woman. She held very definite and somewhat idiosyncratic views on the subject of girls' education, and on leaving the High School she founded a once-famous private school where she put these ideas into practice with considerable success. Though it may appear strange to modern minds, her scheme of education seems to have been admirably adapted to the needs of those girls of the leisured classes for whom it was specifically designed. (Incidentally, in preparation for their leisured lives Miss Soulsby insisted that the girls' weekly time-table should include at least twelve hours of free time.) Her pupils were devoted to her and left school convinced of the value of what they had learnt from her there. They took no examinations and few or none of them thought to go to the University.

During her time at Oxford High School Lucy Soulsby met and made friends with Elizabeth Wordsworth. They went on holidays together; and a warm affection sprang up between them which was to last until the end of Elizabeth's long life. The two women shared a deep religious faith and a wide-ranging intellectual curiosity, although intellectually Elizabeth was the superior both in ability and attainment. 'Yesterday I had a nice long gossip with Miss Soulsby, which is always refreshing,' she wrote on 3 November 1893. 'I call it a gossip but we talked in the most improving way of the coming democracy and how far the precepts of political economy could be reconciled with those of the Sermon on the Mount— and then, in direct contravention of all our principles I went to a sale of dolls!'

Almost alone among headmistresses Lucy Soulsby strongly opposed the petition for the B.A. degree. On this issue Elizabeth Wordsworth found herself in a cleft stick. That women should be allowed to write B.A. after their names seemed to her a matter of little or no importance; the essential point was that women should be given the opportunity to do the necessary work for that degree and to sit the necessary examination. 'If women did the work that was the great thing,' she was to remark; 'sooner or later they would get the credit for it.' The degree was no more than a token of achievement, not the achievement itself; hence the difference between her attitude in 1884 when the point at issue was the opening of examinations to women and now, ten years later, when the cry was for the granting of the B.A. degree. How could she take sides against her personal friend Lucy Soulsby, and Arthur and Bertha Johnson, two of her most faithful helpers at L.M.H. in support of a cause for which she felt so little enthusiasm?

Lack of enthusiasm, however, is by no means the same thing as open opposition. She was not opposed to the granting of degrees for women, and being herself a self-taught classical scholar, she did not regard compulsory Latin and Greek as a hopeless stumbling-block. The majority in favour of the request for the degree was a large one; it would be a mistake for L.M.H. to fall out of step with the A.E.W. and with the other women's Halls. If she were obliged to come down on one side or the other she would be forced to declare herself in favour of petitioning for the granting of the degree. She would have liked to keep clear of the whole affair; but for a person in her position neutrality was an impossible policy.

On 15 December 1894 the Council of the A.E.W. were to debate a resolution 'that the University be asked to admit qualified women students to the B.A., and that a committee be formed to consider the best steps to be taken in the matter.' On the day before this important meeting Elizabeth, who was of course a member of the A.E.W. Council, sent an urgent letter to Bertha Johnson stating her own rather equivocal position:

> I shall be entirely guided on the expediency just now of opening the Degree question by the opinions of the majority of members of the University at our Council. They must know best. The points in my mind are
>
> 1) Certainly let us have the B.A. whenever we can get it.
> 2) We *must* have a certificate for (what at present is the majority) those who are not up to B.A. standard.
> 3) I don't think much of residence (nor do I find head-mistresses do) except at a Hall, and therefore think each Hall may as well keep its own Register till we get full University recognition.
> 4) My chief reason for wanting to get the B.A. settled is that we may have some system to put before headmistresses and intending students.

At the A.E.W. Council meeting the resolution was passed by a large majority. It was also decided that the A.E.W. should keep a register of all women students taking a degree course, and that the Councils of the women's Halls should be asked for their opinion on the degree question. The matter was to be discussed at a meeting of the L.M.H. Council to be held on 14 March. On that date Elizabeth Wordsworth was too unwell to attend. There is no suggestion that her illness was not a genuine one, but it was certainly most convenient. The last thing she wished to do was to express an opinion or cast a vote on the B.A. question; yet, had she attended the meeting, as Principal she would have found it all but impossible to abstain from speaking and voting. Since she could not be present she sent a letter expressing her opinion on another matter on the agenda but making no mention at all of the B.A. By a small majority a motion was passed stating 'that the L.M.H. Council was not in favour of asking the University to give the B.A. Degree to women nor are they in favour of an equivalent Diploma.' The Council thus put themselves in opposition to the Councils of Somerville and St Hugh's, both of which decided in favour of the request for the B.A.

After receiving the views of the various Halls the A.E.W. called a meeting of its full membership for 5 May 1895 to consider the resolution 'that it is desirable that women students who have complied with the statutory regulations as regards residence and examinations be admitted to the B.A. degree.' Eleanor Lodge's brother Richard Lodge tabled an amendment proposing that in addition to granting the degree to those who completed the full B.A. course the University should be asked to give a diploma to those completing a three year alternative course including a Finals examination. By thus providing a way round the obstacle of compulsory Latin and Greek and giving some recognition to students taking Modern Languages and English, Richard Lodge hoped to appease Bertha Johnson and her followers and to unite all the supporters of the women's Halls behind a petition for the B.A. degree. The amendment, he argued, was a friendly not a hostile one, a tactical move rather than a red herring drawn across the path of the original resolution.

Seen in this light the amendment was one which Elizabeth Wordsworth could heartily support. It was, in fact, something of a 'life-saver' to her, giving her an opportunity to speak at the meeting, which she would certainly be expected to do, without expressing too definite an opinion on the main subject at issue. Her speech as seconder was a masterpiece of tact, deliberately vague and digressive, filled with humorous asides designed to turn away wrath, and frequently wandering away from the main issue down more amusing and less dangerous by-paths. Oxford, she declared, should 'show us what to do and pat us on the back when we have done it.' As a place of residence Oxford was 'cold, relaxing, and overcrowded'; but for the presence of the University any sensible woman would prefer to go to Brighton. Women came to Oxford simply and solely because they wanted a university education or the nearest possible equivalent; and those who sought a university education must abide by university regulations, which included the taking of compulsory examinations in Latin and Greek. Those who did this were entitled to recognition by the University. For the present, however, few women could or would abide by those regulations and take those examinations. Professor Lodge's amendment would provide them with a desirable alternative; education should never be allowed to become a bed of Procrustes. She herself had no objection to the proposals put before the meeting provided it was not suggested that women should be allowed to compete for university prizes. 'It would be very bad for girls, who are easily excited, to recite a Newdigate poem, for instance, in a crowded theatre; and, above all, it did not seem fair to founders and benefactors who certainly never intended such an application of their bequests.'

Both the amendment itself and the amended resolution were carried by large majorities. Not all Elizabeth Wordsworth's skill in taking evasive action had availed to obscure the difference in opinion between her and the majority of the L.M.H. Council; she had in fact come down on the side of the B.A. degree, though only by a hair's breadth. 'I should not feel compromised by anything which Miss Wordsworth may do or say,' the Vice-Chairman, W. A. Spooner, wrote to Bertha Johnson on 7 May; 'I am afraid we must concede to her the right we claim for ourselves of forming our own judgement.'

A petition begging for the admission of properly qualified women to the B.A. degree was duly laid before the Hebdomadal Council, a body which is perhaps best described as the Cabinet or Executive Council of the University. In their turn the opponents of the degree presented various counter petitions and memorials. All these documents were laid before a specially appointed committee, which called for evidence from various women prominent in the educational world including, of course, Elizabeth Wordsworth, asking them to answer two specific questions:

1. Whether the exclusion of women from the B.A. degree has been found to injure the professional prospects of women engaged in tuition.
2. Whether the admission of women to the B.A. degree would be likely injuriously to affect the education of women.

Though she appears to have given it verbally Elizabeth Wordsworth drew up her evidence in the form of a letter to the Vice-Chancellor:

In reply to your kind note I only know of one definite instance, viz. the City of London School for Girls, when all the Oxford candidates were 'ruled out' before the election began. But I know that there is a feeling current in a good many circles that the 'lay mind' can grasp nothing but the fact that such and such a person has done 'the same as an Oxford (or Cambridge) man', and that the refinements of the Class List are lost upon it. I cannot but feel that this does affect the popularity of Oxford as a place of education for women, in some degree.

With regard to your second question I may say 'I do not', though I should not wish the B.A. degree to convey (in the case of women) rights to University membership, competition for prizes, or in the future the M.A. degree, and should in many ways therefore prefer a diploma.

Elizabeth's disclaimer of any desire for future admission to the M.A. degree was a tactful move, making the telling point that she had no wish ever to see women admitted to full university membership. Bachelors of Arts have no share in university administration and legislation; they are not, strictly speaking, senior members of the University since only Masters of Arts may vote in Congregation and Convocation.[1]

After examining all the evidence the committee found itself so evenly divided that it could only propose that the Hebdomadal Council should submit some general resolutions to Congregation. Accordingly on 3 March 1896 Congregation met to debate the motion 'that it is desirable, subject to certain conditions, to admit to the degree of B.A. women who have kept residence at Oxford for twelve terms in a place of residence approved by the University and who have passed (under the same conditions as apply to undergraduates) all the examinations required for the degree of B.A.' Matters such as the granting of a diploma for an alternative course or the obligation on women to take an Honours and not a Pass degree were to be dealt with in subsidiary resolutions should the main resolution be passed. It was lost by 215 to 140 votes.

'The campaign for the degree failed, but it failed very peaceably,' wrote Eleanor Lodge. No heads had been broken, nor any friendships either. Elizabeth Wordsworth remained on the best of terms with Bertha Johnson and Lucy Soulsby;

1. Congregation is the assembly of M.A.s who are resident in Oxford and concerned with university teaching and administration; Convocation is the assembly of all M.A.s, called together on special occasions.

and the L.M.H. Council, which had been split in half on the
degree issue, united again very amicably to press forward with
schemes for the enlargement of the Hall.

The seven years from 1889 to 1896 saw L.M.H. develop from
a family party into a formally constituted college. It might be
supposed that Elizabeth Wordsworth would oppose this
change with all her energy. She had always believed profoundly
in the importance of the personal touch, and she had again and
again reiterated her belief that if the Principal were to know
and care for each girl individually the Hall must not contain
more than twenty-five students. Even if she could be brought
to accept the necessity for enlargement she would be expected
to do so with resignation rather than with enthusiasm. In point
of fact, however, she was in the forefront of the drive for more
buildings to accommodate more students; throwing financial
caution to the winds, she defied the doubting and spurred on
the laggardly members of Council.

In this matter, as in so many others, she showed a splendid
if slightly disconcerting inconsistency. Her attitude was,
however, less inconsistent than realistic. One of her more
notable characteristics had always been her ability to accept a
situation as she found it and to make the very best of a *fait
accompli*. L.M.H. had grown beyond the limit that she herself
considered desirable; it was clear that this growth in numbers
would continue. She might not approve of the fact that the
Hall now contained nearly forty students; but there they were,
crowded uncomfortably into the existing buildings, with
inadequate dining-hall, library and kitchen facilities for such
numbers. More and more girls were clamouring for admission;
her kind heart grieved over every deserving and desirable
entrant whom she was obliged to turn away because of the lack
of room. She had already helped in the foundation of two Halls;
to found a third was not practical politics. The only possible
course was to enlarge L.M.H. Though the prospect was not

pleasing to her she could see that it was inevitable, and therefore she accepted it with a good grace. Since she could not put
the clock back she would do everything in her power to support a policy of necessary expansion and to carry it through to
a successful conclusion. It was not in her nature to be lukewarm; she might have said with her mentor Miss Yonge, 'I
don't think I am much given to the sin of accidie.' If L.M.H.
were to have new buildings they must be fine buildings, and
they must be built immediately; she could not abide delay. The
competitive element too may have counted with her. Under
the efficient and businesslike Miss Maitland, who became
Principal in 1890, Somerville had rapidly increased its numbers
and embarked upon an ambitious building programme. Somerville was rising in popular estimation; L.M.H. must not fall
behind.

Faced with an unavoidable increase in numbers Elizabeth
Wordsworth set about revising her theories as to the nature of
a women's college. In her heart of hearts she still believed the
small family unit to be the ideal arrangement, but since it was
no longer a practical one she worked out what she considered
to be the best possible alternative, which she described in an
address given in October 1893 to a Church Congress at
Exeter, her subject being 'First Principles of Women's
Education'. An excellent speaker, Elizabeth was much in demand on such occasions. She enjoyed speaking and, on her
own admission, she never suffered beforehand from the agony
of nerves which afflicts many good speakers. This speech at
Exeter seems to have been one of her most successful efforts:

Directly I got face to face with the audience I felt instinctively
I must not read, so I threw my paper to the winds and made
all sorts of variations to it on the spur of the moment.
Everybody else had been so frightfully grave that I could
not resist a little nonsense which seemed to go down well,

but the climax was reached when, just as I was talking rather eagerly about the necessity for women being graceful and polished, I managed to kick over a horrid and insecurely fastened little brass rod with a red curtain which screened our boots (and a good thing too) from an admiring throng. This thing went bang down on the reporters' table and upset their gravity if not their ink-stands. The delight of the audience can be conceived.

The paper thus delivered was printed later as a pamphlet. It opens with the question, 'Whence are we to get our first principles?' Elizabeth's answer is uncompromising—'In an assembly of Christian women I feel no hesitation in saying, from the Book of Genesis as interpreted by the Church of Christ.' Somewhat surprisingly, she finds in Genesis an exaltation of the nature of woman, who 'is not meant to be merely the feminine of man in the sense in which a hen is the feminine of a cock.' She then turns to a discussion of womanliness, a quality which education is often believed to endanger, if not to destroy. Experience has shown this to be untrue—'we are beginning to see that it is quite possible for a girl to go for two or three years to Cambridge or Oxford, and yet be a womanly woman at the end of it.' Next she gives a description of a women's college, a picture of the new L.M.H. she was now planning. 'My own ideal is a college consisting of moderately-sized groups of students, each of them small enough to have somewhat of a homelike character; while, as in the constitution of the United States, there is a sense of belonging to a great federation, rather than one large building where the numbers preclude any such relations.' Perhaps it was a good thing she could not look into the future; the Hall has in fact developed along different lines.

In that year of 1893 the change which was coming over L.M.H. was symbolized by the transformation of the old

Committee into the more formal Council. In 1889 the Talbots had left Oxford for Leeds. Though he was prevailed upon to remain Chairman, Edward Talbot's absence from Oxford meant that the Vice-Chairman, W. A. Spooner, took the lead both in the day-to-day affairs of the Hall and in the planning of future policy. His famous spoonerisms—Edith Argles heard him lament that his wife should think it necessary to take so many bugs and rags with her when travelling—and his slightly eccentric appearance (one pair of spectacles on his nose, another pushed up to his forehead and a third perched on top of his head) sometimes obscured his remarkable ability both as a scholar and a man of business. For many years he was to be a valuable friend to L.M.H.

In 1889, the year of Talbot's departure, Elizabeth had prodded the Committee into taking a house in Norham Gardens to accommodate the overflow of students. 'We seem likely to have the house if *only* our committee will be a little spirited about it,' she wrote on 29 October of that year; 'but I don't know if I am Hotspur or some individuals, who shall be nameless, the "dish of skimmed milk" of which he complained.' Finally she bought the house herself with money out of her own pocket, and leased it to L.M.H. to be used as 'Wordsworth Hostel', providing rooms for a Vice-Principal and twelve students. Five years later another smaller hostel was opened in Crick Road to house a further seven students. These hostels, however, could only be temporary expedients. On 27 April 1893 the Council, thus named from now onwards, set up a sub-committee, consisting of Spooner, T. H. Warren (President of Magdalen), Charlotte Toynbee, Bertha Johnson and Elizabeth to consider schemes for permanent extensions to the Hall. This committee recommended that St John's College, the ground landlords, be asked to sell to the Hall all the land between Old Hall and the river and northwards as far as the University tennis courts, and that on the site so acquired a complex of new buildings be erected. After considerable negotiation St John's agreed to sell; Reginald Blomfield was chosen as archiect; and an Appeal Fund was opened to help to provide the necessary cash.

At this point in the proceedings Elizabeth Wordsworth went off at a tangent, putting forward a surprising proposal. She gave notice of a motion at the Council meeting on 30 November 'that St Hugh's Hall be amalgamated with L.M.H. under the title of St Hugh's Hostel.' What her reason was for making this suggestion we shall in all probability never know. There is no mention of the scheme in any of her letters nor, oddly enough, in the minutes of St Hugh's Council. We do not even know that she discussed the proposition with Annie Moberly, though surely she must have done so. The only record of it is to be found in the minutes of the Council of L.M.H. Maybe the idea was part of her vision of the new L.M.H. as a large, federated college, a form of institution which would allow of separate units such as St Hugh's maintaining differing standards of fees and accommodation.

The suggested amalgamation was referred to a subcommittee of Council, who reported on 7 June 1894. This committee were of the opinion that L.M.H. stood to gain financially by such a merger but to lose academically, since, in comparison with the better-off girls at L.M.H., a larger proportion of St Hugh's students took a Pass examination, being unable to afford the time and money for a three-year Honours course. It was possible also, the committee concluded, that should the merger take place, 'the tone and average standard would not be quite so select and high.' The motion for amalgamation was defeated by a vote in Council.

If by mischance Annie Moberly ever saw or heard tell of the subcommittee's report its last sentence must have given her cause to feel that insult had been added to injury. Personally, she stood to lose very much by the proposed amalgamation.

If the plan were to go through she would find herself not the Principal of a Hall but the Vice-Principal of a mere hostel, her independence gone and she herself, in the final instance, subject to control by Elizabeth Wordsworth. It is tempting to date her bitter feelings towards Elizabeth from this proposal of amalgamation; but in the absence of any evidence such an idea can be no more than speculative.

Meanwhile, a leaflet appealing for contributions to the L.M.H. building fund had been circulated in the form of a letter from the Principal. It is easy to misunderstand this but to do so is to show a lack of historical perspective. Elizabeth was writing to a generation who unashamedly admitted, and for the most part never thought to question, the existence of class differences. She was appealing for what was then a definitely Church institution, and addressing her appeal to Church people, hence her reference to the struggle for the retention of Church Schools:

> When the Church of England is fighting hard for leave to educate her own children of the poorer classes and the lower middle class, is it not a moment when she should strain every nerve to influence and train those who will be teachers and teachers of teachers? . . . The students at L.M.H. are for the most part daughters of professional men and men engaged in business—in other words, they belong to one of the most influential sections of our modern society. Is the Church to do less for them than she does for her humbler members?

In March 1894 a meeting was held in London in aid of the Appeal, one of the principal speakers being A. J. Balfour, who was reported as making the cautious statement that 'he was not sure that there was not more need for some colleges in the case of women having a distinctively religious character than in the case of men.' The fact that his sister Nora Sidgwick was at this time Principal of Newnham gave Balfour a personal concern in the higher education of women while he had a special interest in L.M.H. through his tie of friendship with the Lyttelton and Talbot families.

No very great sum of money was forthcoming in response to this Appeal. The more prudent members of Council were of the opinion that building should not be started until there was an adequate balance at the bank; Elizabeth, however, was as usual impatient of any delay. At the March meeting, from which she absented herself on the plea of illness, a letter from her was read out urging that a subcommittee be appointed to confer with Blomfield 'and get plans proposed at all events.' Accordingly Blomfield drew up plans which looked far into the future of the Hall. They included not only the block of students' rooms which was all that it was proposed to build immediately, but a more elaborate and ornamental central block containing library, dining-hall and kitchen premises, and beyond that again another block of rooms to be built when and if required. The whole scheme, when completed, would provide accommodation for between seventy and eighty students. The Hall thus planned was the realization of Elizabeth's idea of a federated college, the students to unite in sharing such facilities as library and dining-hall but to live in separate blocks of not more than twenty to twenty-five rooms, each block under the supervision of a Vice-Principal or resident tutor. Various friends of L.M.H. came forward with offers of loans at reduced rates of interest, Elizabeth herself offering a loan of £1,000 on condition that building should be started not later than 1 June 1895. Though this condition was not accepted she was still determined that building must go forward speedily, and at the Council meeting in June she seconded a motion put by A. L. Smith, afterwards Master of Balliol, that work should be begun that autumn on the first block of students' rooms. In consequence, Wordsworth Building, suitably named after the Principal who had been so urgent to see it planned and erected, was ready for occupation by the beginning of the Michaelmas term of 1896.

The official opening on 15 October was overshadowed by the sudden death of Archbishop Benson four days previously. Because she must of necessity attend the opening functions at L.M.H., Elizabeth was unable to be present at his funeral at Canterbury Cathedral. 'It is all very strange, the contrast of our doings here with the great ceremonial there,' she wrote to Dora. She was, however, much pleased by the references to the Archbishop in the speeches made by Francis Paget, Dean of Christ Church, and by Edward Talbot, now Bishop of Rochester. In her own comment to Dora on the subject of Edward Benson's death she quoted, as so often, from her great-uncle's poetry, 'One *cannot* believe that all that mighty heart is lying still—one feels that energy is turned to praise, and perhaps intercession.' Elizabeth's sister, Priscilla Steedman, who was present at the opening party, reported that 'the Vice-Chancellor made a nice little speech in which he said "to know Miss Wordsworth is in itself a liberal education." ' In her own speech Elizabeth praised the staff of L.M.H., spoke of the Archbishop's death, and ended with the phrase from the ninetieth psalm which was always one of her favourite biblical quotations, 'Prosper thou the works of our hands upon us, O prosper thou our handiwork.'

Percy and Priscilla Steedman had now left Yorkshire and taken a house in north Oxford. Their presence was some compensation to Elizabeth for the departure of John and Esther to Salisbury. She still saw much of these dearest of all her relations. In 1892 she had travelled in Ireland with John, attending official functions at Trinity College and Vice-Regal Lodge, sight-seeing at Glendalough, Cashel, and Killarney, and staying as a guest in some of the great Irish country houses. Esther was now too much of an invalid to be able to accompany her husband on such occasions; and her increasing ill-health cast a gloom over the whole family. In August 1893 Elizabeth and Susan went on holiday to Malvern, 'very quiet, which is a rest in itself, only one cannot help one's thoughts being sad ones. Still it is as well to have a quiet time in which to look the future in the face, not only the immediate future, but that far greater and vaster future which is to the other as the sky full of stars is to the pathos and beauty of a sunset.'

In no extant letter does Elizabeth make any mention of Esther's death, which occurred in October 1894, but a year later she wrote a poem to the memory of that beloved sister-in-law, 'O loved, O heart of hearts, O friend of friends!'

Love breathes around thy haunts, still wears thy form
Speaks in thy tones, and gazes through thy eyes;
Thou art not wholly gone—our heart is warm
With love that calls us onward as it flies,
And stops, and beckons, and looks back once more,
And smiles, and lingers, hovering, at the door.

Chapter 9

Lady Margaret Hall in the Nineties

EIGHTEEN NINETY-SIX, the year of the opening of Wordsworth Building, also saw the beginning of a new activity which
was to be of considerable importance in the life of the Hall.
Elizabeth Wordsworth had always encouraged the students to
undertake practical work to help 'the poor'. Gradually these
efforts progressed from tearing up paper for stuffing pillows to
organized social work in a residential settlement in a slum area.
After the pillow stuffing came a plan to invite Oxford shop-
girls to spend an evening a week at the Hall, a form of entertainment which neither hosts nor guests found very enjoyable.
This was superseded by Sunday hymn-singing in the Infirmary
wards, and by the formation of a working-party whose
members spent most of their time making flannel petticoats.
In the eighties various women's colleges banded together to
found a Women's University Settlement in Southwark. Among
old L.M.H. students Edith Argles and Nellie Benson especially
interested themselves in the work of this settlement. From this
experiment grew a wish to have 'a settlement of our very own',
a vision which took shape and form at a meeting held during
the 1896 gaudy. Settlements were a form of social work very
much in the public eye at this period. The first to be founded
was Toynbee Hall in Whitechapel, opened in 1884 and named
after Charlotte Toynbee's husband, a pioneer of social work and
studies. Its success led to the founding of many other settlements connected with schools, colleges or universities, the

idea behind them all being the wish to give to better-off young
people the chance to see 'how the other half lives'. Naturally
the emphasis was on youth work, clubs, Invalid Children's
Aid, country holidays for slum children, and similar activities.
Many of these settlements had a religious basis; the L.M.H.
Settlement in Lambeth, opened at Easter 1897, was from the
first connected with the work of the Church in that district.
Though she was deeply interested in this venture Elizabeth
Wordsworth wisely took no part either in the running of the
Settlement or in the direction of its policy. Its rules, however,
were of her own devising. There were only two of them—the
house must be kept looking pretty and inviting, and all workers
and students living there must have a weekly 'day off'. Edith
Langridge was chosen as the Settlement's first warden; of her
Elizabeth Wordsworth wrote, 'the House at 129 Kennington
Road, so tastefully and suitably furnished, bore as unmistak-
ably the impress of her practical talent as the work and character
of the Settlement did of the spiritual life which she fostered and
stimulated.'

'The average of work has been good and the tone of life within
the Hall could hardly have been better'—so the Annual Report
for 1897–8 described the state of affairs at L.M.H. under the
new order. But, admirable though the 'tone' might be, it was
not quite the same tone as of old. L.M.H. was now divided into
two separate units, Old Hall where the Principal had her rooms
and, across a stretch of lawn, Wordsworth Building, housing
twenty-three students under the supervision of Miss Sellars
and Eleanor Lodge. Although there was a system of inter-
change at dinner the students from the two blocks did not meet
regularly at meals, each block having its own dining-room.
Quite different species of people were sometimes thought to
inhabit the two buildings. A dweller in Old Hall wrote of 'an
alarming, hard efficiency about Wordsworth Building people,

a something which I have since learnt to associate with Cambridge,' and remembered with affection 'the gracious vagueness
which clung to Old Hall and refused to leave it when the
college expanded.' Not all old students had memories of so
distinct a difference; others stressed the fact that to live in
different buildings was no bar to friendship. Nevertheless, the
inhabitants of Old Hall were always to remain a race a little
apart. Elizabeth Wordsworth was so closely connected with
Old Hall that the building became, as it were, permeated by
her personality. Even in the 1920s and 1930s a certain *cachet*
attached to the possession of a room there to the astonishment
of those students who regarded 'gracious vagueness' as no
compensation for discomfort and inconvenience.

The use of Christian names regardless of seniority was still
universal among the students, but this habit, so natural in a
small family group, now seemed slightly forced and difficult.
It would, however, be a great mistake to suppose that the
atmosphere at L.M.H. had suddenly become stiff and formal.
An old student, who was up as late as 1908, recorded her impression of 'a certain delightful casualness', and even remembered 'the front door standing hospitably open at 2 a.m.' A
newcomer, confronted by a formidable list of rules, soon
discovered that many of them were obsolete. One much resented regulation however, remained strictly in force; though lights
were no longer turned out at 11 p.m. all students had to be in
their own rooms by 10.30 p.m.

Chaperonage rules had been slightly relaxed; groups of
girls might go unchaperoned to lectures and classes, but one
girl going on her own must be accompanied by a chaperon.
The actual working of these rules was peculiar; Eglantyne Jebb,
in later life well-known as the founder of the Save the Children
Fund, explained how they were applied in her own case:

I am to coach with Mr Hutton by myself but I have just been

made to write and convey to him that he must alter his hours because someone must be *lecturing next door* at the same time in order to chaperone me! I should have thought that if it was sufficient to be next door it would be sufficient if they came next day.

Some of the more advanced spirits may have felt that the intellectual life of L.M.H. was not sufficiently stimulating, and that the authorities sought to confine thought and speculation within narrow and conventional limits; the majority, however, were quite content to leave daring or unorthodox notions to the more emancipated thinkers of Somerville. In spite of the Principal's tacit disapproval the Suffragette movement was beginning to gain a little ground at the Hall, thanks perhaps to the presence of Kathleen Courtney (1897–1900), Maud Royden (1896–1899) and Ida O'Malley (1893–1896), who were all to become prominent figures in that movement. Where academic work was concerned the standard at L.M.H. remained high. In 1898 Eleanor Lodge's appointment as History Tutor marked the beginning of the system of residential women tutors. For the most part, however, girls continued to be tutored by dons from the men's colleges. This privilege of being taught by some of the most notable Oxford scholars was one which the students themselves greatly valued and something which Elizabeth Wordsworth had always deliberately sought for them.

The increased formality of Council proceedings, and the formation of subcommittees dealing with such matters as the library or finance, were paralleled by the creation of a Students' Committee and the election of a Senior Student, a position previously held automatically by the eldest member of the third year. In this changed atmosphere the relationship between Principal and students inevitably became less personal. The reminiscences of earlier generations are filled with memories of Elizabeth Wordsworth, her witticisms, her opinions, her all-pervasive influence. Accounts of life at L.M.H. between 1896 and 1900 show no such preoccupation with the Principal's sayings and doings; Barbara Gwyer, afterwards Principal of St Hugh's, goes so far as to write, 'In 1900, when I entered L.M.H., Miss Wordsworth was already to a Fresher a more shadowy figure than, for instance, Miss Pearson.'

Elizabeth Wordsworth's influence had of course by no means vanished. To a definite, if diminished, degree it still pervaded the Hall; and certain pupils felt it as a most powerful force. One of them was Eglantyne Jebb. 'I have taken to wandering out into the Parks in the middle of the morning in order to think,' she wrote on 11 November 1898. 'Miss Wordsworth says she does not think; the thoughts come into her head all of a sudden. That is what it is to have genius. When one rakes by main force one's thoughts together from different corners of one's brain, by reasoning, deducing and questioning, the nail does not get hit on the head with such a sharp, concise tap.'

Opportunities for personal contact with the Principal were still frequent. Eglantyne describes the conversation on one such occasion:

Yesterday I had a walk with Miss Wordsworth. I got her to give me ideas for my next essay (on tendencies in modern thought which may be traced to Hobbes). From this she went into a disquisition on modern life in general. We came back in the rain (only my umbrella between us, and that broke as soon as I opened it!) she talking, I listening as usual with intense interest. She dilated, as I think she has some-times done at Bible Class, on selfishness as being the most prominent failing of the present generation, and she traced it partly to the growth of scepticism as regards a future life. I had never before seen the force of 'Let us eat and drink for tomorrow we die' as applied to contemporary history.

Elizabeth Wordsworth continued her practice of taking a student with her when she went on a round of afternoon calls, usually timing the performance of this social duty to coincide with some important event such as a meeting or a concert which all the ladies of Oxford might be expected to attend. On one occasion, when Kathleen Courtney was her companion, the maid who opened the door informed them that her mistress was at home. 'If that is so,' said Elizabeth with a sweet smile, 'I will call again another day.'

She delighted in the company of undergraduates—'I wish people would always put me to sit next undergraduates at dinner-parties; I just *love* them!'—but a shy, unsophisticated youth could find her very alarming. 'Whose young man are you?' she inquired of an undergraduate encountered at an L.M.H. party, and to another she remarked, 'Take a chair, high, low, or broad, like the Church.' Her outspoken comments discouraged confidences; Kathleen Courtney remembered her as 'not the sort of person you would go to in trouble, perhaps because if it were your own fault she would say so.' Though she never intended to hurt, her habit of saying the first thing that came into her head could be painfully disconcerting, especially to the young. Kathleen recalled one conversation:

K.C. May I please go a bicycle-ride with my cousin at Trinity?
E.W. What is his name?
K.C. Furlong.
E.W. Oh, I knew some Furlongs—very rough people they were!

To a student who had done unexpectedly well in Schools she exclaimed, 'Oh, my dear, we expected G— to get a First, but *you*—!' Alarmingly frank herself, she expected and appreciated frankness from other people. She hated to find herself or anyone else described as 'wonderful', and of a fulsome obituary notice in *The Times* she remarked, 'They could not have said more if she had been the Virgin Mary.'

Bicycling was now very much in fashion. Elizabeth equipped herself with a tricycle, a machine more suited to her dignity as Principal, and, with the gardener at hand to help her in mounting and dismounting, practised riding it round the Hall garden until she was sufficiently proficient to venture out on the open road. She much enjoyed going rides with the students, who were considerably disconcerted by her habit of stopping suddenly to point out some object of interest or to deliver herself of a *bon mot*, oblivious of the fact that a rider on three wheels could sit still comfortably while riders on two inevitably fell off. A Sunday spent walking or bicycling in the country was permissible only if it included attendance at a village church—'I don't think that Sunday should be altogether a day of pleasure.' She deprecated Sunday bicycling for another and more unexpected reason—'You girls cannot wear frills and flounces bicycling and I like you to look pretty on Sundays.'

The annual performance of a play was another link between students and Principal, who, not content with writing both words and music, also helped to make the dresses and stage properties. 'Elizabeth made all the Dolly Varden costumes herself, also two dozen paper flowers, beside composing the tune for a lullaby,' Susan Wordsworth wrote of the 1898 performance, adding the comment, 'She looks as if the occupation had been in the nature of a tonic.'

Acting, bicycle rides, social calls, walks and conversation brought individuals into close and informal touch with Elizabeth Wordsworth. For the bulk of the students, however, her influence was now felt chiefly through the medium of chapel services and weekly bible class. To hear her read prayers in her beautiful voice was an unforgettable experience; Barbara Gwyer remembered 'the characteristic cadences of voice' and Gertrude Edwards wrote of 'that blazing spirit and the sound of her delicious voice.' Where her addresses were concerned some students felt that she herself was more remarkable than anything she had to say: 'her bible classes,' wrote C. Luard, 'impressed me more by the transparent fact that religion lay at the root of her life than by anything she actually taught.' But what Elizabeth actually taught was remarkable enough. Her addresses still survive in manuscript, carefully phrased, though untidily written and much corrected. Here at last is the real Elizabeth Wordsworth. Her letters, pamphlets, stories and poems all obscure rather than reveal her personality; but in these addresses she is dealing with something which is to her of such supreme importance that she forgets herself entirely and so forgets to conceal herself. Though she was anything but a commonplace character—'No good person,' said she, 'is ever commonplace'—all, or nearly all, her published writings are commonplace. These unpublished addresses are the very reverse; they are real, and as she herself declares in one of them, 'reality is the answer to the commonplace.'

The long years which she spent helping her father with his Commentary had given Elizabeth Wordsworth an exceptional knowledge of the Bible, and this is apparent on every page of these addresses. She quotes the original Greek and Hebrew, she gives alternative readings from the Septuagint, she discusses in great detail the possible meanings of obscure words or doubtful passages, and she is learned on such matters as dating and authorship. Her approach is by no means obscurantist; she can allow that parts of the Old Testament may be myth rather than history, though personally she herself is always inclined towards belief in a basis of historical fact. And her scholarship is not confined to the Bible itself; her quotations range from the novels of E. F. Benson to the works of St Gregory of Nyssa. On one occasion she goes so far as to cite a passage from a penitential psalm which 'seems to have been translated into a non-semitic language, the Akkadian, belong-

Elizabeth Wordsworth
as Principal, undated photograph

Bertha Johnson (wife of Arthur
Johnson, Fellow of All Souls),
Secretary of L.M.H. and to the
Association for the Education of
Women, 1878–94, afterwards
Head of the Home Students
Society

Elizabeth Wordsworth
April 4th 1909,
the year of her
retirement from L.M.H.

Elizabeth Wordsworth and her
'three Ediths', at the 1906
Gaudy. Left to right, Elizabeth
Wordsworth, Edith Argles,
Edith Langridge, in front,
Edith Pearson

ing to the descendants of Ham.' Some of the most interesting
passages are those in which she compares the Greek point of
view with the Jewish one, Prometheus and Odysseus with Job,
or the attitude of Homer and Sophocles towards the problem
of undeserved suffering with that of Ezekiel or the writer of
the book of Job. One essential difference between Greek and
Hebrew thought she sums up thus: 'While the philosophic
Greek worked his way up through his conception of the Good
to the idea of God, the Jew started with the idea of God and
worked his way down to the conception of Virtue or Wisdom.'

These addresses are as lively as they are learned. Again and
again she drives home her point with some memorable, witty,
or profound saying—'Bach himself would have been powerless
without someone to blow the bellows'; 'Do not let us be rude
because we are real'; 'Should we not be willing to take even an
unspoken hint from God?' She has the knack of condensing a
sermon into two or three short sentences:

> Why do we do even little things badly?
> Because we are not conversant with greatness.
> What is greatness? It is God.

Again and again she recurs to what she describes as 'the sound
counsel summed up in the one word "Wait"', a piece of advice
which comes strangely from someone so little given to hesitation or delay. She herself had waited thirty-eight years before
finding her proper vocation, and she urges the virtue of patience
upon other people, though she is quick to point out that 'it is a
mistaken idea of patience to think of her with folded hands
and listless eyes and downcast head.' Her ideal is the picture of
the child Samuel, 'an attitude of listening, of willingness, of
obedience, not of independent and self-willed action.' And
those who hold themselves in readiness for great works must
never despise ordinary duties, such as the care of some elderly

F

relation or commonplace neighbour—'If you want to hear God's voice you must listen for Eli's.' Everyone, she says, has to wait for God. 'He who has Eternity before Him has no need to be precipitate.' She warns us that 'there is such a thing as forcing the hand of Divine Providence,' and that this is a fault to which women are particularly prone. 'Do not at once try to do something,' she urges, 'wait and see what God does for you.' But waiting, we must not fall asleep, for we must be ready to seize our opportunity when it comes—'God does not flurry us, but He does not, or so it has often seemed to me, give us more than just time enough.'

Most notable of all these addresses is the one for the fifth Sunday in Lent, when one of the lessons for the day is the story of the Burning Bush. She takes as her text a saying attributed to Christ, unrecorded in the Bible but current among the early Christians, 'He that is near me is near fire.' Quotations can give no idea of the quality of this address; it is a whole thing, a burning bush, flaming and alive.

None of the other addresses touches these heights but some of them are remarkable and all of them are interesting. Elizabeth Wordsworth seems to have been especially attracted to the book of Job. She frequently repeated her series of addresses on this subject, re-writing them several times in order to adapt them to her varying audiences. 'The book of Job,' she says, 'is, using the word in its widest sense, a Protestant book.' Protestantism is a form of religion which 'has made man feel that he can never screen himself by any amount of mere religious observance from ultimate and immediate contact with his Maker.' So, in the book of Job, there are no sacred festivals, no priestly caste, no temple or tabernacle, no hint of any kind of religious organization; instead, 'the soul of man is brought face to face with God, it lies open and naked before him as the wide Arabian plains beneath the sky, in sunlight and starlight alike.'

Turning to the behaviour of Job's friends, she argues that they failed him because they were lacking in love—'they caricatured the divine image in man by being so hard and unloving'—and because they had not made proper use of either their brains or their imagination: 'true sympathy needs careful observation, some imaginative power, and a clear and just way of thinking; Job's friends had not the kind of dramatic imagination needed.' Again she stresses the need to wait; 'all the well-meant blunders of Job's friends came from a lack of *waiting.*' Here she is not playing quite fair; elsewhere she points out that these friends had sat on the ground for seven days and seven nights before venturing to speak, and that even then Job himself was the first to break silence. But the virtue of being able to wait was almost an obsession with Elizabeth; she would have agreed with the Swahili proverb, 'Hurry, hurry brings no blessing.'

She does not evade or slur over the unanswerable nature of the problems which lie at the heart of the book of Job—'we must own the fact, and not invent false solutions for the enigma.' In this honest acceptance of intellectual difficulties she sees one of the great glories of the Christian religion:

> Christianity is an absolutely fearless religion. It does not fear to face truth. It loves to face inquiry. It turns nothing off with a joke or a *Que sais-je?*—the saddest word that ever was spoken with a smiling face. It does not profess to understand or explain everything, it can give reverent recognition to many things that it cannot as yet interpret. It is this wonderful courage in Christianity that seems to me the great distinctive mark of its being the absolute religion.

Of quite different quality, but altogether admirable in their way, are the addresses on the Acts of the Apostles. Elizabeth herself recognizes the slightly pedestrian character of that book

—'the Acts of the Apostles, coming after the Gospels, have a somewhat prosaic effect; we feel, if I may say so, as if we had stepped out of a church into a street.' At one time she clearly intended to publish these addresses; the note-book containing them has a title-page pasted in together with a brief introduction dated May 1916:

> The following addresses on the Acts of the Apostles were given to the students of Lady Margaret Hall between the middle of October 1894 and the end of June 1896. Since then they have been carefully revised, and in many places re-written, and it is hoped may be found useful to some teachers and readers who want something more than a brief handbook and yet would find a larger work too erudite and difficult.

It is a great pity that this plan for publication came to nothing; even those whose school-days were darkened by the missionary journeys of St Paul could not fail to enjoy these lively addresses. Conveniently forgetting all about the 'practical lessons' of the proposed title Elizabeth Wordsworth paints a vivid picture of the world of the first century A.D. Her knowledge is immense, her enthusiasm unflagging. She quotes from Aesop, Horace, Seneca, Tacitus, Virgil, Ovid, and, at secondhand, Juvenal ('a satire so coarse as to be quite unreadable except in extracts'); she even cites what appear to be sailing directions from *The Mediterranean Pilot* to explain the exact locality of St Paul's shipwreck. She knows and tells us all about the private lives of such characters as Felix and Festus, Agrippa and Bernice; she describes how they went about the small actions of everyday life, such as the rubbing out of a wax tablet with the blunt end of a stylus. She compares Gallio, who 'cared for none of those things', to an 'Indian civil servant, an Oxford man of good family and thoroughly up-to-date culture' faced by a mob of Hindus or Mahammedans denouncing some harmless fanatic who had outraged their religious susceptibilities. Like Gallio, this type of Englishman is to be blamed not because he fails to recognize a saint when he sees one, but because he does not make sufficient effort to understand and sympathize with the religious ideas of the races he governs:

It would have been too much to have expected of Gallio that he should see in St Paul all that we see in him, but it was not too much to expect that he should take the trouble to enter into the feelings and understand the position of a race as numerous and as influential as the Jews.

Elizabeth Wordsworth's addresses are good to read, but they must have been far better to listen to when all the charm of voice and gesture and personality was added to their intrinsic interest. Perhaps C. Luard was right after all in her judgement; perhaps the speaker was fundamentally more impressive than the spoken word. 'Life is always running into infinity,' says Elizabeth in the address for Trinity Sunday; 'we ought to gravitate back to God as easily as we put foot to the ground.' All through these addresses her mind is turning towards infinity; effortlessly and inevitably she gravitates back to God.

Chapter 10

The New Century

In 1900 Elizabeth Wordsworth received a legacy which caused her to make a considerable change in her way of life. Some years previously she had tried to buy Gunfield, the house next door to Old Hall, for use as an extension to L.M.H. The owner, a Miss Jephson, refused to part with her home during her lifetime, but when she died in 1900 it was found that she had left Gunfield not to L.M.H. but personally to Elizabeth, who made it over to the Council, insisting that Miss Jephson had intended it for the benefit of the Hall. The Council decided to use Gunfield as a Principal's residence and leased it back to Elizabeth who, finding herself thus possessed of a large house and garden, decided to make her permanent home in Oxford.

The death of the old family nurse, Janet McCraw, made it easier for her to cut her connection with Lincoln. Before leaving the house in Pottergate she enjoyed a reunion there with old friends when Robert Hugh Benson, now an Anglican clergyman, preached in Lincoln cathedral. On Easter Day 1900 she wrote Priscilla Steedman an account of the occasion:

I had the pleasure of introducing Hugh Benson to the Bishop.[1] They looked very picturesque having their tea together in the window-seat, the Bishop in his purple cassock. It was a

1. Edward King, now a member of L.M.H. Council.

strange taking up of old memories, the boy fitfully so like (and yet very unlike) his father, Minnie her old self (with a difference), we just going to leave Pottergate and having her in this house for the first and last time, seeing Hugh in the pulpit his father had so often filled (he did *very well indeed*, I may say) and then in the evening going to the cemetery and seeing the new stone on Janet's grave, and the Leekes with their daffodil crosses and Susan with a wealth of daffodils and ivy, and behind all this peace, the thought of the war, and those poor men at Mafeking.

Like Queen Victoria, Elizabeth refused to admit to depression about the Boer War:

I don't feel so hopeless about the war as some people do. People like the Rector of Exeter and Mr Spooner make themselves almost ill over it but I can't get rid of the feeling that God has work for England yet and that all this is meant to chasten, not to crush us. Indeed, we may say that of all trouble, national and personal.

Although Elizabeth and Susan Wordsworth were now to break up their joint household and go their several ways they were still to spend frequent holidays together. In August 1900 they went on pious pilgrimage to Tintern Abbey to visit the scenes made famous by their great-uncle. Their experience there was very much more down-to-earth than his had been— 'we were caught in a pouring rain at Tintern but managed to console ourselves with tea.' The move to Gunfield followed, where Elizabeth established herself with two maids and a cook to look after her and the four students who were to have rooms in the house. Other students came over in relays to dinner, while she herself dined every week either in Old Hall or Wordsworth, and, of course, attended chapel, thus maintaining a personal connection both with students and staff. Nevertheless, the move separated her physically from the day-to-day life of the Hall and emphasized the change from those early days when Principal and students had lived together as a happy family party.

The Principal's move to Gunfield coincided with the twenty-first anniversary of the opening of the Hall. Over a hundred old students attended the coming-of-age gaudy held during the first week of October 1900. Priscilla Steedman wrote to Dora Leeke describing the service in chapel at which Edward Talbot preached a sermon 'with a very graceful and delicate allusion to Elizabeth's work at L.M.H.; no stranger could have grasped that it meant her, but every student must have felt that it was intended for her.' A series of luncheons and dinner-parties was followed by a big 'At Home' and a Settlement meeting. Priscilla described Elizabeth as happy and thankful, though tired and almost overwhelmed at the sight of so many old students and friends of L.M.H., 'all owning how much they are indebted to her.'

The Annual Report for 1900 surveyed the twenty-one years of the Hall's existence and found the retrospect a happy one:

On looking back for that length of time there are many positive blessings to be thankful for in the growth and prosperity of the Hall, its academic distinctions, and the useful work and satisfactory character of the students. But perhaps we are apt to forget the negative as well as the positive side of our blessings—the immunity from serious illness and accident, the fact that there has been not one single death or one painful or distressing incident in all those years of residence, that life has flowed on as brightly and as calmly as the waters of the Cherwell itself so close beneath our windows. It would be hardly too much to say that harmony has been one of the main characteristics of the academic life,

and a singular absence of friction and a general friendliness
and kindness of tone one of its best features.

Elizabeth Wordsworth herself looked back over those twenty-
one years with thankfulness tempered with nostalgia. 'It is nice
to think you keep up your old love of Oxford and the Hall,'
she wrote to Gertrude Edwards. 'I sometimes look back on
those palmy days when we were fewer in numbers and really
knew one another better, but I ought not to grumble, for we
have much to be thankful for both in the old state of things
and in the new one.' Gertrude Edwards had recently suffered
a series of bereavements, and out of her own experience of
sorrow Elizabeth wrote to comfort the younger woman—'I
am sure you must *unspeakably* miss some of those whom you
have had to part with in the last few years; still the number of
miles from home gets fewer at each succeeding milestone in
life, and when you come to be as old as I am you won't reckon
from your partings but think how rapidly you approach the
last milestone that precedes the meeting, please God.'

The death of Queen Victoria in January 1901 meant the end
of an era and a change in the appearance of many familiar
things in everyday use. Elizabeth Wordsworth was so moved
by the disappearance of the Queen's head from the postage
stamps that she wrote a poem on the subject, beginning,

> Farewell, dear face, which we have known
> Familiar as our mother's own.

These verses proved to be one of her most successful and
popular literary efforts. They were widely read both at home
and abroad; she was delighted when a friend told her of an
encounter with an Italian waiter who kept a copy in his pocket
to show to English visitors as proof of his devotion to Queen
Victoria.

In the month of the Queen's death Elizabeth met two old
acquaintances from the pioneering days of women's education.
Robert Bridges took a short lease of a furnished house near the
Hall, and Mrs Humphry Ward visited Oxford to give a series
of lectures which Elizabeth criticized as being good in matter
but inadequate in delivery. 'I can't say I care about Mrs
Humphry Ward as a writer,' she was once heard to remark. 'I
like her as a woman. She doesn't write full of her delight in
people as Jane Austen does. I say, out of the abundance of the
note-book Mrs Ward—!' A few months later she was delighted
to be asked out to dinner to meet Arthur Balfour and John
Morley, but to her great disappointment she had no chance of
real conversation with either of these celebrities—'Mr B. (a
handsome likeness of his caricatures) was just at that aggra-
vating distance, two places off, where one could occasionally
catch half-sentences in his very clear and musical voice.' She
was much taken by John Morley's 'thoughtful, intellectual,
sincere face', little as she approved of his Liberal views—'I
dare say I shouldn't like Mr Morley's opinions, but his face
somehow impressed me more than A.J.B.'s; it has more force
and feeling in it perhaps.'

At Oxford dinner-parties Elizabeth Wordsworth's entry
into the room still aroused a little stir of pleasurable expectation. She was a brilliant talker, but, unlike many good talkers,
she could be relied upon not to raise awkward questions though
she could not always refrain from correcting an obvious error.
Nothing annoyed her more than an inaccurate quotation. On
one occasion she was taken in to dinner by the Beit Professor
of History. 'You know, my dear,' she confided to the friend
who was sharing her four-wheeler for the homeward journey
after this party, 'we began talking about the Sermon on the
Mount, and he twice quoted "Consider the lilies of the *valley*".
It's quite extraordinary to me. He can't be really educated—I
suppose he's some London man—but it shows such a *sloppy*

mind.' 'Well, one must not be uncharitable,' she concluded magnanimously; 'perhaps his bark is worse than his Beit.' At another dinner-party the wife of the philosopher William James attempted a definition of pragmatism—'I think it means, "By their *works* you shall know them".' She paused, and then repeated with obvious satisfaction, 'Yes, yes, by their *works* ...' Elizabeth could contain herself no longer: in a clear ringing voice she exclaimed, 'Fruits!'

With increasing years Elizabeth Wordsworth's idiosyncrasies became more rather than less pronounced. She made no attempt to alter her business method, or lack of method, to suit the growing volume and complication of Hall affairs. Even the devoted Eleanor Lodge was provoked into admitting that the Principal could sometimes be very embarrassing to work with; cheques would be used as book-markers, important correspondence kept in an old shoe-box, lost scholarship papers discovered under her bed. Boredom was something she could not and would not tolerate. She would walk out of a committee or a Council meeting if the proceedings threatened to become tedious, returning when a more interesting subject came up for discussion, and at L.M.H. garden-parties, if she felt that her visitors were dallying too long, she would have the dinner-bell rung early in order to speed the parting guests.

Her horror of boredom and her liking for good conversation made her particularly appreciative of a remarkable young woman who in 1904 joined the staff of L.M.H. as English tutor. Grace Hadow was an excellent talker who could never become a bore, and very soon she had won Elizabeth's confidence. Other members of staff found Grace Hadow a good person to use as go-between if they wished to get the Principal's approval for some innovation, or to enlist her sympathy over difficulties arising from a clash of twentieth-century notions with the older traditions of the Hall. Elizabeth Wordsworth was no die-hard. Her own outlook, however, was not even that of the nineties; she remained essentially a mid-Victorian. The Hall was so entirely her creation and reflected her personality so faithfully that it was in danger of appearing old-fashioned. How was L.M.H. to keep itself up-to-date and abreast of modern ideas, and yet preserve its own special and subtle ethos, to use a good Tractarian expression? The problem was solved by turning the difficulty into a jest. Were the inhabitants of L.M.H. labelled 'ladylike'? Very well then, ladylike they would be, and make a good joke of it; nobody must suppose that they took themselves too seriously. Solemnity was foreign to Elizabeth Wordsworth's nature and therefore foreign to L.M.H., which was always a place where laughter bubbled up easily. According to Helena Deneke, who knew the Hall well at this period of its history, 'it would have been difficult to have escaped being happy there.'

Elizabeth's concern and affection for her own family never slackened. John Wordsworth had married again in 1896, his bride being Mary Anne Frances Williams. In the summer of 1902 Elizabeth and Susan spent a holiday with him in Switzerland. His wife did not accompany them; there were already two babies in the nursery at Salisbury and a third was expected. The two sons of Elizabeth's other brother Christopher were both up at Cambridge where in 1904 she saw them take their degrees. 'Little did I think when I stayed at Trinity in the sixties that I was to re-visit it in the next century as the aunt of a "Wrangler",' she wrote to Dora, adding a remark which shows how little concerned she had been in those far-off days with the subject of women's education: 'I think I should have felt rather ill if anyone had told me that I should have a girl cousin in the Classical Tripos at Newnham which I suppose had hardly come into existence then.'

Not only had she a girl cousin at Newnham; much nearer home she had already had a niece at L.M.H. reading Greats and finally taking a First, much to her aunt's delight. Christopher Wordsworth's daughter Ruth had come up in 1896. As a shy school-girl she had been both embarrassed and hurt by the vagaries of an aunt who said and did odd things in public and whose criticisms were more candid than tactful. Now at Oxford she saw her eccentric relative as a revered and respected public figure, and found that the one-time critic had become an affectionate sympathizer, quick to praise, and ready, on occasion, to turn a blind eye to faults and failings. She learnt to relish the outspokenness which had previously been a cause of offence, and to enjoy the robust, at times almost ribald, humour which could be a stumbling-block to weaker spirits. There was no touch of irreverence in this uninhibited mixture of the sacred and the profane. 'She was not easily shocked,' Ruth wrote of her aunt, 'because her own sense of the unseen was coupled with a hilarious attraction to homely details which sometimes rather shocked her herself, and perhaps reminded her of the "Elizabeth's" that must have been said to her so often in childhood.' Ruth also discovered that her aunt would never carp at the young, though she might criticize them; her profound belief in a divine providence forbade her to indulge in cheap pessimism about the future of the world or the behaviour of the younger generation.

On leaving L.M.H. Ruth was to give great satisfaction to her aunt by going out to teach in Japan as a missionary. Teaching was one of the few professions in which women were not merely tolerated but welcomed because of the chronic shortage of women teachers. Winifred Peck described her contemporaries at L.M.H. as divided into 'those who meant to earn their living and those whom we described, not always aptly, I fear, as Home Sunbeams.' For nine girls out of ten earning a living could only mean teaching. Elizabeth Wordsworth had always resolutely refused to allow L.M.H. to be regarded as a reservoir of teachers—in her heart of hearts she cherished a secret sympathy for the Sunbeams—but she made an exception in favour of teaching in missions or Church schools, and she could see nothing odd in the conception of a women's college as primarily a training ground for Church workers. In a letter to *The Guardian* she stressed both difficulties and achievements in that direction and claimed that Church people had shown themselves as neither generous not grateful in their failure to support the higher education of women:

At Lady Margaret and at St Hugh's Halls we have had for the best of thirty years to make our way in the teeth of financial obstructions which might easily have been removed for the price of half-a-dozen motor-cars. Yet, in despite of this we have four Lady Margaret Hall students now engaged in missionary work in India, several more in South Africa, and others preparing to go out; while St Hugh's has also furnished its quota, one holding an important post in Japan. It is heartrending to us to have to refuse time after time applications for workers in the mission field, to say nothing of what is required for Home missions. We seem to be expected to make bricks without straw. We have met with very little support from Church people as a whole (though there are not a few honourable exceptions), we are cut off from many scholarships and endowments by the fact of our being denominational, and yet Church people seem to expect us to be ready to provide efficient helpers for good works at home and abroad at the shortest possible notice.

Elizabeth Wordsworth had always been deeply interested in religious education and aware of the inadequacy and inefficiency of existing methods of teaching. As far back as 1893 she had written to *The Guardian* pointing out the need for women teachers 'trained in such subjects as evidences, textual knowledge of Holy Scriptures (which in some cases might well include some knowledge of one or both of the original languages) and some acquaintance with the great Fathers and Anglican Divines.' Had the Church authorities taken her words to heart more might have been done to change an attitude typical of her own day and still all too prevalent some seventy years later—'we have never been taught to see how the very intellect and knowledge which our secular studies tend to develop has any part or lot in our religious life.'

'We want to catch the very ablest women of the rising generation,' Elizabeth Wordsworth wrote, 'and to "level up" their theological education to the standards reached in other subjects.' In 1893 the opening of the Honours School of Theology might have been taken as an encouragement to those who sought just such a 'levelling up'. The first woman to take a First in Theology was Ethel Romanes, an L.M.H. student who achieved this distinction in 1902. On going down from Oxford 'Fritz' Romanes, as she was always called, joined the Anglican community at Wantage, a decision not wholly approved by Elizabeth Wordsworth, who believed that nuns were inclined to give too little attention to the things of the intellect.

In her opinion, the first necessity in dealing with the problem of religious education was to teach the teachers. With that end in view she helped to found the Oxford Society for the Religious Instruction of Women Teachers in Secondary Schools, a body which organized holiday courses held in L.M.H. and planned 'to give students and young mistresses the stimulus of personal contact with university teachers.' These university teachers were for the most part theologians of very high standing, including such men as William Sanday, John Wordsworth, and Leighton Pullan.

Coming down from secondary to primary school level Elizabeth Wordsworth was rather surprisingly in favour of closer cooperation between the various denominations, arguing that 'much is gained in charity while nothing is sacrificed in principle by that strongest of all influences, personal contact, being habitual between us and our Nonconformist brethren.' She cited her own experience at Oxford as proof of this point:

> Having for nearly twenty years worked on a body by which university education is given equally to students (such as the majority at L.M.H.) who profess definite religious opinions and to others who do not, I can only say that there has been *absolutely no friction* on subjects connected with religion, and that I have never felt anything but satisfaction in working with colleagues of widely differing shades of religious opinion in matters which happily afford a common ground.

The body to which she refers is clearly the A.E.W.; at L.M.H. she could have had no experience of working with colleagues of widely differing shades of religious opinion since no one could be elected to Council who was not a member of the Church of England, and until 1921 a similar restriction applied to staff appointments.

The first decade of the twentieth century saw a real advance in the progress of women's education at Oxford, a step forward towards the ultimate goal of their admittance to full membership of the University. Lord Curzon, who was installed as Chancellor in 1907, proved himself to be the first holder of that office to give genuine support and encouragement to the women's cause. 'I have always meant to put forward Women's Degrees,' he wrote. 'The University can take it or reject it, but I shall certainly put it forward.' In 1909 he published *A Letter on Principles and Methods of University Reform*, a publication known as 'the Scarlet Letter' because of the colour of its binding. In this letter, which Elizabeth Wordsworth praised as 'lucid, interesting, and opportune', he strongly advocated among other proposed innovations the granting of degrees to women. In June of the same year the Hebdomadal Council passed a resolution stating that 'the Council is in favour of bringing before Congregation at an early date the question of admitting women to degrees upon the lines laid down in the Chancellor's memorandum.' There, for the moment, the matter was allowed to rest. The women's supporters feared to press the degree question further lest it should interfere with a proposal to set up a University Delegacy for Women which should include both men and women members under the presidency of the Vice-Chancellor. Such a Delegacy was in fact established in 1910 and continued to deal with matters affecting women students until the final granting of degrees took place ten years later.

The University had by this time come to accept, and on the whole to approve, the existence of women's colleges; it was clear that they were no passing experiment but a permanent feature of Oxford life. More and more girls were applying for admission; and, though the opening of Wordsworth Building had done something to ease the pressure, the accommodation at L.M.H. was still cramped and inadequate. Elizabeth Wordsworth was determined to press on as speedily as possible with the completion of Blomfield's designs for the enlargement of the Hall. Fortunately for L.M.H. she was not afflicted with Emily Davies's almost pathological passion for bricks and mortar, but she has nevertheless been described as 'a keen spender' who was not to be deterred by any pettifogging consideration of hard financial facts. In 1908 her insistence on the necessity to begin building immediately led to the resignation of three members of Council, among them the ex-Treasurer, R. F. Dale, who was convinced that in the existing state of the Hall's finances such a policy could only lead to disaster. Blithely disregarding this expert opinion, Elizabeth proposed on 13 June that building be started 'not later than 25 March 1909.' Her motion was carried; by the proposed date, work was in progress on the central block containing library,

dining-hall, kitchens and accommodation for the Principal.
As soon as this was completed work was to start on the second
block of students' rooms.

Determined though Elizabeth Wordsworth was to see the
new L.M.H. housed in dignified and adequate buildings, in her
heart of hearts she still preferred the old order. Perhaps she
had been the more enthusiastic about building because she
knew that she herself would never have to preside as Principal
over the enlarged Hall. It was becoming apparent that her very
personal and haphazard methods, which had so exactly suited
the spirit of L.M.H. in the eighties and nineties, were ill adapted
to the needs of a larger and more modern institution. In 1908
the change in the character of the Hall was symbolized by the
abandonment of the time-honoured custom of performing one
of the Principal's own plays, and the substitution of a production of Lyly's *Campaspe*, which was so carefully researched and
rehearsed as to win the distinction of a long and favourable
review in *The Times*. One of the chief promoters of this performance was Evelyn Jamison, an old student who had returned
to L.M.H. the previous year as Domestic Bursar and Principal's
Secretary. She was in charge of catering and domestic management and was responsible for the care of the students' health,
while to her secretarial work she added the duties of Hall
Librarian. For all this she was paid the princely salary of sixty
pounds a year. Though she admirably discharged these
comparatively commonplace tasks Evelyn Jamison's real gifts
lay elsewhere. In 1903 Somerville awarded her a travelling
Fellowship, which enabled her to spend four years at the
British School in Rome and to pursue that study of the art and
history of medieval Sicily and Southern Italy which was to
become her life's work. Back at L.M.H., first as History Tutor
and then as Vice-Principal, she inspired many generations of
pupils with at least a little of her zeal for perfection both in
accuracy of scholarship and in the composition of English

prose, finding time meanwhile to continue with the writing and research which were to bring her many academic honours and to make her name well-known among medieval historians.

'Jimmie' loved and served Elizabeth Wordsworth with a deep and perceptive devotion. Although not unembarrassed by the Principal's idiosyncrasies, she could see them as the reverse side of 'her supreme quality of the unexpected'. Other more precise and less appreciative members of the Senior Common Room did not suffer these things so gladly, finding themselves particularly annoyed by Elizabeth Wordsworth's total disregard for the letter of the law when it clashed with personal considerations. On one occasion, when she had given a student leave to stay away out of Oxford twice in one term— 'an excellent plan, she thought it'—Edith Pearson was provoked into the comment, 'the Principal of course does not know the rules.'

Elizabeth herself was finding less and less pleasure in the work in which she had once so much delighted. She could never reconcile herself to dealing with students in the mass rather than with girls as individuals, a necessity forced upon her by the increase in numbers. 'I am rather like an old piece blotting-paper; I cannot absorb so many new students,' she remarked to Gemma Bailey. Committee work she had always disliked and shamelessly dodged whenever possible; now it had become an almost intolerable burden. In September 1906 she wrote to Ruth Wordsworth complaining of 'those damp headachy, autumnal times when the three-and-twenty freshers lie heavily on my soul and committees embitter the afternoons.' With regret not unmixed with relief she realized that the time had come for retirement.

Her official letter of resignation was dated 8 October 1908 and addressed to Bertha Johnson as secretary of Council: 'Much as it costs me to take a step which my present age seems to render almost imperative yet my predominant feeling is one of great thankfulness for the health by which I have been enabled to remain at my post without (so far as I can remember) the break of a single term for nearly thirty years; and I am not less profoundly grateful for the kindness, forbearance and sympathy which I have received from the Council, tutors, and students during that time, especially, dear Mrs Johnson, from yourself, with whom I have been associated from the very beginning of the work.'

Her resignation was to take effect at the close of the academic year of 1908–09. When the news became public a flood of letters flowed in upon her, each one filled with regret, affection, and memories. 'I remember how most of the other authorities I have known were liked, at the best, as part of an institution,' wrote Winifred Peck, 'and how you were loved just as yourself.' Not one writer thought to mention Elizabeth Wordsworth's contribution to the cause of women's education but all stressed the extraordinary impact made on them by her personality—'You were the centre and mainspring of our life'; 'No one helped me as much as you did'; 'You are so entirely the centre and essence of L.M.H.'; 'There is no end to the wise things you have taught us often in ways as witty as wise.' The general feeling was summed up very justly by Francis Wylie, member of Council, brother, husband and father of three old L.M.H. students, and himself a man known all over the world for his work in connection with the Rhodes Trust: 'There is no shadow of doubt as to what has given the Hall its command over public confidence—it has been your presence at its head; nor as to what has given to the Hall itself its "tone"—that also has been your presence at its head.' He ended his letter by voicing the general feeling of gratitude 'for all you have done through the early critical times to give to the Hall a character and distinction it could hardly in any other way have obtained.'

The task of finding a successor to such a personality was obviously a difficult one. Out of ten candidates who applied for the post the final choice lay between Henrietta Jex-Blake, a member of a family well-known in academic circles and herself headmistress of a girls' school, Gertrude Edwards, now headmistress of a school in Bloemfontein, and a Miss Vernon-Harcourt, daughter of Augustus Vernon-Harcourt, a leading Oxford scientist. Henrietta Jex-Blake was elected by a majority of ten over five, a result disappointing to Elizabeth Wordsworth, who would have liked to have seen her own old student Gertrude Edwards as her successor. She was, however, prepared to give a hearty welcome to the chosen candidate, and on the very day of the election she sent a warm letter of congratulation to Henrietta Jex-Blake, inviting her to stay for a few days at Gunfield during the coming term. The new Principal was a shy woman, not gifted with her predecessor's ready wit; there were times when, to put it bluntly, Elizabeth Wordsworth could not resist the temptation to score off her. Relations between them, however, were always cordial if never close. Elizabeth particularly admired Henrietta Jex-Blake's taste in dress—'Not that I mean smartness, *that* is usually odious, but a ladylike suitability, that's what I call good dressing.' Interested though she was in clothes Elizabeth had neither the time nor the patience necessary to achieve such elegance for herself; 'My idea of Elysium,' she was once heard to remark, 'is a place where you can get nice clothes without having to take any trouble about them.'

Elizabeth Wordsworth had already decided to make her home in Oxford, and with that end in view she had bought a house in Rawlinson Road next door to Percy and Priscilla Steedman. Gifts came showering in upon her to help with the furnishing and adornment of her new home; past and present students of the Hall presented her with a pair of silver candlesticks as a personal gift and planned to panel the new dining-hall at L.M.H. as a permanent commemoration of her years as Principal.

On 25 June Elizabeth walked over to the Hall for 'my very, very last meal, and very last chapel.' (In point of fact she was to dine there frequently during the next twenty years and to attend chapel on numberless occasions.) She had never been one to indulge in vain regrets for the past and she did not grieve overmuch at the coming of the inevitable end. 'I am thankful to Nature for giving me a forward-looking disposition,' she wrote to Ruth Wordsworth on this day of farewells. 'Certainly I don't take at all after Lot's wife—not that I wish to compare dear old L.M.H. to Sodom.'

Chapter 11

Retirement

AFTER a pleasant holiday in Normandy Elizabeth Wordsworth returned to Oxford to settle into her new home. The
neighbourhood which she had chosen was not a romantic or
beautiful one; she herself described north Oxford as 'the very
baldest prose'. Number Twelve Rawlinson Road was neither a
comfortable nor a pretty house; but so long as she had room for
her many books and for the few pictures which she specially
valued she asked for nothing more, not even a comfortable
sofa or chair. A true Wordsworth, she looked for beauty out
of doors in the things of nature. Each returning spring brought
a renewal of delight and energy. 'If it weren't for her age and
my respect for her,' one old student wrote in 1911, 'I would
say that spring made her inclined to kick up her heels.'
The show of snowdrops and crocuses in her strip of suburban
garden gave her acute pleasure—'the crocuses in the garden are
a joy, almost a gospel.' She particularly loved her flowering
cherry-tree and would spend hours standing beneath it looking
up at the mass of blossom against the blue sky.

The discomfort of her house was not due to any lack of
domestic help. She was a person who had the art of attaching
servants to her and winning their loyal and devoted affection.
The chief prop of the Rawlinson Road household was Kate,
who had been cook at Gunfield for many years. Another maid
rejoiced in the name of Annie Jane Jones, 'in itself,' wrote her

mistress, 'a guarantee of respectability.' With an adequate staff
Elizabeth could entertain as much as she wished, giving small
dinner-parties for Oxford friends and welcoming old students
to lunch or tea. Every now and again she would take girls to
live with her in the house, supervising their studies and introducing them to the pleasures of Oxford life. Her first boarders
were two girls from South Africa. The prospect of their arrival
caused her some perturbation—'I only hope they won't be
too popular with Rhodes scholars and the youth of South
Africa generally; I feel as if my drawing-room were going to
turn into a haunt of colonial undergraduates.' In the event she
found the Miss Ramsbottoms such congenial guests that she
parted from them with real regret—'Such nice girls, and with
so much individuality, not at all like a pair of shoes, just repeti-
tions of the same pattern.' Later, two daughters of the famous
scientist, Sir Oliver Lodge, whose sister Eleanor was now
Vice-Principal of L.M.H., came to live with her for a while and
to be coached by her in Latin.

She particularly enjoyed any such chance to exercise her
gift for teaching, finding, as she told Gertrude Edwards, that
'teaching the old things to a new listener seems to make them
new to oneself.' As well as these occasional coachings she held
bible classes for young children, for school-girls and, later on,
for her own friends and contemporaries. The standard of
scholarship which she imposed on these classes was a fairly
high one. 'Today, for the first time in my life,' she wrote to
her brother Christopher on 16 November 1913, 'I have read a
few pages of Whiston's *Josephus* which has bided its time all
these years on a lower shelf in my drawing-room. Of course I
was only getting it up for a class.' At one time she organized
Browning readings for a group of German students, whose
mishandling of the English language caused her acute pain—
'It's all I can do to keep myself from rising and snatching the
book from their hands. But it shan't happen again. No, no! *I*

do all the reading now. Much more satisfactory, to me at any rate.'

Entertaining, teaching, writing magazine articles, occasionally lecturing or speaking, and, of course, reading omnivorously, Elizabeth Wordsworth did not find time hanging heavily on her hands. The extra leisure given her by retirement meant that she had more opportunity to enjoy the company of her much-loved relations. Nineteen-twelve was to be a year of grief in the Wordsworth family. When Elizabeth and Susan were on holiday together in August in the Lake District they received news of the sudden and unexpected death of their brother John. A few months later a proposal that his memorial should take the form of a recumbent figure in Salisbury cathedral met with Elizabeth's outspoken disapproval—'There was nothing recumbent about him; energy was the dominating note of his character.' In November another blow fell. For some time Susan had been ailing; and when Elizabeth took her to see Sir Bertram Dawson[1] he diagnosed inoperable cancer of the lung. For the short while that remained to her Susan made her home with Elizabeth, who watched over her lovingly until her death in the early days of the new year. A friend who called to condole murmured some conventional phrase about the comfort of knowing that Susan was at peace. Elizabeth looked up, her face suddenly radiant—'Oh, so much, *much* more than *that*!'

Priscilla Steedman had died some time previously, but the near neighbourhood of her husband Percy and their children was a constant pleasure to Elizabeth. Of the remaining brothers and sisters Mary Trebeck was already a widow, Christopher had become Chancellor of Salisbury diocese, and Dora Leeke and her husband were still living in Lincoln.

Visits to old friends were a source of great pleasure to

1. Later Lord Dawson of Penn.

Elizabeth. In the summer of 1912, when staying with the Benson family at Tremans, their attractive if uncomfortable home in Sussex, she wrote Mary Trebeck a letter containing a typical piece of descriptive writing:

> Rarely do I remember such a beautiful evening as last. Minnie and I went out and paced the terrace about seven-thirty beneath a row of glorious Scotch firs which stretched down over the path towards the lawn. The red boughs literally *glowed* in the sunset and stood out from the foliage with unusual distinctness. At the bottom of the lawn was the old red-grey Elizabethan house. Close to the path where we were walking up and down were tall swaying grasses and sorrel heads all alive with light. If one looked across beyond the corner of the house there was a perfect bit of pearly sunset sky with soft greens and greys in between. It is difficult to describe the effect of the contrast between this delicate bit of sky and the brilliant ruddy gold of the fir boughs, so forceful and definite and contorted in their shapes—and all the while *how* the birds were singing!

In different vein in this same letter she pokes gentle fun at the rapturous reception Robert Hugh had received in America and at the arrival home of Fred, the only 'worldly' member of the family, complete with man-servant and motor-car.

The Suffragette movement was one of the chief questions of the day during these years immediately preceding the outbreak of the First World War. Elizabeth Wordsworth had never been outspoken in her dislike of that movement, but dislike it she did none the less. She disapproved most of all of any suggestion of women's right to equality with men in the ministry of the Church. The old L.M.H. student, Maude Royden, was a pioneer in this direction. Of her Elizabeth Wordsworth wrote with studied moderation, 'I don't think she is quite as wise as well-meaning,' excusing Maude Royden's preaching in the City Temple on the ground that 'one can't call it preaching in a *church*.' Later, she expressed more definite disapproval:

> I am sorry Maude Royden defied the Bishop. Even if it were defensible on legal grounds it was not 'behaving like a lady'. A mere hint of his wish ought to have been enough.

On 4 August 1914 Elizabeth Wordsworth chanced to be staying in an old house under the shadow of Durham cathedral. Like most of her fellow countrymen she had been taken completely by surprise by the outbreak of war; as late as 27 July she had written Dora a letter containing no hint or foreboding of the coming catastrophe. A spinster in her seventies, she had no one especially near or dear to her involved in the fighting; her concern was general rather than personal, and her reaction to the war was the conventional one of her class and generation. For the next four years her letters are full of the usual wartime topics, Belgian refugees, ships sunk by U-boats, difficulties of travel, shortages of all sorts, and on a deeper and more tragic level, 'the terrible reading of the casualty lists.' The nearest she herself came to hostilities was 'a *slight* air-raid' on Oxford, a raid so slight that no guns were fired and no bombs dropped. At her age war-work was of necessity limited to such occupations as making sand-bags and reading Dickens aloud to wounded soldiers in hospital.

Yet though her personal involvement in the war was small, as a thinking and feeling person of necessity she shared in the common burden of suffering. When faced by the horrors of the news from the Front, or exasperated by the petty, nagging difficulties of civilian wartime life she turned, as always, to find comfort and consolation in the Bible and the Greek classics. On 18 September 1915 she wrote urging Dora to

encourage her husband and sons, in spite of the pressure of
wartime occupations, to make time for the reading of Aeschy-
lus:

> I suppose neither Edward nor the boys have any time for the
> classics. I wish they would look once more at *The Persae* of
> Aeschylus. There is a long speech by the ghost of Darius
> (who appears at Susa after the battle of Salamis) and the
> concluding portion of it might have been written apropos of
> the present war—it is a *grand* thing and almost up to the
> level of parts of the Old Testament. The part I mean is that
> which begins by describing the sacrilege of the Persians in
> Greece (Belgium!), the mass of dead piled up, a voiceless
> witness against human presumption etc. (lines 806–830). I
> expect you will laugh at me but really when one feels as if
> everything were down in the depths of commonplace it is a
> refreshment to take up a book of this kind—one can't
> *always* be making sand-bags. And Aeschylus is at times
> almost as wonderful as Ezekiel, parts of which I have been
> reading at prayers (though how far the new parlour-maid
> takes it in perhaps one had better not inquire).

The war had not put a stop to all building activity. The new
central block of Lady Margaret Hall had been opened in 1910
by Lord Curzon, the first occasion when a Chancellor of the
University had paid an official visit to a women's college. Work
was then started on the second block of students' rooms, which
was completed in 1915 and christened Toynbee. A year later
St Hugh's abandoned its motley collection of houses in Norham Gardens and moved to fine new buildings on a spacious
site within a few minutes' walk of Elizabeth Wordsworth's
own house. The occasion was naturally a source of great
satisfaction to her—'I never expected to see my dream so
delightfully realized'—though she was much disappointed

that a slight illness prevented her from attending the opening
of the new chapel.

The year 1917 and the early months of 1918 were overshadowed by bad news from the war-fronts, and by the deaths
of many old friends, including Henry Scott-Holland, James
Strachan-Davidson, and, nearer and dearer, Minnie Benson.
With the years Minnie had mellowed; as Elizabeth said of her,
'it was not perhaps till after her widowhood that the full beauty
of her character came out.' Though naturally she missed her
friends Elizabeth was not unduly saddened or depressed. Her
philosophy of life had taught her to accept death—'all the sad
parting seems like a mere parenthesis.' A passage in *Essays Old
and New*, a collection of articles and addresses which she
published in 1919, gives what might be described as her
secular, as opposed to her religious, views on death and
bereavement:

Ideally, our friends are perfect; actually they only hint at,
and suggest, future perfection. Suppose your friend has
died, and you know that in this world he is lost to you for
ever. Immediately the image of him, or her, rises before you
more beautiful than life; it is to you what the phantasm of
the absent Helen was to Menelaus. At few moments of actual
life did he or she reach that absolute perfection which this
image of the memory possesses. Suppose, for instance, that
your friend is unexpectedly restored to you, by recovery
from a 'fatal' illness, by escape from shipwreck or imprison-
ment. When the old familiar life recommences, do you not
once more become conscious of little rubs and annoyances
which had affected your intercourse in former days? Perhaps even when Helen came back to Sparta, Menelaus may
have felt—despite her divine origin—that she had her little
imperfections. The 'real' always interferes—more or less—
with the ideal. Or perhaps it would be more true to say that

the 'actual', the 'phenomenal', interfered with the true, inward reality.

As might be expected from any such collection, the essays in this book are of very uneven quality. Nearly all of them, however, contain some pithy remark or pregnant reflection that stays in the memory. Take, for instance, this passage from a not particularly notable essay on Christopher Columbus:

> The great men of the world have always walked on two feet —the foot of Reason and the foot of Enthusiasm. The little ones very often hop only on one leg. And there is a stage in human progress when the fervour of the enthusiast is as necessary as the logic of the thinker. We want light and we want fire.

'The Lilac Bush', the last and perhaps most attractive of the essays, includes one typically Wordsworthian passage:

> How miraculously beautiful, for instance, is a yellow crocus open to the February sunshine! And yet we could often count on the fingers even of one hand the days in which in any spring we have beheld this delightful revelation in perfection. Yet when once you have seen a crocus in the act—one might almost say of adoration—it becomes a treasure—a possession for ever, a haunting, oft-recurrent vision to the contemplative mind.

One essay is entitled 'The English Church and the English Character'. On first reading it would seem that Elizabeth Wordsworth seriously believed that the English Church existed simply to produce English gentlemen—'the English gentleman is what he is to a great extent because she has ruled over his home, his boyhood and his adolescence.' This is, in fact, an unfair criticism; but the interest of the essay lies less in its main theme than in its comments and asides, such as the description of 'that truly English temperament which has a kind of instinctive perception rather than a logical conviction of what ought to be done,' or a caution which is at least as relevant to the Church of England today as it was when Elizabeth Wordsworth wrote it, 'In seeking to adapt our forms of service to the popular needs of a new age let us see that we do it by way of a real enrichment, not by making them poorer.' The Church as a whole, and not merely its services, must be able to meet the intellectual needs of intelligent and educated English men and women:

We may say the Church of England is very like the noblest poetry. Our greatest poets in their highest moods will never be popular. A foolish music-hall song has for its little day incalculably more vogue than *Paradise Lost*—but what would the greatest minds of our country have been without our highest poetry? It is surely a note of 'the true Church' that she has nothing vulgar or mean or petty or ephemeral about her, and that she possesses the power of appealing not only to humble and simple hearts but to men of the highest intellect and the finest culture.

Some people would see Elizabeth Wordsworth's apologia for the Anglican Church as a piece of intellectual, almost of aristocratic, snobbery. Her early preoccupation with school-teaching and with 'good works', however, gives the lie to the theory that she was neglectful of the religious needs of 'humble and simple hearts'; but, having been so much concerned with higher education, and living for so long in university circles, it was natural that she should lay particular stress on the intellectual side of religion.

In 1915 Elizabeth Wordsworth had resigned from the Council of St Hugh's, but she remained a member of the L.M.H. Council until 1922. She thus retained an official connection with the Hall, but she sat on none of the Council committees and seems to have taken no very active part in its proceedings, though she continued to preside over the annual meetings of the L.M.H. Settlement. 'I am rather like Mr Wilmot in *The Vicar of Wakefield*,' she had written on 10 November 1913. 'One virtue he had in perfection and that was prudence, too often the only one which is left us at seventy-two.' Prudence now demanded that she should be a benevolent onlooker rather than an active participant in the affairs of the college over which she had ruled for so long; 'she never lost interest,' wrote Eleanor Lodge, 'but she never criticized or interfered.' Every now and again she would be asked to give an address in chapel, and occasionally she would invite students to dine with her, reading aloud to them after dinner from some old favourite such as *Cranford* or one of Jane Austen's novels.

Apart from such occasions her closest links with L.M.H. during the twenties were through the daughters of friends or relations who came up as students. The presence of John Wordsworth's two daughters, Faith and Salome, was a special pleasure to her. She delighted in their company, which she liked to enjoy without interruption. If other visitors chanced to be present when either of these girls called on her she would turn to her guests with a beaming smile—'Well, I have enjoyed our talk very much, and now I want to talk to my niece; will you please go?' Elinor Frere, a young cousin whose 'pleasant company' Elizabeth had already enjoyed several times, came up to the Hall in 1924. A frequent visitor to Rawlinson Road, she was interested and a little amused by various questions put to her about life at L.M.H. in the 1920s, a typical query being, 'Do you ever sit round the fire of an evening doing your sewing whilst someone reads aloud?' Sometimes Elizabeth would

Charlotte Toynbee,
widow of the sociologist
Arthur Toynbee and Treasurer of
L.M.H. 1883–1920

William Archibald Spooner,
Warden of New College,
Chairman of the L.M.H. Council,
1901–07

Elizabeth Wordsworth
in her D.C.L. gown at
the Degree Ceremony, 1928

H.R.H. the Duchess of York
presenting Elizabeth
Wordsworth with the insignia
of the D.B.E. at the Jubilee
garden-party, 1928

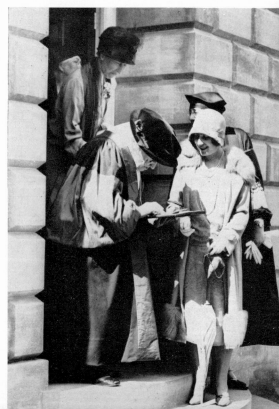

recite page after page of Homer, finding in Elinor, who was reading Honour Mods, a particularly appreciative audience. Another favourite visitor was Edward Benson's niece, Kitty McDowall, an Old Student of L.M.H., who had come up in 1896. Afterwards Mrs Esdaile, she was to become famous under that name as the pioneer of the study of English monumental sculpture. 'She reminds me so much of her uncle in many little ways,' Elizabeth wrote of her, 'a sort of eagerness and keenness and enthusiasm about everything.'

In October 1919 came the fortieth anniversary of the opening of L.M.H. During the celebrations which marked this occasion, Elizabeth Wordsworth was presented with an illuminated address signed by many past and present members of the Hall. The writer of this address simply and felicitously expressed the general feeling of love and loyalty:

> We rejoice to see the steady growth and honourable standing of the Hall. We know that from the first you inspired its destiny and made its interests your own. As we think of those forty years gone by you are in all our thoughts. To you therefore we bring our loyal homage today.

On 3 June of the following year, 1920, more celebrations were held to commemorate Elizabeth Wordsworth's eightieth birthday. 'The sun shone and the world in general looked most amiable,' she wrote of this great day. Her old cook Kate, now retired, 'trotted up looking very pink and flushed, all the way from St Aldates (Beersheba to Dan)' to bring a birthday cake. Other friends sent armfuls of flowers and such welcome presents as Bezique cards. Bezique had become a favourite occupation, to be played with intense seriousness and an undisguised determination to win. Her more earnest friends looked rather askance at this preoccupation with a mere game; but Elizabeth herself held that at the age of eighty, she was

G

entitled to waste time playing cards. 'Moralists speak severely of "killing time",' she had written in an essay entitled 'A Plea for Fetish Worship'; 'but really time has to be killed, or at least put under chloroform now and then.' Later in the day came a tea-party at L.M.H. with more birthday cake, followed by the presentation of a cheque to be given to the fund for the building of a permanent chapel, and the more personal gift of a marabou stole. In her speech of thanks Elizabeth described the warm stole as a symbol of the warmth of affection which she felt all around her, and spoke of the scheme to build a worthy chapel as a recognition of the paramount importance of the spiritual life. 'It is because of that recognition that I am thankful to be united with you here today; after all, it is our sense of the unseen which binds us together.'

The year 1921 was a troubled one in the history of the Hall. In January the difficult question of 'Church principles' came up before the Council, causing much dissension. When in 1913 the Hall had become a non-profit-making joint stock company it had been necessary for legal reasons to form an Association of Senior Members whose chief function was to elect the members of Council and to hold an Annual General Meeting to receive a report and audited accounts. This Association could also on occasion call a Special General Meeting to consider any particular problem. In November 1920 a letter signed by twenty-six members of the Association was laid before Council, asking that such a Special General Meeting be called 'to consider whether it is still desirable that the rule limiting membership of the Council to members of the Church of England should remain part of the Articles of Association.' A Special General Meeting of the Association was accordingly called for 29 January 1921, but unfortunately no minutes seem to have survived. Apparently, however, this meeting passed a resolution proposing that membership of Council should no longer be confined to members of the Church of England. At the Council meeting held on 26 February Dr Joseph Wells, chairman of Council and Warden of Wadham, proposed that the resolution passed by the Special General Meeting should be submitted to a postal vote by the full membership of the Association. Elizabeth Wordsworth seconded his motion. It was defeated; and in its place Council passed a motion accepting the resolution put forward by the Special General Meeting, whereupon Dr Wells resigned from his position as chairman. In May, however, the Association held another meeting at which this decision was reversed. 'It is a great weight off my mind,' Elizabeth wrote on 18 May, 'that at an L.M.H. Council[1] meeting last Saturday we gave (I hope) a final quietus to those tiresome resolutions about admitting non-Church people to our Council. I am afraid the younger generation regret it, but hope with them years may bring the philosophic mind.'

Meanwhile Miss Jex-Blake had sent in her resignation. Elizabeth Wordsworth was deeply concerned about the choice of a successor, believing that the whole future of the Hall might hang upon the character and abilities of the new Principal. On 22 April she wrote joyfully, 'I hope we have got the right woman in Miss Grier.' It was a choice that she was never to regret.

These important events in the history of L.M.H. were put in the shade by the interest and excitement of greater doings in the University itself. During the war women had worked side by side with men in farms and factories, even in the armed forces. They had proved the justice of their claim to be treated as responsible citizens, and they won their reward in June 1918

1. The word 'Council' must be a slip of the pen; the meeting was one of the Association attended, of course, by members of Council who were the only people allowed to vote on this particular motion. The meeting passed another motion abolishing the Church qualification in the case of members of the tutorial staff.

when a Bill was passed giving them the franchise. Though
Cambridge was to remain obdurate, Oxford University was
logical enough to admit that where the vote had been granted
degrees could not be withheld. Already the wartime demand for
more doctors had led to women's admission to the First
Examination for the degree of Bachelor of Medicine, one of
the few important examinations which had remained closed
to them. Now they were to be permitted to take all university
examinations and to hold university degrees. An Amendment
to the Sex Disqualification Act gave Oxford University the
power to make the required changes; and finally in May 1920 a
statute was passed admitting women to full membership of the
University.

In no letter of Elizabeth Wordsworth's is there any mention
of this final victory for the cause of the higher education of
women. This curious omission may be due to the fact that
most of her surviving letters are written to her brothers and
sisters and are therefore chiefly concerned with matters of
personal or family interest; another possible explanation may
be the casual forgetfulness of old age. Nevertheless, it is strange
and perhaps significant that she should make no reference to an
event of such obvious importance, and one which might be
regarded as setting the seal of success on the work to which
she had devoted her life. In a letter written in July 1920, to
congratulate (or rather to condole with) her niece on a Second
in History Finals, she makes no mention of the fact that Faith
will be one of the very first L.M.H. students to write the letters
B.A. after their names and to take their degree with full ceremonial in the Sheldonian; instead, she states once again what
she believes to be the true object of an Oxford education: 'You
have got (which after all is the real thing) a great mass of
historical and economical [*sic*] ideas in your mind besides (what
Oxford is supposed to impart to her sons and daughters) a
sense of style and the power of expression.'

Having passed no examinations Elizabeth Wordsworth herself was not qualified to receive the ordinary B.A. degree. She was, however, to be granted a degree that was very much out of the ordinary. As the *Brown Book* recorded in happy phraseology, 'The University has done itself the honour, since degrees were opened to women, of conferring degrees on three women only, Her Majesty the Queen, who received the D.C.L., and Miss Wordsworth and Mrs T. H. Green, who received the Honorary M.A.' In a letter to Dora dated 2 June Elizabeth typically and deliberately played down the importance of the honour which is to be given her:

> You will be amused to hear that the University has just offered me an M.A. degree *honoris causa*—which means that you need not pay any fees. It is not of the smallest use to me, at my time of life, to be an M.A., but I thought it would be ungracious to refuse, so I have accepted it and I expect it will be 'nuts' to Dr Godley, the Public Orator, who has to present me, as he will be able to poke any amount of fun at me in Latin.

On 25 October Elizabeth Wordsworth drove to the Convocation House to receive the degree of Master of Arts, *honoris causa*. She went escorted by the Principals of St Hugh's, St Hilda's and the Home Students—all three of them old students of L.M.H.—and, representing L.M.H. itself, Lynda Grier and Evelyn Jamison. Old students had planned to present her with a silk gown and hood, a gift which she had firmly but gratefully refused, asking that the money collected for this purpose should be given to the funds of the Settlement. Instead, she went carefully and correctly dressed—Evelyn Jamison had supervised the business of robing—in the official gown which belonged to the Principal of L.M.H., Eleanor Lodge's cap, and Evelyn Jamison's own hood. Robed thus, and with her marabou stole thrown over her shoulders to keep her warm, she waited for a moment or two in the vestibule of the Convocation House, a figure reminiscent of a Rembrandt portrait. As she entered, preceded by the four Bedells, all the members of Convocation rose spontaneously to their feet, a welcome never before extended to anyone, however distinguished. To the disappointment of many of those present the Public Orator made an unusually short Latin speech, having been warned that he must not keep an old lady standing too long. Nothing, however, could detract from the happy solemnity of the ceremony. Three days later Elizabeth wrote a characteristic account to Dora:

> I am told the scene in the Convocation House was really very picturesque. I had an exceptionally good welcome (so they say) and everyone seemed pleased, but I could not help thinking of the old story of George III, who when someone told him how much they had enjoyed the Coronation procession replied, 'Oh, Mr So-and-So, pity me! I only saw the back of the coachman.' I saw the back of the four Esquire Bedells who came to conduct me, also the dais on which the bigwigs were sitting, and had a consciousness of Dr Godley's scarlet gown beside me, also of the Vice-Chancellor taking off his cap, but not much more.

Underneath the deliberate self-mockery sounds a deep note of pleasure and satisfaction. Though it was ironical that she, who had cared so little for degrees, should find herself thus honoured, no one had done more to deserve this recognition. She had given her life to the business of educating women and to the work of building up Lady Margaret Hall into a place where they might learn to understand and value a tradition of 'true religion and sound learning.' Her wit and wisdom and, above all, the appeal of her personality, had done much to reconcile

Oxford opinion to the admittance of women to university membership. No one could object to the presence of academic women if the academic woman resembled Elizabeth Wordsworth. Of all Oxford women she was the best known and the best loved, and she had earned her right to a triumph.

Chapter 12

'An Old Age Serene and Bright'

ELEVEN YEARS of life remained to Elizabeth Wordsworth, 'An old age serene and bright/And lovely as a Lapland night.' Her instinct had always been to look forward; now, in extreme old age, she looked forward to death, facing it as she had faced life with lively curiosity and a certain humour. For her death was now the most interesting of all subjects; she discussed it freely and frequently with her friends as she had always discussed any subject that interested her. She was too realistic to attempt to evade the issue or to pretend to a complete assurance which she did not feel. But now she spoke with a new tenderness. In conversation with Kathleen Thicknesse, Warden of the L.M.H. Settlement, she compared man's entrance into the next world with the birth of a baby into this one:

> We don't expect too much of it at first and we don't try to tell it everything at once. It just lies there and coos a little and smiles and sometimes cries a little, and we are quite content—yes, I think we shall be very gently treated there.

Her wit and intelligence sparkled as brightly as ever, and so did her mischievous sense of humour. 'I sit here,' she remarked to A. E. Levett, 'so close to eternity, never quite tired of the old game of shocking my relations.' In conversation with her niece Salome she admitted that when she was young she would have liked to marry, 'but when I see the old gentlemen my friends have to sit opposite to at meals every day of their lives I am quite glad that I remained single.' The historian E. L. Woodward recorded one of her more deflating remarks made when she was over eighty-eight:

> I once heard someone read Tennyson's 'Tithonus' aloud in the presence of Dame Elizabeth Wordsworth. The reader almost broke down with emotion:
>
> > The woods decay, the woods decay and fall,
> > The vapours weep their burdens to the ground,
> > Man comes and tills the fields and lies beneath,
> > And after many a summer dies the swan.
>
> Dame Elizabeth relieved the strain by saying in the clear tones of a woman Born to be Queen, 'I always think that one of the greatest alleviations of old age has been the invention of false teeth.'

In earlier years this caustic humour had sometimes obscured her essentially warm heart. Now, however, her overflowing affection was her most obvious characteristic. 'Love' is the word most frequently mentioned in connection with her in her old age. 'How genuinely she loved us!' Ruth Wordsworth exclaimed; E. Mitchell wrote of her 'vast large-heartedness,' C. Luard of 'that last gift of a loving heart'; and the obituary article written by Evelyn Jamison ends with a reference to 'her depth, her brightness, her power of loving'. Her warm-heartedness expressed itself in her gestures; she would fling her arms in greeting round the neck of an old student. 'We called it her praying hug,' wrote E. M. Belcher. 'It was such a long embrace that we were quite sure she was praying for us and sometimes felt a little embarrassed. We loved it, though.'

Even in her very last years Elizabeth Wordsworth never

thought to opt out of life; 'one does not want to sit still in a
train and watch everything go past one,' she wrote three weeks
before her death. She grieved over the death of old friends but
she took their departure as a sign that the time had come to
look for new ones—'One wants to build up some new friendships for the ranks of the old ones are thinning rapidly.' Those
old friends who remained she cherished ever more closely. 'I
shall always look back on your visit here as a gleam of sunshine
in this particularly sunless year,' she wrote in 1925 to Gertrude
Edwards. 'Horace Walpole was pretty right when he said "Our
best sunshine in England is made of Newcastle coal", but he
might have added, "Better still, what we find in the faces of
our friends".'

Mary Trebeck died in 1926 leaving Dora Leeke as her only
surviving sister. However, as she herself put it, 'I am glad to
think not only of the fading leaves but of the young buds'; and
nothing gave her more pleasure than news of the birth of a
great-nephew or great-niece. Perhaps the best loved of the
intermediate generation was Ruth Wordsworth, now far away
in Japan. Two other nieces were living abroad; Salome had
married a doctor working in India, and Faith had gone to
teach in West Africa where she met and married William
Tolfree. At home next door in Rawlinson Road were Margaret
and Susan Steedman. Of Susan her aunt wrote, 'Susie is one of
the persons who cannot be judged by common rules and I am
such a very conventional person that I can no more understand her than a barn-door fowl can understand a swallow.'
The comparison is strangely inapt; about Elizabeth Wordsworth there was nothing of the staid barn-door fowl but a great
deal of the swooping, skimming swallow, flying so swiftly
between earth and heaven.

Elizabeth Wordsworth's travels abroad ended with the
First World War. Holidays were now spent at some such place
as Brighton or Llanfairfechan in North Wales where she

greatly enjoyed 'the fine dark head of Penmaenmawr, the delicious little roadside brook and those pink flowers, the great expanse of sea with its changing skies, the well-filled church, Mr W.D.'s eloquence, and all our pleasant walks, or rather, saunters.' In the spring of 1924 she spent a week at Winchester with an Old Student called Evelyn Waters. At an Oxford tea-party given in her honour during this holiday someone repeated the story of two Victorian ladies attending a performance of *Antony and Cleopatra* and the one remarking to the other, 'Ah, how unlike the domestic life of our own beloved Queen!' Elizabeth Wordsworth promptly countered this old chestnut— 'And it is still more difficult to imagine the Prince Consort in the role of Antony.' On pious pilgrimage to Hursley she described how, on her first visit there, she had walked with Charlotte Yonge along the winding lane from Otterbourne. As she gathered primroses growing near Keble's grave she quoted *The Christian Year* and made a curious comparison between Keble's verses for St Matthew's Day and her great-uncle's famous sonnet composed on Westminster Bridge, 'Earth has not anything to show more fair.'

William Wordsworth had recently become a subject of renewed discussion and criticism. In 1922 the publication of Emile Legouis' *Wordsworth and Annette Vallon* had given to the world the facts about Wordsworth's early love affair and the birth of his illegitimate daughter Caroline. Elizabeth's father had at first intended to include the story, which had never been a closely-guarded secret, in his official biography of the poet, but instead had inserted only a brief reference to Wordsworth as 'encompassed with many and great temptations' during his stay in France. In a letter to Edward Quillinan[1] the Bishop explained why he had finally decided to omit any reference to Annette:

1. Husband to Wordsworth's daughter Dora.

As it is I have suggested such extenuating circumstances as the case admits of, and thus endeavoured to guard his memory, and to prevent his lapse being perverted into an example for leading others astray. I believe that David (who was inspired) is a better guide in these matters than any living adviser; and I am confident that the departed spirit, if he is cognisant of what is done on earth, would desire that the subject should be so treated as under all circumstances of the case seems most conducive to the divine honour and the good of men's souls.

When the story of Annette was made public, Bishop Wordsworth's policy of silence came in for considerable criticism. Wishing to defend her father's memory Elizabeth suggested to her cousin Gordon Wordsworth that the letter to Quillinan should be published as giving the explanation for this reticence. She added with a worldly wisdom lacking to the simple-minded Bishop that it would be as well to omit the reference to King David—'one cannot say that the two cases were parallel.' Gordon Wordsworth wisely decided against this course of action; Bishop Wordsworth's remarkable epistle remained unpublished until 1965 when it appeared in Mary Moorman's classic biography of the poet. Elizabeth Wordsworth never believed in hushing things up; when some members of the family objected to the publication of Crabb Robinson's correspondence she retorted that the letters could hardly reveal any harmful secrets and that in any case they would be read by very few people. She had always known of her great-uncle's love affair and now in old age she felt free to speak openly and often of Annette.

Both physically and mentally she was still active enough to enjoy the intellectual pleasures of life in Oxford, meetings, lectures, even an occasional theatre. At eighty-four years of age transport problems presented no difficulty to her; on

5 July 1924 she wrote to her brother Christopher inviting him to stay with her for a Church Congress to be held in Oxford later that year—'We can always get about in buses if the distance is beyond our walking power.' 'Miss Wordsworth's bible classes' had become a north Oxford institution; she would expound to 'a group of old grannies like myself' such abstruse subjects as the authorship of the Epistle to the Hebrews, occasionally providing a little relaxation in the form of tea with delicious cakes (her guests were always supplied with excellent food) followed by a reading of *Cranford*. Books were not so much a pleasure to her as a necessity of life. 'I think old age has a great deal to be said for it,' she wrote in December 1922, 'I love the leisure to read old books and after Hugh Walpole's *The Cathedral* turn to *Hamlet* again with a great sense of refreshment.' Her reading ranged from Homer through Froissart, Bossuet and Madame de Sévigné, to such modern books as Streeter's *Reality* and the biography of Lord Shaftesbury by her old pupil, Barbara Bradby, now Barbara Hammond. She described Lytton Strachey's *Queen Victoria* as 'hardly a book to buy but interesting to read.' When feeling ill or out of sorts she turned to an old favourite and, like many another Charlotte Yonge enthusiast, took refuge with the May family and *The Daisy Chain*.

She had always been a lover of poetry though her taste in this respect was an idiosyncratic one. In a letter to Gertrude Edwards dated 26 October 1927 she set out her likes and dislikes:

Dare I own to you that I simply can't read either *Hyperion* or *Endymion*?—though I love the shorter poems and expect that I shall like his letters. I suppose it is the same thing that makes me not care so *very* much for Spenser. I like poetry like Milton's sonnets that shows you the ideal in actual life, and have the most intense admiration for Gray's Elegy.

Rudyard Kipling is the only modern poet I really care for—
well, set me down a heretic and have done with it.

Shakespeare she read constantly though complaining of his
coarseness and comparing him unfavourably in this respect
with Homer. Like so many of her generation she was an enthusiastic admirer of Browning. Tennyson she also appreciated,
one passage from *In Memoriam* giving her especial pleasure:

> And if along with these should come
> 　The man I held as half-divine,
> 　Should strike a sudden hand in mine,
> And ask a thousand things of home,
>
> And I perceived no hint of change,
> 　No hint of death in all his frame,
> 　But found him all in all the same,
> I should not feel it to be strange.

'That,' she would declare, 'is exactly how it seems to me—"I
should not feel it to be strange".' 'I can't make up my mind
what to think about modern French poetry,' she wrote on 21
February 1921. 'It is like turning over a portfolio of charming
water-colour drawings. One gets a little cloyed with sunsets
and flowers, the sea and so forth. They seem to have a delicious
lot of words and not a very big range of ideas. One becomes
too conscious of the artist, the colour-box; and I hark back to
La Fontaine's fables, which I suppose are not poetry at all.'

Though she was made an Honorary Fellow of L.M.H. and
Honorary Vice-President of St Hugh's after her retirement
from the L.M.H. Council in 1922, she no longer had any close
official connection with either college. Except in the earliest
years of its existence she had taken very little part in the affairs

of St Hugh's. It would seem that she had been deliberately cold-shouldered by the authorities of the college she had founded; according to Annie Rogers, 'she was very much ignored by the Principal and Council until B. E. Gwyer took control.' Maybe it was thought essential to stress the fact that St Hugh's was an entirely independent body and not an appendage of L.M.H., which some people might have believed it to be had it been in any way under the influence or control of Elizabeth Wordsworth. Wisely, she accepted the position as she found it, making no attempt to assert herself and giving neither hint nor sign of resentment.

When, however, a serious crisis arose at St Hugh's Elizabeth Wordsworth inevitably found herself involved. Because 'The St Hugh's Row' has passed into Oxford legend it is difficult to disentangle fact from fiction. One of Elizabeth's last acts as a member of St Hugh's Council had been to second a motion appointing an old L.M.H. student, E. M. Jourdain, to succeed Annie Moberly as Principal. The arrival of the new Principal marked an immediate improvement in Elizabeth Wordsworth's relationship with St Hugh's College, as it was now to become. On 17 November 1915 during Eleanor Jourdain's first year in office, she was among the guests at the St Hugh's Night dinner held to mark the festival of the College's patron saint. Her eye chanced to fall on a student in a very pretty red dress (red had always been Elizabeth's favourite colour) and she asked to have the girl introduced to her. Young Joan Evans, later famous both as archaeologist and historian, made such a good impression that she was invited to Rawlinson Road. When she dined there, of course wearing the same red frock, her hostess chanced to remark that, although she was the founder of St Hugh's, that St Hugh's Night dinner had been the very first occasion on which she had been invited to dine officially in College.

Though Eleanor Jourdain was much to be commended for

her efforts to bring about a better relationship between St Hugh's and its founder, in her dealings with other people she was not so happy; as Elizabeth herself wrote, 'it seems as if the Principal and tutors could not see their way to acting harmoniously together.' Though part of the trouble was of course due to a clash of personalities, an important principle was also at stake. The real issue was not the disagreement between Eleanor Jourdain and Cecilia Ady but a profound difference of opinion between Principal and tutors as to the powers and position of members of the Senior Common Room. At St Hugh's, as at L.M.H. and Somerville, all authority had originally rested with the Principal and Council. Tutors had no authority for the reason that in those early days there were no tutors, the A.E.W. being in control of all educational matters. Gradually with the appointment of residential tutors and the growth of the tutorial system, the members of the Senior Common Room came to be associated with the Principal in the control and management of college affairs. When women were granted full membership of the University many people felt that the time had come to make the government of women's colleges approximate more closely to the traditional pattern of the Head of the House acting in concert with the resident Fellows. At St Hugh's, however, more old-fashioned ideas prevailed. Eleanor Jourdain was against granting any measure of authority to the tutors. The younger tutors naturally resented her attitude and sought to gain some right to a voice in the running of the college. The general feeling of dissatisfaction came to a head in the Michaelmas term of 1923. On 19 November Eleanor Jourdain sent for Cecilia Ady, an able and popular History tutor who had been at St Hugh's for fourteen years, accused her of disloyalty, informed her that her contract with the college was not to be renewed, and pressed her hard to resign of her own free will, which Cecilia Ady rightly refused to do. Five tutors immediately resigned in protest and while the

Council, by a single vote, passed a motion in support of Eleanor Jourdain's action, the majority both in the Senior and the Junior Common Room sided with Cecilia Ady. So did the University as a whole, outside tutors, both men and women, refusing to take pupils from St Hugh's unless and until she was reinstated.

Elizabeth Wordsworth endeavoured to remain impartial, though admitting that 'E. Jourdain has been, to say the least of it, very injudicious in trying to get rid of an excellent tutor.' Neither Eleanor Jourdain nor Cecilia Ady appears to have sought her advice; but Annie Rogers, now a Fellow of St Hugh's, appealed to her to intervene. She did so, but apparently with no success. A brief sentence in a letter written by Annie Rogers twelve years later is the only record of this episode—'At the time of the St Hugh's row I did appeal to her and she rose to the occasion but I don't think she had any effect on Miss Jourdain.' Nothing, in fact, was to have any effect on Miss Jourdain until the Council finally decided to ask the Chancellor, Lord Curzon, to institute an official inquiry. The Report resulting from this inquiry exonerated Cecilia Ady, and hinted also that the tutors ought to be given more power and that it might be as well to appoint a new Principal. A day after the publication of this report Eleanor Jourdain died from a heart attack.

Elizabeth Wordsworth believed that the repercussions of this unhappy affair would do great harm to the reputation and standing of Oxford women's colleges in general. Though her fears proved unfounded St Hugh's itself had received a blow from which it would take a long time to recover. The immediate problem to be solved was the appointment of a new Principal; it would not be easy to find someone prepared to take up the task of restoring order and good-feeling to a distraught and disorganized college. Elizabeth Wordsworth was therefore the more delighted when yet another old L.M.H. student, Barbara

Gwyer, consented to accept the unenviable position. In the difficult situation facing her Barbara Gwyer naturally turned for counsel and support to the founder of St Hugh's, who had also been her own Principal at L.M.H. In Elizabeth Wordsworth she found someone who could not only give her wise advice but also provide much needed spiritual refreshment and relaxation, someone who 'discoursed that wisdom which is original, authoritative, not "as the scribes".'[1] For Elizabeth herself this friendship with Barbara Gwyer meant a strengthening of her connection with St Hugh's; in her old age she came to know more about the college she had founded than she had ever done since those early days when she and Annie Moberly had been in complete control. As a happy postscript to this unhappy affair Elizabeth lunched at St Hugh's on 17 November 1924 and afterwards gave a brief address to the students saying nothing of old troubles.

At L.M.H. the situation was a happier one. Elizabeth Wordsworth was on the best of terms with Lynda Grier, thoroughly approving of her as Principal. 'Miss Grier called yesterday afternoon and was nicer than ever,' she wrote on 25 February 1923. 'I am getting very fond of her and so glad that she is where she is.' Nevertheless, she viewed the continued expansion of L.M.H. with very mixed feelings. Shortly before she resigned from the Council she was heard to remark, 'If they are going to consider extensions at the L.M.H. Council meeting tomorrow then I am against it.' Looking at this large, formally-organized institution, so different from the small Hall over which she had presided, she fell to wondering how she herself would deal with the problems of managing such a large body of students. As usual, her conclusion was a practical one: 'with a Hall too big for real knowledge of everybody the thing

1. 'Elizabeth Wordsworth' from *Exhortations in St Hugh's College Chapel* by B. E. Gwyer, Blackwell, 1936.

of course would be to concentrate on the third year, tell the first year you hoped to get to know them better later, and meanwhile establish a real relationship with the third year.' The vital feature of university education was personal contact, the impact of mind upon mind. Since the head of a large college could not hope to know every student intimately this business of personal contact must be left to the tutors. 'That's what they are there for,' she maintained. 'If the tutors won't do this the college will fail; it *must* be held together by personal influence and sympathy.' The friendliness which had been so notable a feature of life at L.M.H. in the early days must continue to characterize the Hall—'In an institution apart from friendliness there is nothing between anarchy and red-tape.'

If she could not bring herself to feel really enthusiastic about the remarkable growth of L.M.H. neither did she show any interest in the question of the increasing numbers of women in the University as a whole. In 1927 a Statute was promulgated putting a strict limit on the number of women students, a decision which the supporters of women's education regarded as a severe set-back. Elizabeth, however, remained unperturbed, perhaps secretly a little pleased—'the women were beaten on the limitation question at Oxford; I can't say I mind.'

The L.M.H. annual gaudy was always a particularly happy time for her, an occasion when she would meet old friends and perhaps give a talk in Common Room or an address in chapel. At the 1923 gaudy there was much rejoicing when it was announced that the Council had succeeded in buying the freehold of the site of Old Hall and some outlying portions of land, thus giving permanent security to the Hall and making it possible to plan confidently for the future. On Sunday afternoon Elizabeth Wordsworth attended a tea-party in Toynbee Common Room and afterwards spoke to the assembled old students. She began with a very brief reference to the news

which was in everybody's mind, merely remarking that she felt
as if she had been nursing a baby which had suddenly and quite
unexpectedly turned into a grown-up person. Then her
wrinkled face lit up with sudden energy and enthusiasm as she
urged her audience to take a larger view of life:

> I don't want you to have just your little parts and cues; I
> want you to study the whole play. Every big drama deserves
> study as a whole, and life is the greatest drama and there is
> the greatest of dramatists guiding it and shaping it. Remem-
> ber we have only a part, perhaps a little part, but we must
> look to the whole and rejoice when someone else with a
> bigger part does well, rejoice too when the whole play goes
> well, and be very proud to be allowed to have a part in it.

The year 1928 saw the fiftieth anniversary of the founding of
L.M.H. The University chose this Golden Jubilee as a fitting
occasion on which to bestow on Elizabeth Wordsworth the
Honorary Degree of Doctor of Civil Law, 'making a Scarlet
Woman of me at my age, Mr Vice-Chancellor,' she jested in
reference to the colour of the D.C.L. gown. At the Encaenia,
contrary to custom, a chair was provided for her so that she
could sit during the Latin oration by the Public Orator. As the
tiny, bent figure painfully and slowly climbed the steps towards
the Vice-Chancellor's pulpit the Vice-Chancellor himself
came down to give her the support of his arm. Smiling, bowing,
waving, tired and aged and yet 'so humbly happy', she took
her seat at his right hand while the Sheldonian Theatre rang
with applause.

Another honour awaited her at the L.M.H. Golden Jubilee
celebrations held at the end of June. In the recent Honours list
she had been appointed a Dame of the Order of the British
Empire. When she wrote to accept the honour she had pointed
out that she was too old to attend an investiture at Buckingham

Palace and had asked instead that the insignia should be posted to her 'in a cardboard box'. Now she was to receive it in more dignified fashion at the hands of H.R.H. the Duchess of York,[1] the guest of honour at the Jubilee celebrations.

Elizabeth Wordsworth was too old and frail to be present at the official Jubilee lunch at which the Archbishop of York, proposing the toast of the Hall, referred to her as 'the embodiment of the traditions for which this college stands.' After lunch a small body of friends gathered on the lawn outside Lodge Common Room to watch the old lady, splendid in her scarlet D.C.L. gown, come out on to the steps ready for the investiture. So small and bent was she that for convenience' sake at the actual ceremony she stood on the top step above the Duchess. The loyal deference shown by age to youth and the charming courtesy of youth towards age made the occasion a particularly moving one. This festival day ended with a large official dinner in Oxford Town Hall. Again, Elizabeth Wordsworth did not feel able to attend; but instead every guest on arrival at their place found a rose tucked into their table napkin and beside it a printed letter bearing her signature. Her last formal message and farewell to the generations of L.M.H. students must be quoted in full:

I cannot allow this unique opportunity to pass without a few words of greeting to those old students whom I already know and love, and to those whom I am sure I should have loved, had I had the opportunity of knowing them.

In some ways we most of us have some thoughts in common, at this time. Most of us, it is to be feared, have some sense of sins, negligences, and ignorances, which—could we have our time here over again—we should try to avoid, of failures and faults for which we should try to make

1. Now H.M. Queen Elizabeth the Queen Mother.

amends. But these are matters rather for private thought than for public expression. On the other hand our sense of thankfulness is one that can be shared with others, and we rejoice in doing so.

Few of us can remember our start here on an October Sunday in 1879, with a party of only eight students—a ninth was soon afterwards added—in the humble villa now known as 'Old Hall'. When I look round at the fine buildings and the beautiful grounds which we now possess I feel almost as if some enchantment had been at work. It was 'a day of small things', but I at least can never forget to be grateful to the members of our original Council, to the distinguished University men who gave us so generously of their time and educational gifts, and to many Oxford ladies who helped us in a variety of ways. I cannot mention names, it would be invidious, and yet I must make an exception in the case of Mrs Arthur Johnson, whose remarkable powers, ready sympathy, and unfailing energy were unstintingly bestowed upon us.

Alas, how many of these, as well as of our first band of students, have already passed away. And this brings me to another thought. Every generation of students has its own sacred memories of friends who have passed into the unseen world. Their names will occur, I know, to their contemporaries. Surely we may give thanks for the living—for friendships begun here, some lasting long after the Oxford days were over? Friendships of a lifetime?

I am sure we shall all feel that our blessings also involve our responsibilities. Do we ever think what it is to belong to a great country—perhaps at the present time, the most influential in the world? To have grown up in the midst of a high civilization, and of Christian traditions—may I not say, of Christian faith?

In the case of most of us to have had kind parents, good

homes amid circumstances, if not of wealth, yet not those of extreme poverty? To have, on the whole, good health, good faculties, good surroundings?

Is it nothing to have been, for two or three years, brought into contact with a place like Oxford, so rich in historical associations, in noble traditions, in learning, in beauty and in art? A place whose pavements have been trodden by some of the noblest of Englishmen, whose very air seems to vibrate with ennobling thoughts and aspiration? To have had opportunities of study, access to lectures, to libraries, to talk, to discussion—to have had leisure to benefit by all these things? What return are we making for them?

The ancient Greeks had a saying, 'Sparta has fallen to thy lot, see that thou adorn her.' We too, may say, 'The lot has fallen unto me in a fair ground. Yea, I have a goodly heritage.' That He who has thus called us may enable us to walk worthy of our calling, is the earnest prayer of your affectionate old friend

E. WORDSWORTH.

Elizabeth Wordsworth was now eighty-eight. When writing letters she would still quote from *The Odyssey* in the original Greek, adding the caution 'I don't feel sure of the accents', because she could no longer see well enough to use a lexicon. Her eyes were now so dim that she could barely read; and the firm handwriting had degenerated into an illegible scrawl. When kind friends offered to read aloud to her she would indicate the exact position of the book on her shelves and the precise passage she wanted to hear. 'Get down that Life of Carteret,' she demanded of one friend. 'I think that those two young officers in the Levant died with the same Greek lines upon their lips as Carteret did, and I must make sure.' The task of a reader was not an easy one; among the books she chose were Grimm's Fairy Stories in 'plat-Deutsch', 'that new

French book on Thucydides', and various books in Spanish. Katharine Esdaile called one day to find her sitting at a table with a copy of the Vulgate open before her—'Here you are! Just get the Hebrew lexicon from over there and take the Septuagint for yourself. I am sure the *firmamentum* of the Vulgate is a mistranslation; solidity is the very last quality suggested by the sky. Let's look it up.' In lighter moments *Vanity Fair* was a special favourite, often chosen for reading aloud 'because I shall soon see people like Shakespeare and Milton but I shall not see Becky Sharp.'

In extreme old age Elizabeth Wordsworth could still charm the young. Katharine Esdaile had asked if her son, who was then up at Oxford, might call to pay his respects. 'What? Why should he want to meet an old pyramid like me?' was the reply. But call he did and, after much conversation on such topics as Kant or the Romantic Movement, came away declaring this old lady to be the best company in Oxford. Other visitors found some of her habits odd and slightly disconcerting. When talking to friends she would suddenly rise to her feet and wander out of the room and into the garden for a breath of fresh air, returning in a minute or two to take up the conversation exactly where she had broken it off. Like most old people she found it hard to remember names, but she found ways and means of overcoming this difficulty—'at my age I can do the diplomatic mumble as well as anyone.' Boredom, however, was something which she had never been able to conceal and with the years her dislike of bores became more rather than less evident—'I am afraid I have never mastered the art of looking *surreptitiously* at my watch.'

Throughout the bitter winter of 1927–8 she was content to spend much of her time dozing quietly in a chair by the fireside, but with the coming of warmer weather she was out again every day, rambling about north Oxford and causing considerable alarm to friends and relations. She would stand still in the middle of the road talking to herself, regardless of passing traffic, before darting off aimlessly first in one direction, then in another. She believed that the road drains were a menace to health if they remained blocked even for a short while, and would spend much time poking her walking-stick down between the bars of the grids, clearing away mud and dead leaves. These eccentricities of behaviour were no indication of any kind or degree of mental decay; her mind remained clear as crystal. On her ninetieth birthday the Principal, Fellows and members of Council at L.M.H. presented a Latin address to her, *Domina illustrissima et dilectissima*. She listened intently as it was read aloud by Cyril Bailey, then Chairman of Council. 'A most interesting use of the subjunctive,' she commented as he finished, 'yes, Mr Bailey, a *beautiful* subjunctive.'

But though her intellect might remain undimmed, inexorably the dark was closing in upon her. 'Alas, I can hardly do more than spell out a few verses in a very large print Bible,' she wrote on 7 January 1931; 'luckily I have a very good memory and know a good deal by heart.' The world outside was becoming a strange place full of problems she had never thought to be asked to face. Frugal though she was both by nature and by upbringing, she had always taken for granted that certain things would be provided for her as if by nature; she might query expenditure on luxuries but she never considered, perhaps had not even known, the price of the necessities of life. Now in the bleak economic climate of the thirties these horrid financial questions raised their heads for the first time. Elizabeth Wordsworth, however, could always find interest and entertainment in any new situation; shortages and rising prices brought a small but welcome spark of excitement into her life. 'I must say that to experience the discomforts of poverty in my old age was a thing I didn't anticipate,' she remarked in the cheerful tones of someone making a surprising but exhilarating discovery; 'To have trouble in getting coals! And legs of mutton! Things one never even thought about!' In a letter written in September 1931 she described one of her more remarkable economies:

> I have dug out a very old pre-war dress which is, or was, rather a handsome one, and now that the old fashions are back again it really does not look half bad. So with a little taking-in at the waist I have adopted it as my Sunday frock.

She had always been interested in clothes, though not in fashion, delighting especially in bright colours. In 1878, when first appointed Principal, she had assumed the dignity of a cap. She continued to wear one to the end of her life, but she wore her caps with a difference. 'To the uninitiated eye it looks like a bundle of flowers tied together by a ribbon of velvet and then a row of lace all round,' Gertrude Bell had written of one of these caps. 'It's very, very little (and you know Miss Wordsworth's head is very wide and large) and generally it's crooked.' Now in her old age she still chose to add a touch of frivolity to her caps, brightening them with a bow of scarlet ribbon.

At the beginning of 1932 Elizabeth Wordsworth fell ill with a bad chill. She made a good recovery, and when the summer came she was well enough to attend her last L.M.H. gaudy. She was sitting in the Hall garden, so frail and shrivelled that it seemed as if the least puff of wind would blow her away, when someone placed a three-month-old baby in her lap. As she crooned over it and the child crowed back delightedly the two together made a picture of age and youth which the onlookers were never to forget.

On Elizabeth Wordsworth's ninety-second birthday her old pupil Elizabeth Lea, now Mrs Joseph Wright, called to bring her a bunch of flowers. The bent, frail body huddled into an old frock and a crochet shawl was in curious contrast to the undimmed sparkle of the mind. 'She is so inspiring, so other-worldly,' Elizabeth Wright recorded, 'it helps one to know that the after-life is real, and the present shaping of our souls for their future the only thing that matters,' and, to another correspondent, 'her mind is as active as ever and, what is still more remarkable at her age, she can express her beautiful thoughts with all her accustomed freshness and vigour.'

On this birthday occasion Elizabeth Wordsworth's mind turned to childhood days and to the earliest of all her birthdays —'You know, I don't think I ever gave so much pleasure in my life as I did by being born! I was the first grandchild, and all my young aunts and people were in raptures over this baby.' Three weeks later Elizabeth Wright was again at Rawlinson Road, this time with Louise Creighton whose marriage had marked the first eruption of women into the closed circle of Oxford society. Elizabeth Wordsworth would not allow either of her guests to pour out but, brandishing the teapot in a dangerously dramatic manner, she launched into animated conversation. A bowl of red poppies was contrasted with a bunch of roses brought by Elizabeth Wright—'They are all one colour, might have been made of paper. But those roses are like music to me, modulated; look at the shades of colour in each! Those poppies are like jazz.' She went on to talk of the changed order in Europe, the vanishing of so many crowned heads, and all the new inventions she had seen in the course of her life—'If some prophet had told me when I was a girl that all this would happen in my life-time I should have said "Is thy servant a dog that I should believe all this?" '

Later in the summer she enjoyed the pleasure of a visit from Maud Holgate, one-time bursar of L.M.H. Together they spent an afternoon with Edith Argles, one of the oldest and dearest of L.M.H. friends, now living in retirement near Oxford at Bagley Wood. On 6 November Elizabeth Wright called once more at Rawlinson Road. Bent, shrivelled and frail though her body might be, Elizabeth Wordsworth's spirit still soared free from any touch of decay—'her mind is like a phoenix.' Though admitting that she was sleeping badly and 'feeling very sorry for myself' she refused to dwell on the unavoidable trials of old age but instead turned back to the past to count up the many blessings of her long life. These, her last recorded reminiscences, reflected her attitude towards society and life in general. Class-conscious she was not, because like others of that vanished generation she took class completely for granted; she was, of course, a lady, and she was also a very humble Christian. She began by speaking of her home, her parents, and above all, of her old nurse, Janet McCraw—'She was a lady in the real sense of the word; I don't mean birth, I mean what she was.' She went on to talk of early days at L.M.H. and of the Oxford men she had known long ago—Pusey, Liddon, Scott-Holland—lamenting that the race of giants was no more. 'But,' she added, as always confident and hopeful of the future, 'perhaps the great men are going about and we don't recognize them. In the same way I often think that though our servants seem very stupid to us, in the next world we shall find that they are really much better than ourselves.' Her face lit up as she threw out her hands in an eager gesture—'Oh, in the next world we shall see quite a difference in values.'

Elizabeth Wright's visit had to be cut short because her hostess was expecting a group of ladies to arrive for a reading of one of Trollope's novels. A fortnight later, on a cold, wet, autumn day, Elizabeth Wordsworth held another of these readings, the chosen book this time being *Pendennis*. She followed the reading with her usual bible class, taking Hebrew poetry as her subject. She spoke first of Psalm 107, mentioning in this connection a brilliant young doctor whose recent death had saddened Oxford, and then she turned to the passage from Psalm 45, 'The king's daughter is all glorious within, her clothing is of wrought gold.' 'You and I are weaving that garment,' she commented; 'our lives are, or should be, strands in that pure gold.' Thus unwittingly she spoke her own epitaph. That evening she collapsed. When her devoted maids tried to be of some help she told them firmly to leave her alone; she was going to die and nothing that they could do would be of any use. Her sister Dora came immediately so that she might have one of her own family with her till the end. For a day or two she lingered, her mind perfectly clear, her body in no pain; then on 30 November, St Andrew's Day as she herself would have noted, quietly and with complete composure she faded out of life.

Elizabeth Wordsworth

by E. M. Jamison

Part I 1840 – 1858: Foundations

Ancestry and birth

Elizabeth Wordsworth had the rare distinction of being at once the perfect representative of her generation and upbringing and the possessor of an individuality completely her own. Out of no other circle could she have sprung, but she was not in bondage to it. Her character developed in originality and independence throughout her life, and yet it never lost the first impress stamped upon it. The earlier portion of a life is often the most significant and interesting, while in later years a man or woman becomes merely a representative, although in some special way, it may be, of the position or profession reached in maturity. 'As is the case with all springtides, it possesses a fascination which the summer cannot boast; the latter may be beautiful, dignified, satisfactory, but the delicious surprises of April are no longer there.'[1] So could Elizabeth Wordsworth write of her great uncle 'the Poet'; but with her, surprises came later than the April of her life. The fineness of intellect, the quickness of warm sympathy and affection, the seriousness of purpose were there from the earliest years, but not until she was nearly thirty did the other aspects of her genius begin to show themselves; the gift for writing, the wit and unexpected humorous reactions, the creative power all the more effective

---

1. E.W., *William Wordsworth*, 1891, p. 130.

for being largely unconscious, and the ever growing illumination of religious faith. The earlier period of her life was that of her family and background; the later is *sui generis*, when through the awakening power of a great friendship, and later with the opportunity of leadership in a new field, when she was thrown on her own resources, she became entirely herself. Yet no tinge of professionalism ever coloured her exercise of a profession. Throughout her life the training of childhood and early youth provided the stable warp into which she wove the many-coloured threads of her own achievement.

She was born a hundred years ago, on 22 June 1840, the eldest child of Christopher Wordsworth, then headmaster of Harrow, later Canon of Westminster and Bishop of Lincoln, and his wife, Susannah Hatley Frere. Her father was the youngest surviving son of another Christopher, Master of Trinity College, Cambridge, and of Priscilla Lloyd of the great Quaker banking family of Dolobran and Birmingham. The Wordsworths came of good old north country stock settled for centuries in Yorkshire, and later in Westmorland and Cumberland. 'They belonged,'[1] to quote once more the subject of this memoir, 'to the class which produces farmers, attorneys, clergy, tradesmen, soldiers and sailors, and which, while obliged to depend on its own exertions, is nevertheless rarely exposed to the shifts and struggles of poverty; a class which commands respect while it does not relieve its members from the necessity of independent action, or expose them to the temptations incident to great wealth and luxury, and obliges them to develop whatever is in them.' At the beginning of the last century the destiny of the family was fulfilled in a startling way by the children of John Wordsworth, the Cockermouth lawyer, and his wife, Anne Cookson. The genius of William Wordsworth and Dorothy, his sister, brought them

1. ibid., p. 6.

universal fame; and their youngest brother Christopher, through his brains and grit, reached a sober academic eminence as Master of Trinity.

In spite of narrow circumstances Christopher, like William, had gone up to Cambridge. There, the early training of school-days passed at Hawkshead, in the freedom of the Coniston fells, was strengthened by the discipline of the University in classics and mathematics, and broadened by travel in Europe. The high church tradition of the older type brought a steadying influence; and with it there went a sympathy for all that was good in others and a tolerance for those who dissented in religion. The plain living and simplicity of manners which marked the family continued long after the attainment of assured position, and some wealth brought with it the dignified standards of the professional and merchant class in the nineteenth century. Here were the elements which formed the essential heritage of the next generations; religious conviction; habit of humane learning; instinctive feeling for natural beauty; and a poet's insight and power of expression. With it all went family affection and dutifulness, independence and integrity in word and deed.

Of no less importance in the strands of inheritance was the contribution of Priscilla Lloyd, of whom her husband wrote: 'her understanding is exceedingly good . . . All her feelings are deep, severe and profound.'[1] In certain respects she brought to her sons but an added measure of the qualities inherent in the Wordsworths. The sense of reality in religion was strong in her family, which had suffered for its Quaker belief, and the love of ancient literature and the writing of verse were remarkable in her father, Charles Lloyd of Bingley House, the translator of Homer and Horace. Even more strongly did the

---

1. J. H. Overton and E.W., *Christopher Wordsworth, Bishop of Lincoln*, 1888, p. 7.

H

poetic strain show itself in her brother, another Charles, himself a poet and the friend of poets, the ally of Charles Lamb and of the Lake School. It was probably from this side of his ancestry that Priscilla's youngest son, named like his father, Christopher, drew his passionate devotion to Horace, the secular author whose words were oftenest on his lips, and whose works were at his side as he lay dying. This devotion he handed on to his daughter Elizabeth, who turned instinctively to the poet of Venusia to cap an illustration or point a conversation. This clear line of devout Horatians is the more interesting in view of the conflict of evidence as to William Wordsworth's sentiment. His great-niece records his saying: 'Horace is my great favourite, I love him dearly';[1] but in 1809 Charles Lloyd the younger joined him with Coleridge and Southey as having 'next to a contempt for Horace'.[2] Priscilla's descendants have ever been ready to attribute their gifts of verse-making and hymn-writing to their Lloyd forebears, gifts which found expression in the Bishop of Lincoln and his children, Elizabeth and John. But the Wordsworth contribution, derived perhaps from the Cooksons, cannot wholly be left out of the account. Another, more particular, endowment came to Elizabeth from her Lloyd grandmother in the quick observation, the keen interest in people, the incisive judgement, together with the instinct for direct and lively expression with pen or brush and pencil. Drawing was Priscilla's only accomplishment, since Quaker practice did 'not admit of fashionable accomplishments,'[3] and this she handed on in full measure. There are extant, moreover, pungent letters, alive with vigorous insight, such as she wrote to her brother Robert: 'Lamb would not I think by any means be a person to take up your abode with. He is too much like yourself—he would encourage

1. E.W., *William Wordsworth*, p. 201.
2. E. V. Lucas, *Charles Lamb and the Lloyds*, 1898, p. 233.
3. *Christopher Wordsworth*, loc. cit.

those feelings which it certainly is your duty to suppress';[1] or to her sister-in-law about her brother Charles's plan to translate Alfieri: 'I am sorry that I cannot either like or approve Alfieri. The stories are so atrocious, as rather to *disgust* than to excite sympathy—and the style so inharmonious as by no means to add to its attractions.'[2] But the letters about her sons, especially the little Christopher, show all her humour and detachment and withal the warmth of a deep reserved affection. 'As to poor Christy, his attractions are but small for he wants most of the *graces* of mind and body. He is quite an oddity, but I find enough to love in him. He is a great darling with his parents.'[3] Three years later she noted: 'Little Christy discovers a great fondness for learning';[4] and again: 'Christy's eyes glisten with interest'[5] in the Book of Judith. He 'has quite a warlike spirit—nothing he delights in so much as Chevy Chase, or anything about war and fighting. It is curious to observe the very different tastes of children as their minds open—and very interesting to listen to their different views of the same subject.' Priscilla Lloyd did not live to see her son grow up and fulfil her reading of his character.

Christopher Wordsworth, with his eager questing intelligence and his readiness to give battle for any cause in which he believed, had a brilliant career at Winchester and Trinity College, Cambridge. He won almost every classical honour open to him and he was elected Fellow of his college. His solutions of textual problems were accepted throughout the world of learning and he was the first scholar to transcribe the *Graffiti* of Pompeii. Besides his linguistic flair, he was endowed in rich measure with the 'sense of country' and the sense of the

1. *Charles Lamb and the Lloyds*, p. 99.
2. ibid., p. 256, n. 2.
3. *Christopher Wordsworth*, p. 9.
4. ibid., p. 9.
5. ibid., p. 10.

unity of history, which had full scope in his travels in Greece. They resulted in two books of considerable weight: *Athens and Attica* and *Greece, pictorial, descriptive, and historical*, both of which went through many editions. But very soon he turned his back on humane learning and gave himself up to pastoral work and biblical studies. His mind was not speculative but in essence historical and practical; and his ultimate object was to draw out the moral and devotional content of the Holy Scriptures. Once the firm assertion of fact was reached, the debate was over. This was the reason for his settled faith and its fulfilment in a saintly life, and it was the basis of his ecclesiastical standpoint. He had a convinced belief in the English Church at once Catholic and Reformed; Catholic from historical necessity; Reformed, as the moral corollary of the Faith. He based himself on the Fathers of the Early Church and on the Caroline Divines, accepting the old High Church position with its standards of seemly liturgical services and sober, yet heartfelt, devotion. He had many links with the Tractarian movement but his roots were in a more ancient tradition. With all his love of beauty and order in worship he had little patience with unhistorical 'Ritualism'. The rooting in tradition had its natural flowering in daily practice, and gave a dignified simplicity and unselfconsciousness to the religion of him and his children. It was so much a part of their life that they took it for granted.

The English Church, in Christopher Wordsworth's view, had a special mission to bring about reunion at home and reform abroad. He made a plan, for which the times were as yet unready, for the return of the Wesleyan Methodists to the Church, and he had high hopes for the reformation of the Catholic Church in Italy and France in the period between 1850 and 1870. The actual course of events, ending in the declaration of papal infallibility, was a bitter blow. It put the seal on his reprobation of the Roman Church; and while he helped the Old Catholic movement in Germany, he turned resolutely to the crying problems of his own church and country. All this has been set down here because of its effect on Elizabeth Wordsworth. Her father poured out his ideas, hopes and plans with passionate intensity, and his temper of mind left its mark upon her point of view. Her mind was no more speculative than his, but it was less historical and logical. This had two very opposite results. It sometimes happened that opinions which he had based on careful study of the facts were accepted by her because she had been brought up in them, and they became for her prejudices. On the other hand, since she depended little on reasoned evidence her faith was a matter of personal intuitive conviction and moral certainty.

In 1838 Christopher Wordsworth, then headmaster of Harrow, married Susannah Hatley Frere. She was the second daughter of George Frere, a solicitor in the grand manner of the firm of Frere, Foster & Co., and of Elizabeth Raper Grant of Highland ancestry. Mr George Frere came of a family with a long record of distinguished service to church and state and learning. He and his wife belonged to the same wealthy and cultured circle, remarkable also for its unending kindliness and charity, as Mrs Hoare, the widow of the Quaker banker, Samuel Hoare, but herself a church-woman. She was the great friend of Priscilla Lloyd, and she had given what was in truth a second home to the three motherless Wordsworth boys. At her house at Hampstead they spent much of their vacations, and her thought for them is witnessed by her constant gifts and a vast pile of mutual correspondence. Men and women well-known in the literary and musical worlds frequented the parties at 'The Heath', and William Wordsworth stayed there when he went to London. Not the least of the benefits due to Mrs Hoare's good offices was the meeting of Christopher Wordsworth and his future wife at one of the parties.

All the descriptions of Susannah Frere, and her portraits, insist on the loveliness of her clear complexion and finely modelled features; straight nose, lips at once firm and tender; wide blue eyes whose gaze seems fixed with unwavering affection on husband and children. In temperament, devoutness and tenderness were matched by a reserve which forbade all extravagant expression of feeling; she had musical gifts and taste in literature; her practical ability undertook the management of a large household in such a way that her husband was spared all friction. Her sympathy and sound judgement never failed him, 'her whole delight was to be his handmaid.'[1] So much did he depend on her head and pen that he confessed she had spoiled him 'for a wise, solitary, severe old divine'.[2] Always unobtrusive, she seemed somewhat withdrawn especially in later life owing to slight deafness, but her presence in the background gave constant support by her 'firmness, strength and self-possession'. Her courage never flinched from any duty to be done, or service to be rendered, and that without a thought for herself. It was an ideal marriage: 'their married happiness was as near perfection as anything on this side of Eden could be.'[3] And yet in every characteristic of mind and body they were wholly contrasted. As complements one of the other their opposite personalities found their full realization and reconciliation. It was in this harmony of diversity that the family of five daughters and two sons was to grow up, united by strong affection and yet differing in natural qualities and acquired interests. Some of them had more affinity with their father, others with their mother. But granted the framework of the family and the outlook and beliefs of their parents, which they accepted wholeheartedly, they were never constrained by parental pressure to fit a rigid common mould, and

1. Jane Frere in J.H.O. and E.W., *Christopher Wordsworth*, p. 90.
2. Christopher Wordsworth in ibid., p. 99.
3. ibid., p. 87.

they developed on divergent lines. Looking back after some forty years, Elizabeth Wordsworth could write to her sister Priscilla: 'How we ever all lived together in one nursery— John with his codexes, you with your bandages, Mary with her county society and I with my Higher Education—to say nothing of the rest of the family and *their* tastes—all in embryo—I can't imagine.'[1] The children differed indeed in character and interests, but their unity of fundamental outlook saved them from corroding friction within the family.

Elizabeth, the first child, was born in the small house at Harrow to which her father moved after the headmaster's house had been burned down shortly before his marriage. Her birth was the occasion of much midsummer delight, and the letters interchanged by members of the family dispel once for all, so far as they at any rate were concerned, the commonplaces about early Victorian stiffness and reserve. The headmaster wrote to his mother-in-law, Mrs George Frere, on

> June 24, i.e. John Baptists Day
> and two days after your granddaughter's
> birth

This is all very pleasant, is it not? And it is a sober pleasure too, which seems likely, by God's mercy, to last. We are going on wonderfully well . . . I really do think baby a very respectable looking young lady, and quite equal to the average of babies, and hope you, who know more about babies will think so too. It was a great pleasure to see my father here yesterday morning from Bedford Square, and we look forward to another visit from him soon with you and the two aunts, Anne and Judith, to whom pray give my best love. Lizzy is writing so many letters that I am afraid she

1. Letter lent by Mrs Leeke—E.W. to her sister Priscilla, 3 July 1885.

will wear herself out. She takes excellent care of the household and makes a very good Susan.

Yours affectionately,
Christ[r.] Wordsworth[1]

'Lizzy', the Wordsworth children's 'Aunt Lissey' was their mother's eldest sister, Elizabeth, in charge of the Harrow household for the time being. She was to have a big share in their affections and their daily life especially after they all went to live at Stanford-in-the-Vale. Anne and Judith were the two youngest of the sisters; Judith married Dean Merivale of Ely and so brought about the close connection of Wordsworths and Merivales; Anne married her cousin, Captain John Frere, and to her Elizabeth Wordsworth was bound by a special tie of warm sympathy and community of outlook. A letter written on 23 June by Anne to her sister Lissey sounds so wholly modern a note that it might have been written a century later by any young aunt thrilled by the birth of her first niece, although her counterpart today would have used the telephone for a lengthy gossip, and we should have no record of it. But Aunt Anne's letter was for the time entirely up-to-date in that affixed to it was one of the new penny stamps with Queen Victoria's head on it. The subject of the letter, the niece in question, belonged to the earliest generation to know the famous stamp from the very beginning of life, and more than sixty years on, when the Queen died, she could write:

Farewell, dear face, which we have known
Familiar as our mother's own,
Through Life's long chequered years the same,
Far reaching as the English name![2]

1. Letter lent by Mrs Leeke.
2. E.W., *Poems and Plays*, Oxford, 1931, p. 54.

In this present year of grace 'the dear face' has returned in the commemoration issue which marks the centenary of the adhesive stamp and with it the birth of Elizabeth Wordsworth.

But to go back to Aunt Anne's letter:[1]

My dearest Liss,

I cannot help writing a word to say, how entirely happy your good news has made me, and how very kind you are to write such a long letter—I am so afraid you will have written too much, and do wish I could have been there to help . . . It is like a pleasant dream—Aunt Anne and Aunt Judith sound very well, don't you think? As to Aunt Lissy, Uncles John, George and Bartle, we are well enough used to think them agreeable titles. My dear love to Christ.ʳ· and Susan. I am wild to have somebody else to tell the news to, tho' I assure you our kind friends here were most agreeably sympathetic. Shall we get the frock done in time? . . . I wonder whether Grandpapa did go down to see the Baby yesterday. I am a very long way from Harrow I find . . . I shall write no more rigmarole, for I could go on for ever, and as I shall certainly write about nothing else I may as well close here.

Take care of yourself my dear Aunt. I have long settled that the Baby is to be Elizabeth. Pray don't let them call it Sarah if you can help it.

Always your affect. Co Aunt
Anne Frere

Elizabeth she was in fact christened after her grandmother Frere, although there was far less Frere than Wordsworth in her makeup. Her godmother was Miss Hoare, step-daughter of

1. Lent by Mrs Leeke. Found tucked into E.W.'s own copy of *Glimpses*, having been sent to her by Miss E. Frere.

Mrs Hoare, the old friend of both families; and the Wordsworth blessing came from Great-uncle William in a letter
written probably in July and ending:

> With love to Susan, and kisses to the Baby, in which
> Mary and Dora unite, ever
> > Your affectionate Uncle
> > Wm. Wordsworth.[1]

Perhaps it was with the kisses that there descended a portion of
'The Poet's' genius.

Environment

When Elizabeth was four years old, her father was appointed
Canon of Westminster and left Harrow. Her only memory was
of a brilliant bed of nasturtiums in the garden. Even so early
did her passionate delight in colour make itself felt. A couple
of years later the misery she endured on the death of her
grandfather Wordsworth was caused by her black frock; and
once she wanted to go in a particular carriage because it had
red wheels. But if the Harrow house sank into a very distant
background, No. 4 Little Cloister left an impress that was
always present with her. The Wordsworths occupied the old
house from 1845 till they went to Riseholme in 1869; but from
1851 their real home was in the country because the Canon
held, together with the Canonry, the chapter living of
Stanford-in-the-Vale cum Goosey in Berkshire. There they
spent eight months in the year, and four months in Little
Cloister; Elizabeth Wordsworth's life was to be passed in
places of ancient beauty: Westminster, the Vale of the White
Horse, Lincoln, Oxford.

Westminster from the first put its spell upon her; the great

---

1. E. de Selincourt (ed.), *Letters of William and Dorothy Wordsworth:
The Later Years*, Oxford, 1939, p. 1030–31.

church brought home to the small child the consciousness that Divine Service was for enjoyment rather than endurance. She was to spend hours in dreaming and sketching in the Abbey and its precincts, engulfed in 'the intense and almost human relation that arises between such a building and those who grow up beside it.'[1] Little Cloister with its pseudo-classical arcade of golden stone is itself a refuge of quietness from the surrounding city, where 'the life of today, of yesterday is beating and throbbing, streaming and struggling with eager and passionate animation.'[2] In the cloister garth a single tree with slanting trunk stands guard, like a sentinel with sloped rifle, over against the Abbey behind. No. 4 had, and still has, all the attractions, and some of the practical drawbacks, of a very old building with its foundations in a remote past, and the marks of the changes and additions of all the ages since. It was once part of the monks' infirmary, and the Norman arches of St Catherine's Chapel, where St Hugh of Lincoln was consecrated, enclose one side of the little courtyard in front of the house. Within, the entrance hall still shows the small hewn panels of the sixteenth century, but the stained glass in the new manner of the mid-nineteenth century, which Mr James Powell made for the windows into the courtyard, has vanished before yet more modern love of clear light. With the glass has gone also the inscription chosen by Canon Wordsworth, '*Domus Dei porta coeli*'. The hall leads to a long dining-room with the tall windows and the gracious panelling of the eighteenth century; next came the Canon's study with 'a door which opened on to the College garden (the old infirmary garden of the monks) . . . the four lawns divided by paths, where the canons of Westminster and their families used to take their Sunday stroll,'[3] and where somewhat later the families began

1. Grant Lloyd (E.W.), *Thornwell Abbas*, 1876, I., p. 115.
2. ibid., p. 117.
3. J.H.O. and E.W., *Christopher Wordsworth*, p. 110.

to play croquet. In the background is an old high wall, the tower of the Jewel House a little to the east, and on the west the Jacobean dormitory of Westminster School. Between the Canon's house and the College Garden was a strip of private garden of which her mother could write for Elizabeth's twelfth birthday: 'the trees are in leaf and clean after the rain; the borders . . . are edged with Virginia Stock in full blow which looks very cheerful; there are a few Tiger Lilies, Stocks and Wallflowers out; and Chrysanthemums planted ready for their turn.'[1] Indoors, from the entrance hall a splendid staircase of carved mahogany went up to the great drawing-room with its pale-green panels and chimney-piece, which last was held in special affection by the Wordsworth children because the fable of the Fox and the Crane was carved there. Next door was the schoolroom, also panelled; on the floor above were the bedrooms and finally there was the nursery looking out on the college garden. It was presided over by Janet McCraw, the most unselfish and devoted friend of them all throughout her long life.

In 1845 four children already occupied the nursery; Elizabeth, the eldest; Priscilla (Mrs P. A. Steedman) born in 184?; John (Bishop of Salisbury) born in 1843; and Mary (Mrs Trebeck) in 1845. At Westminster the three youngest members of the family were born; Susannah (head of the Grey Ladies) in 1846; Christopher (Canon of Salisbury) in 1848; and lastly, Dora (Mrs E. T. Leeke) in 1852. Three years after the move Westminster was attacked by a great typhoid epidemic caused by ill-conceived plans of sanitary reform. The three eldest children fell victims to the fever and their 'little cropped heads long bore witness to the dangers they had undergone.'[2] For a time they were sent away to Blackheath and later to

---

1. Letter lent by Mrs Leeke.
2. *Glimpses*, p. 10.

Southend where their Frere relations looked after them. The children all recovered; but death came very near them when their cousin Louisa Frere died. She was the baby Christopher's god-mother, and his baptism had taken place only a short time before the epidemic broke out. The children found their companionship in each other, as often happens in a large family, and were the less dependent on other friends of their own age.

At first their relations with each other were determined, as was natural, by proximity of age, and Elizabeth had always a close link with her next sister Priscilla; she felt keenly the break which was caused when her childhood's companion went in 1867(?) to nurse at King's College Hospital, but she had no 'special' sister to the exclusion of the rest. As time went on she shared Mary's interests in drawing and sketching, and ultimately she was drawn close to Susan, who in the early Westminster days was still reckoned among the younger ones. They in their turn grew up into an equality of intercourse. John, only three years younger than Elizabeth, had almost from the first a great part in her life, and his Oxford career was to lead to hers. She looked forward also with eagerness to playing with her cousin Charlotte, only a year older than herself, at Mrs Hoare's house at Hampstead. Charlotte's mother had died when the child was born, and her father, Charles Wordsworth, later Bishop of St Andrews, left her for long periods in the care of his own boyhood's friend. She stayed, too, at the Cloisters from time to time, and, later on, her small half-brothers paid visits to their contemporaries, the younger Wordsworth children. Older visitors left a very definite impression on Elizabeth: there was Joshua Watson, one of the co-founders of the National Society and the Additional Curates' Society, who was remembered as 'a bright, playful and most kindly old gentleman—always doing something for somebody, from generous gifts of money to little presents' to the children; and there were many relatives and connections, Hoares and Mannings, Selwyns and Powells and Freres. On one occasion her father wrote to her humorously that he had seen about thirty Freres that day. Alas, that she remembered nothing of the visit of William Wordsworth when she was seven years old.

The nursery régime inculcated hardiness: a cold bath daily continued to be Elizabeth's habit throughout her ninety-two years, and fresh air and a walk every morning were to her essentials of living. There was no luxury or indulgence of the flesh; on the contrary there was self-denial in small things, and endless help given to those in poverty or any kind of distress. And yet withal there was a dignified household routine, enough servants, plenty of plain food and other necessaries. The absence of such things was unthinkable and Elizabeth expressed her fundamental point of view when she exclaimed in reference to the rationing of fuel and food during the First World War: 'I must say that to experience the discomforts of poverty in my old age was a thing I did *not* anticipate! To have trouble in getting Coals! and Legs of Mutton!! Things one never even thought about!' And all the time she was re-using the envelopes of letters she had received, and denying herself the 'luxuries' of a penny bus fare or cherries at 6*d*. a lb., and in consequence giving away substantial sums here and there wherever cases of need came to her notice.

The occupation of the vicarage of Stanford-in-the-Vale began in 1851, on a morning in May which displayed to the children, who had till then known the country chiefly in July or August, all the marvels of the English spring in the Vale of the White Horse. Stanford is a big village lying off the high road midway between Challow and Faringdon. The houses, not picturesque but plain and well-proportioned, built here of old red-brick and there of grey stone in jostling neighbour-liness, are not untypical of the Vale. The long street bending round corners rises slowly to the ancient church of St Denys with its square, solid tower. Beyond the churchyard, through the green gate in the wall, is the vicarage, a house of small distinction plastered in grey rough cast. Canon Wordsworth added to it a gabled wing containing long rooms with great bow-windows, which looked out over the stretches of wide green meadows beyond. The garden was not large, but it had boxed parterres and lawns and a small orchard. To the west it was marked off by a row of great elms. All round the garden went the 'vicar's walk' leading to a low stone seat set in the ivied wall. There the vicar would go to meditate in view of the White Horse and the long line of downland closing the prospect to the south; or on Sundays after church he would walk fast along the garden paths, expounding to guests and children his views on St John's Apocalypse, or some other topic on his mind. So narrow were the paths that 'there was need of a perpetual skipping or jumping on the part of the girls in order to keep within earshot of their father.'[1] In front of his new wing he had planted a cedar of Lebanon; and he had put one of his favourite inscriptions on the lintel of the front door: '*Nisi Dominus aedificaverit domum, vanus est labor aedificantium eam.*' There were other texts, too, put about the house: on the rafters of the dining-room, 'whether ye eat or drink ... do all to the Glory of God'; and in the store-closet the words '*Μάρθα Μάρθα*' gave pause to the mistress of the household. The habit of recollection was certainly impressed on the family and their guests.

The rooms at the vicarage were bare and plainly furnished, but there were some prints on the walls, and there were books everywhere. The study 'walls are covered by books and book-shelves, and in the centre was a table loaded with open books

---

1. Dean Burgon's reflections in J.H.O. and E.W., *Christopher Wordsworth*, p. 522.

while books in all positions cover the floor and furniture,'[1] ready for the vicar's consultation in his great work of commenting on the Holy Scriptures. That was his constant occupation in the comparative leisure of Stanford, pursued by him for nearly twenty years; and the whole family helped.

The daily experience at the vicarage was of plain living and hard working. It was informed by a good conscience towards God and their neighbour; mutual confidence and respect towards each other; happiness in the simple pleasures of the country; contacts with notable personalities who came to stay. Indoors and out there was space for individual growth. For many years they had no carriage; a pony-trap drawn by 'poor little Jessie in the old brown harness' helped them to get about and there were ponies or horses for the boys to ride; but for the most part they walked in large companies on the Faringdon road, or through the fields and over ditches and stiles taking note of men, beasts and flowers. All her life Elizabeth had the seeing eye and the observing mind, registering images of orchards foaming with white and pink blossom; high banks blue with veronica; the molten sea of buttercups motionless upon the meadows until it broke in the white surf of parsley against the hedgerows. These were visions of enduring things, as valid now as then; but the scenes and festivals of village life in which the Wordsworth children rejoiced belong to a vanished past. In the early days at Stanford, refusing to be ousted by the National School, there was a dame's school kept by old Nanny Grundy in a cottage on the green. 'Each child brought a brick to sit upon and, when they were naughty, they were pinned by the skirt to the cushion on which the old lady sat. When they were very bad indeed, she called them "little unbelievers."'[2] There were carol-singers, and mummers

---

1. E. W. Watson, *Life of Bishop John Wordsworth*, 1915, p. 17, quoting reminiscences of Bishop John.
2. *Glimpses*, p. 25.

who played their parts at Christmas in the vicarage dining-room; there was, greatest excitement of all, 'Club Day, when the benefit club'[1] marched about the village with a band and a banner; the stewards had heavy poles painted blue, with red knobs, and decorated at the top with bunches of lilac, peonies and laburnum. The band accompanied them in church 'to the Old Hundredth and Happy the man whose tender care Relieves the poor distressed'; and then they danced on the vicarage lawn, all of them men, in their hats and Sunday blacks, solemnly hopping and turning between the flower-beds, in preparation for the great feast in the schoolroom, which was shared by the vicar and his curates. The vicar also made a point of holding his tithe dinner complete with punch bowl and ladle, when in person he received from the farmers the vicarial tithes instead of letting them be paid through a lawyer. Some of the old women still came to church on Sunday in scarlet cloak, black coal-scuttle bonnet, white frill and velvet shoes; the younger women wore sun-bonnets and the men smock frocks. In the year in which the Wordsworths went to Stanford, Mr Pusey, the first landowner in the parish to make allotments on his land, took all his allotment holders to the Great Exhibition and presented them in their smock frocks to Queen Victoria in Hyde Park.[2] The vision of a confirmation in the ancient church white with the young women's caps and the young men's smocks could never be forgotten. Parish occasions meant contact with the outer world; neighbouring clergy came, and the Bishop. He was Samuel Wilberforce who often stayed at the vicarage, and impressed on Elizabeth his magnetic personality, 'his fascinatingly ugly face, large mouth, thick wavy hair and irresistible manner, his quick powers of observation, his courtesy and his unfailing

1. *Glimpses*, p. 23.
2. Lewin G. Maine, *A Berkshire Village*, Oxford and London, 1866, p. 94.

humour. You could never forget he was in the room, he dominated every society in which he was to be found.'[1] On one
occasion, Mary Wordsworth at the age of nine, 'strewed the
Bishop's path to church with primroses, whereupon it was
observed that Bishops' paths were oftener strewn with thorns
than flowers,' as Elizabeth reported at the time.

The parish of Stanford-cum-Goosey was large and scattered:
there was no single squire, but instead many small landlords
and a population recruited to a great extent from those who had
failed to make good on more fortunate estates. Housing was
bad, wages low, sickness chronic, conduct indifferent; the work
of regeneration was crying out to be taken in hand. The church
was restored, and Canon Wordsworth was able to indulge his
taste for stained glass by filling the vacant top light of the east
window with a panel showing Our Lord enthroned on the
Gospels. This became a subject of ardent discussion in the
family; according to Elizabeth in a letter written to Mr Watson
in March 1854: 'we did not quite like it at first.'[2] The high
pews were replaced by open benches and the vicar's tact
eventually carried all the parishioners with him in the change.
Services became more frequent; Holy Communion was celebrated on alternate Sundays; the offices were read on some
of the weekdays. The music was of the simplest; there was no
organ, and the singing of the metrical psalms and the canticles
was started by an old wooden pitch pipe, until it was replaced
by a more efficient set of silvery pipes. The vicar's superb
reading of the services and his inspired sermons made no less
an impression on his hearers because they were often above
their heads. There was regular catechizing in church, his own
children standing up to answer with the rest; and his teaching
in preparation for Confirmation was so lucid that light could
not fail to fall on the candidates. The work in church was fol-

1. *Glimpses*, p. 35.
2. Lent by the Rev. Christopher Wordsworth *per* K. M. Thicknesse.

lowed up by almost daily teaching in the National School on his part and his curates'; his children took a share in the Sunday school from an early age—Mrs Wordsworth, away at Westminster, wrote to Elizabeth when she was twelve anxiously hoping that they had 'had a good school this morning and that John and Mary were both able to take a Class.'[1] The teachers were aged only nine and seven! A little later Elizabeth and her sisters spent many an odd half-hour in the National School doing their 'best to impart the most elementary knowledge to some not very orderly children.' Visiting the whole and the sick formed a large part of the vicar's pastoral work, and he and his family really knew each of his parishioners as an individual. Aunt Lissey after her father's death came to live at Stanford, first at the old gothic cottage beyond the vicarage, later on at the Curate's house, and then at the stately eighteenth-century 'Rectory House' across the road. Here she made a home for orphans of the clergy, and gave herself to evangelistic work in the parish. She laboured without stint to reach the half-awakened consciences of the parishioners and to bring help in every difficulty. It was not only spiritual help that came from the vicarage and Rectory House. Mrs Wordsworth had a storeroom full of good things and homely remedies; and Elizabeth on leaving Stanford could contrast it humorously with Riseholme, 'where *we* are the parish: no poor people, no broth, no tracts, no flannel'[2]; but she could also recall with warm feeling 'Plummer and William Varney and dear old fat Mrs Winch and Mr Proctor in the ascendant.'[3] The villagers were her friends, and she never forgot 'the great kindness and friendliness'[4] of the Stanford farmers and their wives for whom the vicarage family had a warm regard.

1. Lent by Mrs Leeke.
2. Letter (lent by Mrs Leeke) to Dora at school, 11 March 1869.
3. Letter to Susan for her birthday, 13 May 1874, lent by Mrs Leeke.
4. *Glimpses*, p. 25.

Life was not without its small humours and minor tragedies.
A letter from Miss Irving, the children's governess, opens so
wide a window on a cross section of daily routine that it must
be quoted in great part.[1]

Stanford Vicarage
2 June 1856

My dear Elizabeth,

You contrived to write me such a long letter after we had
parted only a few hours, that I feel I ought to be able to send
you a folio at least, now that nearly three days have past, but
I can only promise to go on till Charles comes for letters.
After you were out of sight on Saturday, I returned to my
calico in the drawing-room followed by a troop all open-
mouthed, demanding 'May we go to Mrs Cornwall's now.'
Having said the required yes, the four[2] set off in a great
bustle and soon returned with various packages, and saying
that Mrs Cornwall was *so* glad of their help, and hoped so
much they would come back again for more. This was
delightful as you may imagine, and they made three expedi-
tions before 12½ o'clock, at which hour having finished my
cutting I went out and with Dora's[3] help got a nosegay for
Miss Hobhouse's room. (She had been out all this time with
your Aunt.) Then we had dinner, and then it began to rain,
but not enough to keep me from my singing class, where I
had a large attendance. After it was over I went in to Mrs
Strattons to make an oration, as she had sent up Mira with
the work so that I could not do it here, but I was again
baulked, for I found the whole family sitting round the fire,
full dressed in honour of a very round faced son, who had
come home for the day, so I had not the heart to hurt the

1. From Miss Margaret Irving to E.W. (lent by Mrs Leeke).
2. John, Mary, Susan and Christopher, aged 13 to 8.
3. Aged 4.

mother's feelings in the midst of such a domestic scene. On my return home, I found Miss Hobhouse comfortably reclined on the drawing-room sofa, the children having a great game of play in the schoolroom and passage, and Miss Frere reported to be at her house. So I went there to see if I could help, and a scene of greater confusion and discomfort you cannot well imagine. Miss Frere's things were coming *out*, and Mrs Cornwall's were going *in*, little baskets, little boxes, and little trays being the means of transport. The rain was hopeless—it soaked people through in no time—they all came in and shook themselves like dogs in the passages. Mrs Cornwall was backwards and forwards, guiding Edwin Embling and his donkey, and unloading the little cart of its curious looking packages which were all put on the kitchen floor. At the kitchen table I sat, making the inventory, putting down things as Miss Frere called them out. But having no Isabella, nobody knew how many plates and cups there *ought* to be, so that the business went on in this style:

Miss F:	3 grey plates—one cracked—(set down)
Sus^a Varney:	Please Ma'am here's another grey plate in the scullery—(added to list)
Miss F:	10 cups and saucers 3 large knives, I small fork
Jane Wicks:	Please Ma'am I've found 2 grey plates in Elizabeth. (Figure altered to 6)
Mary Ann Varney:	Oh, here's lots of knives in the cupboard—(all the figures altered)

and so on. I thought we should never end. I came away at $5\frac{1}{2}$ and got ready for dinner at $\frac{1}{4}6$. But Aunt Lissey did not appear till 6, then she hurried over her meat, and in spite of all remonstrance went off to school. Nobody was there to help her. Mrs Cornwall was too tired to go, and Mr Hepher could hardly have got through the wet. She had about 14 boys and said she got through very well. Miss Hobhouse and the children and I played at sundry games round the fire till she came back to tea at 8, when we got her to sit in the arm chair and be comfortable till bedtime. She was very tired yesterday, but looks quite well today. Yesterday we went to School and Church as usual. Mr Cornwall preached about Joel. . . . In the afternoon Mr Romanis preached on the same subject . . . I heard the collects etc. *before* Tea—and after Tea they all set to work to tell Aunt Lissey about the baby house, a fruitful subject as you are aware. Today everybody was up remarkably early, and got on with lessons and business in a very agreeable way. Miss Hobhouse and Miss Frere sat out in the garden from soon after breakfast till luncheon. We did lessons and music as usual and went for a walk towards Hatford. The children too were out after breakfast a little while, while I ordered dinner and did Monday morning work. Miss Hobhouse went away at 3, and Aunt Lissey went to the Station with her intending to walk back. She has not appeared yet. We have been at lessons till 4, and now I am very near upon post time . . . There is a feast prepared for me in a tent which I must contrive to eat before teatime.

Our very best love to Papa and Mama and Priscilla, and
    Believe me
            My dear Eliz[th]
                Yours very affec[ly]
                    Margaret E. Irving

Another letter[1] to Elizabeth, this time written by her father almost at the end of the Stanford days, has its own significance.

1. Lent by Mrs Leeke.

In the midst of his preoccupation with the Commentary and the dark shadow of the coming Vatican Council, he could yet find time for a lively account of the arrival of Charles Keen, the man servant, in the study weighed down with some bad news to tell. 'We have lost our old pig' was the burden of the disclosure. 'She was quite well last night at ten o'clock when you were at prayers, and when I came in the morning early I found her lying dead—and a litter of nine little pigs running about in the stye just born. To the rescue came Dora after breakfast, with a baby's sucking bottle filled with milk, and Mama in the pigstye (very clean with fresh straw) down on her knees, trying to feed the little pigs out of the bottle, and with very good success.' St Frideswide came immediately to the vicar's mind, and he ended the letter to his daughter, 'You will have here a good subject for a poem as you come along by the train. Also we all look for your help and Mary's in trying to rear this interesting little family.'

A quick perception of the humour to be found in the small incongruities of life, and entertainment in the odd juxtapositions of people and things was characteristic of the Wordsworths, as it was of their contemporaries of like intellectual and social standing.

But in the long run it was the sense of life as a serious thing that prevailed over the humour and happiness of the country. To Elizabeth there came 'glimpses of drunkenness and vice which till then had been unknown to [her], except through the medium of books.'[1] Coming as they did at the age when childhood was passing—she was eleven years old when the sixteen years at Stanford began—and life was beginning to be seen from the grown-up point of view, she never forgot some of the depressing influences of those first few years of village life. And it was not only village life that was depressing:

1. *Glimpses*, pp. 18–19.

Canon Wordsworth poured out to his wife and friends, and also to his children, because they were constantly with him, everything that he had on his mind, and he never 'talked down' to them. In these years he was preoccupied with many things that cried for reformation in the world and the Church; consequently they 'grew up under a rather uneasy sense of some sort of crisis hanging over [their] heads.' Westminster Abbey, which was restored and enriched in 1847, was still hemmed in by crowded, crooked, dirty streets; Victoria Street was not yet built; the two parishes of St Margaret's and St John's, held by Canons of Westminster, contained between them some 52,000 souls. The Canon had much to do with founding the Westminster Spiritual Aid Fund to build churches and schools, and with planning St John's House to provide sick-nursing for the poor of Westminster. This was a home for the nursing sisters under a clergyman Master, with Miss Frere as Lady Superintendent. It was characteristic of Canon Wordsworth's outlook, as it was of his eldest daughter's after him, that there were no vows of celibacy and no severance of family ties for the sisters. Besides all these schemes, there was anxiety on account of the Chartist Movement, the Gorham Controversy, Manning's secession to Rome, and the question of the 'Canada Reserves'.

In the outer world there were grave events; the Revolutions in Europe in 1848; the Crimean War; the Indian Mutiny. Many friends and relatives were in the Crimea and India, and this brought the troubles there very close to the Wordsworths. Of particular interest to the Canon was the condition of religion abroad, and this led him to spend August and September of 1853 in Paris, taking with him his wife and the two eldest girls, then aged twelve and thirteen. Elizabeth always remembered the visit to the Abbé Migne, who produced the vast collections of the *Patrologia Latina* and *Graeca*; he asked whether she and Priscilla learned Latin, and questioned them in that language;[1] and she remembered also her first French play *Le Consulat et l'Empire*,[2] a sort of glorification of Napoleon with plenty of gunpowder in it, and a procession of the monks of St Bernard.

In the life of the Church at home Canon Wordsworth devoted himself with all his ardour to the revival of Convocation, and after its first meeting on 5 November 1852, he worked unceasingly as a proctor in the Lower House of the Province of Canterbury for many reforms; the Prayer Book; Ecclesiastical Discipline; Courts of Appeal; the extension of the Episcopate. The reaction on Elizabeth of her father's absorbing interest in Convocation is shown in a letter[3] written by her just after its first prorogation:

Nov[r] 15th 1852
Stanford

My dear Papa,

We were all very much interested by the Speeches in Convocation, though when it broke up, I could not quite see what became of your grievances but I suppose they were put off till the next time. *I* could not understand it all by any means, as I suppose you know, and I wish I could understand more of it than I did.

Do you not think there might be a prayer for Convocation in the service as well as for Parliament? Or at least a sentence relating to it in the Prayer for the latter?

I have been reading about Sir Roger de Coverley in the *Quarterly Review* and I liked some of it very much. Mamma has been reading *The Merry Wives of Windsor* to us in the evening, and is now half way in *The Taming of the Shrew*.

I went into the kitchen-garden yesterday—the vicar's

1. Christopher Wordsworth, *Notes at Paris*, London, 1854, p. 38.
2. *Glimpses*, p. 20.
3. Lent by Mrs Leeke.

border is 'boxed' all down, and I hope it will soon be raked and made decent.

I am going to set to work and copy some Heads that Miss Irving has got in her Portfolio, whenever I have finished this letter.

The garden is beginning to look very destitute indeed.

Cindy had a war the other night with some four-footed creature or other, and has scratched her face most woefully.

Will you give my love to Grandpapa and Aunt Lissey and believe me

Your affectionate Child
Elizth Wordsworth

The slight thin child, with her father's eager deep-set eyes, short well-shaped nose and wide mouth, was using her mind to its utmost stretch, yet with a disarming humbleness, to make his interests her own. But she found her escape from hard problems by way of Sir Roger de Coverley, the tidying of the kitchen garden, and the nocturnal adventures of the vicarage cat, to say nothing of the *Merry Wives of Windsor* and the *Taming of the Shrew*, a somewhat surprising choice by Mrs Wordsworth for reading aloud, when the eldest member of the audience was but twelve. In another field, that of aesthetic taste, Elizabeth found relief in her love of bright colours and childish pleasure in 'pretty' trifles from the rich though sombre tones and austere forms of the Gothic revival which had aroused her father's enthusiasm. It is plain that she experienced to the full the secret satisfaction felt by all children who are brought up in an artistic convention beyond their grasp, in the presents she received from the more wealthy friends of the family and in the luxury of Mrs Hoare's house at Hampstead and her rich furs and fine carriage. She always remembered Mr Watson's gifts to her and her sister Priscilla of 'two cardboard boxes (receptacles of new cambric handkerchiefs) with coloured pictures outside, which we considered the acme of loveliness!'[1] And she delighted in the 'Easter eggs, black, yellow, crimson or purple, with white designs scratched upon them'[2] by the skill of old James Dixon at Rydal. But the pleasure with her was not merely one common to most children; it sprang from a deep-seated sentiment for gay things, and a light-heartedness which went side by side with a truly serious outlook, justifying the self-appraisement that she had 'gone dancing through life'.[3]

It was the year before the move to Stanford, when Elizabeth was ten years old, that the whole family spent the summer at Rydal after the death of 'the Poet'. The children stayed in Mrs Irving's cottage with their governess, their parents at Rydal Mount, while Canon Wordsworth was carrying out his task as literary executor, arranging for the publication of *The Prelude*, and writing *The Memoirs of William Wordsworth*.[4] The summer in the north made a very definite impression on Elizabeth; she kept always the vision of the incomparable beauty of the mountains and the picture of the gracious homely household presided over by Aunt Wordsworth. One vivid memory was of 'the big dish or soup-plate, with a little nosegay in it for each guest', which used to appear at the mid-day meal on Sunday, and she remembered also the delights of boating and fishing with her cousins, William's grandsons. There were games with the rough-haired terrier, Pepper, and as a set-off against all this, there remained the unattractive thought of Rydal Chapel, 'with its high pews and horrible little four-legged stools, which did duty for hassocks,' and, when they were upset, left their painful marks on childish knees and

1. *Glimpses*, p. 9.
2. ibid.. p, 15.
3. *per* Ruth Wordsworth, *Brown Book*.
4. *Glimpses*, pp. 14–16.

shins. It was a poor substitute for the Abbey Church of Westminster.

Besides 'Aunt Wordsworth', 'Aunt Dorothy' was there in
old age, her mental powers brought low by the attack of
meningitis many years before. But she was still able to go round
the garden in her chair in company of a tame robin, and to sit
by the parlour fire in tears at the memories called up when her
nephew, the Canon, was reading Beattie's *Minstrel*. A letter
from 'Aunt Wordsworth'[1] fills in with its fine strokes the
picture of the Poet's wife and sister in their last days together:

Rydal Mount
Dec[r] 26th —53

My dear Nieces, Elizabeth and Priscilla,

Your dear Old Auntie, having got a little cold, is not in
the humour to use her pen today—so you must be contented
with a few lines from me, to thank you for her, for the nice
slippers which arrived safely on the morning of her 82[d]
birthday—and she will be well pleased to find the comfort
of them when she goes out—which, tho' we have beautiful
weather, must not be today. I am afraid *you* are kept
within doors by snow, from the reports we see in the news-
papers—The tops of our highest hills, I am told, are covered,
but we have had none in the Valley.

I have not been out, except that I hobbled down to
Chapel yesterday, for more than ten days—having before I
reached home, after a brisk, long walk, without either *twist*,
slip, or *stumble* was siezed [sic] by a sudden pain shot into
my left knee, which has kept me almost to my chair ever
since, but the lameness is going off and I trust I shall be all
right again in a few days.

Your Cousin Jane is, if all be well, to meet her *Madeira*

---

1. Lent by Mrs Leeke.

friend at the Waterloo Station tomorrow—at whose house I suppose she may stay a week or 10 days. But I dare say your Mamma knows about her movements. I have not yet seen any of her Brothers. Their Father wished to have them all at home on Christmas day.

It was a great pleasure to me dear Eliz. to receive your letter and to hear such a nice account of sweet little Dora, and of your all being well. Give my tenderest love to your dear Mamma and say that I shall write to her soon—she, and you all will be busy again, preparing to remove to the Cloisters, where I so lately past a happy time as one of you, and where I trust your Cousin Jane may be with you again. Love to Miss Irving and God bless and send you all a happy new year prays your affec^{te} Aunt

M. Wordsworth

Dorothy died little more than a year after this letter was written, and the writer of it in 1859. There was a strong likeness between Dorothy, as she had been at the height of her brilliance, and her nephew, Canon Christopher,[1] a likeness which was inherited by her great-niece Elizabeth. There was the same square face, the blue-grey eyes, full of shrewd and humorous observation, and the wide mouth which could, if she chose, give effective utterance to it. She had a slight figure, rapid in its movements, an active intelligence impatient of boredom, a common sense expressed with devastating frankness, and a quick sympathy and warm heart 'surely never exceeded by any of God's creatures.'[2] There is a story told of Dorothy, which would have been no less characteristic of Elizabeth who records it. Her brother and Mrs Hemans were having a discussion, no doubt on art or literature, and equally

1. E.W., *William Wordsworth*, pp. 41–2.
2. J.H.O. and E.W., *Christopher Wordsworth*, p. 130.

no doubt the discussion was banal and humourless; Dorothy in the background was tearing up breadths of calico. (Who that in childhood has ever heard it, can forget the shriek of tortured calico?) 'My dear Dorothy,' began the poet in his slow expostulating tones, 'my *dear* Dorothy!' 'Well!' quickly responded she, 'at all events *I'm* doing something useful, which is more than *you* are!'[1]

Besides the close contact with the Rydal household in its simplicity and affection, the summer of 1850 gave occasion for visits to relatives on the Lloyd side, the Braithwaites of Kendal. For all that they were Quakers, Elizabeth's memory was not of simplicity and country nosegays before the Sunday meal but of 'the rather formidable pause, instead of saying grace, when the dinner was put on the table; and the sober rich dresses of the ladies, with caps and white muslin fichus.'[2] There was an acquaintance, too, with Mr Quillinan and his two daughters, who lived at Loughrigg Holm on the banks of the Rotha. Mr Quillinan, whose second wife had been the Poet's daughter, Dora, did not make as favourable an impression on the small child Elizabeth as he did on Matthew Arnold, although he introduced her to Browning by reading aloud the 'Pied Piper'. The Arnold family at Fox Howe, on the other hand, with their good looks and their lovely house, excited all her admiration and the wedding of Miss Jane Arnold and Mr W. E. Forster was a most memorable treat.

The early impression made by the fells and tarns was deepened for Elizabeth by later visits to the Lakes, in 1870 and again in 1876, when she expressed the treasure of remembrance in the poem which begins:

Great twins of Langdale, giants of the West
Still in our household speech, our thoughts and dreams

1. E.W., *William Wordsworth*, p. 42, n.1.
2. *Glimpses*, p. 17.

Have ye lived on, and still in glory dressed
By one rich sunset's unforgotten beams
Through six long years, and now like amethyst
Darkly you greet us through the soft grey mist.[1]

Yet once again she was to see the north country, and this time in 1903 it was family piety which inspired the lines on the grave of her great-grandfather, John Wordsworth, at Cockermouth:

'Tis six score years ago, this very year,
   Since o'er yon grave the funeral words were said;
Four boys, untimely orphans, standing near,
   Bleak wintry sky o'er each uncovered head.

And she, the little maid, whose ready tears
   Fall o'er the mourning weeds, so black, and new,
God knows through what a waste of homeless years
   'Tis her's to wander, ere her home she view![2]

The sense of beauty and the sense of kinship were very strong, but I do not think that Elizabeth Wordsworth ever felt herself a north countrywoman. Her birth and education in the south overcame the pull of ancestry. Her spiritual home was not among the dales of Cumbria, but in the abbeys, parsonages and cathedrals of the Midlands. At Westminster and at Stanford she grew up, the outer world of practical and political experience impinging at many points on the family routine, and later on Lincoln and Oxford made their own contribution.

Education
Education began early for Elizabeth: she acknowledged that

1. E.W., *Poems and Plays*, p. 61 (written 25 July 1876).
2. ibid., p. 22.

her real educators were her parents and other relatives, especially her father. When she was born he confessed to his disappointment that she was not at once like *that* (pointing to the Child in the Holy Family by Vandyke), and able to run about and be talked to.[1] He certainly began to talk to and instruct her as soon as ever she was able to profit by it, making her repeat a list of bishops and their sees ('Who was St Augustine?' etc., and ending with 'Who was John Lyon?'—Answer: 'Founder of Harrow School') to earn some fruit at dessert when she was four years old. And he continued to talk to her all his life. His was the type of mind which feels an imperious need to discuss every problem no matter with whom, wife, children, friends; to make them his anvils, as he called it. He found the stimulus to his thought in the impact of another mind, whether or not it was as informed and mature as his own; but he invariably respected it as equal with his own. There was no talking down or simplifying, and no difference in his approach to man or woman, boy or girl, expert or ignoramus. Miss Edith Pearson recalled a visit she paid as a girl in her early twenties to Riseholme, near the end of the Bishop's life, and the way in which he turned to her in complete simplicity for her opinion on a difficult point of theology. It was this free and equal intercourse with an acute and eager mind and trained intelligence that gave an indelible character to Elizabeth Wordsworth's outlook. It meant that she was never a feminist in the accepted sense of the word. Because in her own experience there had been, where things of the mind were concerned, neither male nor female, old nor young, she felt no necessity to fight a battle for the freedom to learn for women as such; and she was often regarded as lukewarm in the struggle for women's equality in Oxford. Her ideal was for man and woman together, the ideal of her own home, 'for Adam would have

---

1. Anne Frere in *Life of Christopher Wordsworth*, p. 91–2.

been a poor creature without Eve.'[1] In the same way, in her dealings with students at Lady Margaret Hall, although she might and did think them foolish and inexperienced in practical life, yet in things of the mind and spirit, in matters of learning and principle, they were met on equal terms.

In her upbringing Elizabeth Wordsworth suffered from no theories on her father's part in regard to girls' education, and she and her sisters learnt as a matter of course, just as her brothers did, those things that for him had proved the indispensable mental equipment. Latin was the foundation, and to the end of her life if she wanted to know what part of speech an English word was she had to turn it into Latin. The Latin poets, and Horace in particular, were her natural companions, although Ovid left her cold. The gift for languages was inbred and remarkable. French and Italian were learnt at home as a matter of course, German at school, and her father could write to her there when she was sixteen: 'You may send me a letter in Italian, or French, if you write in German, do not write it in those florid characters which are not intelligible to me.'[2] These beginnings were supplemented by journeys abroad in which her father was in close touch with certain ecclesiastical circles in France, Italy, Germany and Switzerland. The study of modern languages meant the beginning of the study of the classics in several literatures. The foundation was laid for the wide knowledge of later days, a knowledge so fully assimilated that it entered into the very life-stream of her mind. So too did English literature, which came to her, not through systematic reading, but by free access to many books. Greek she learnt on her own initiative; the rudiments came incidentally from the Greek Testament which the Canon liked to do with his family on Sunday evenings. 'It was pretty easy to construe the epistle

1. *per* M. Coate.
2. Letter lent by Mrs Leeke.

I

or gospel for the day, when one knew the English by heart,' she wrote many years later, 'but our dear father's mind was much more intent on theology than grammar, which he seemed to expect one to know by intuition. Happily, however, our brother John came to the rescue, and a few old grammars and school books of his were pressed into the service.'[1] Elizabeth read Homer in Clarke's edition and, with the aid of the Latin translation and a grammar and dictionary, she plodded through the entire *Iliad* (all but the catalogue of ships), and probably the *Odyssey* also at the rate of about fifty lines a day. She never regretted the time thus spent, but she reflected how lucky modern girls were to have things made easy for them. History was to a great extent absorbed through contact with the buildings and the art of the past, and through the lives of great men. The personal and artistic heritage was always her means of approach, and she had an unconscious philosophy of history in that she was sensitive to the continued connection of kings and saints and heroes with the scenes of their former life, and through these scenes she had a strong sense of the community of human lives past and present. This comes out clearly in such poems as 'On the Portrait of Charles V at Madrid' or 'St Cecilia' in Rome.[2] She needed something tangible to bring up the past, and she had little liking for the history of laws and institutions, while she was thoroughly impatient of detailed research and the investigation of subjects and periods that she thought useless. It is a paradox that anyone who had such a vivid appreciation of medieval architecture and medieval literature should have thought the study of medieval history sheer waste of time. Hers was a mind which worked in pictures and, from the image which she formed, reached conviction in a flash of intuition. She once said that she was incapable of

1. *Glimpses*, p. 43.
2. *Poems and Plays*, 1931, p. 17; *St Christopher and other Poems*, 1890, p. 53.

thinking, and conscious reasoning was rarely the basis of her conclusions.

Mathematics and natural science were wholly left out of the education of the young Wordsworths. They 'did just know that the earth went round the sun, and if hard put to it could perhaps have explained the cause of an eclipse.'[1] The reason for this big omission was no prejudice against scientific knowledge on their father's part; but he was not interested in these branches of learning. Had he been a mathematician and not a classical scholar and theologian, his daughter's training would have been in other disciplines. The lack of any formal teaching was filled to a certain extent by Elizabeth's naturally observant and inquiring mind, and by her gift for drawing, so far at any rate as plants and birds were concerned. She kept her eyes open and drew what she saw, always asking insistent questions in order to understand the biological how and why. Knowledge of 'country life and simple primitive human nature'[2] came from the daily experience of a country clergy family, but the first excitement caused by the theories of Darwin and Huxley seems to have passed her by.

Books were to Elizabeth Wordsworth the obvious sources of knowledge and inspiration: 'When once you have taught a boy or girl to read, you have put the key of knowledge into their hands, and they can follow their own peculiar bent.'[3] This is her solution of the whole problem of education; and it is very interesting to trace her peculiar bent in her reading, or rather in the reading that seemed after many years to have had a significance for her. Her imagination as a child was seized by the traditional fairy tales and by such treasures for all time as *Don Quixote*, the *Pilgrim's Progress* and *Robinson Crusoe*. Shakespeare was an essential part of her education—she bought

1. *Glimpses*, p. 48.
2. ibid., p. 42.
3. ibid., p. 41.

a Shakespeare for herself with a present from Mrs Hoare, to whom she owed her introduction to Miss Edgeworth's *Tales*. A Milton of her own was a gift from her mother; Homer came to her in Pope's version before she read him in Greek. Wordsworth was a family possession and his attitude to God and nature sank deeply into her mind; a first acquaintance with Browning was gained through the 'Pied Piper of Hamelin'; and when she was thirteen the *Antiquary* and the *Lay of the Last Ministrel* set the spell of Walter Scott upon her.

The books that were 'epoch-making' for her between the ages of fourteen and eighteen were compounded of standard works of the seventeenth and eighteenth centuries and some of the most recent works that were being published from year to year.[1] Butler's *Analogy of Religion* impressed on her the reasonable sanity of his point of view, which became characteristic of her own; Humphrey Prideaux's *The Old and New Testament connected in the history of the Jews and neighbouring nations* appeared in new annotated editions in 1845 and 1858, and in spite of his length and dry presentation, his wealth of precise information about the (to her) obscure successors of Alexander the Great appealed to this side of her mind, while the references to the life of the Prophetess Anna gratified a taste already apparent for the homely and the incongruous. The fifties of the nineteenth century were marked by the appearance of many notable books. Dean Trench of Westminster's *On the Study of Words*, which came out in 1851, answered the needs of her strong philological bent; Macaulay's *Essays* (1843) were eagerly read by a girl who all her life was to have a vivid interest in people. Of contemporary novels, the *Heir of Redclyffe* (1853) struck her as the most significant in the appeal it made not only to her as a girl, but equally to a large section

1. *Glimpses*, p. 29.

of English upper middle class cultivated society. The book was popular with soldiers, scholars, artists and public men, and Charlotte Yonge achieved a first success that was repeated in many novels for nearly half a century. There is no doubt her outlook corresponded with the religious awakening of the Tractarian movement and the ardent desire for social reform; she had the faculty of clear characterization and the reproduction of the details of the daily life proper to her readers, but it can only have been her inborn gift for telling a story that outweighed what seems today the intolerable sententiousness and high-falutin' tone of much of her writing. It would have been good to know whether Elizabeth Wordsworth read much of the great contemporary novelists while she was still in the schoolroom—Dickens and Thackeray; Charles Kingsley and Trollope; the Brontës, George Eliot and Mrs Gaskell. Of the writers of an earlier generation, she was definitely captured by Scott; but when did she come to know her real first favourite of later years, Jane Austen, a far finer artist, as she herself acknowledged, than Charlotte Yonge?

The training in the faith and worship of the Church and the knowledge of the Bible was so closely woven into the texture of life, that it is someting of a misnomer to speak of Elizabeth's religious education. That would suggest that it was a subject like others in a curriculum. On the contrary, from earliest years the daily use of family prayers, and on Sundays and Holy Days of Divine Service in church seemed part of the natural order of things, and familiarity with the words of Holy Scripture and the liturgy bred a deep unchanging devotion. Definite dogmatic teaching was received through the medium of the Catechism, whether in the public catechizing in church of all the children of the village, or in the Canon's instructions in his own home. At the same time his children 'had been unconsciously imbibing both from Wordsworth and Ruskin the belief that the Being who created this wonderful physical universe with all its beauty was the same Being to whom we owe our moral and spiritual life.'[1] A contrast to both these presentations of religion was provided by Bishop Butler. His guarded statements and his axiom that 'probability is the guide of life' were something of a shock after the confident faith in which she had been reared, but she recognized with gratitude that the *Analogy* and the *Sermons* let in a new light on her mind when the idea dawned of God's method of working in human life and passions in the world of actual events. This influence came just about the time that she was confirmed by Bishop Blomfield on 18 February (Quinquagesima Sunday) 1855.

The year 1857, which was spent at school at Brighton, did not carry her religious training much further. It 'consisted of our learning some passages of Scripture by heart for repetition, for which I have always been grateful; in a dull little reading of "James on the Collects" on Sundays between breakfast and church; and I rather think we had some papers of questions given us to answer in writing, at a class in the evening or afternoon, as well as some good little S.P.C.K. story books dealt out to us as Sunday reading, but I doubt if anyone read them much. We used to go to All Saints' Church, which, if not exciting, was certainly not "extreme".'[2]

Of much greater significance was the home occupation of copying out for the press the various portions of Canon Wordsworth's Commentary, first on the New, and then on the Old Testament, and then in looking over the proof sheets and verifying every Scripture reference. In the process his children gained an unrivalled knowledge of the Biblical text, as well as a severe secretarial training. On 3 May 1856, Canon Wordsworth could write to the sixteen-year-old Elizabeth:

1. *Glimpses*, p. 29.
2. *Glimpses*, p. 38.

'Thanks for your help in looking out the references. I wish you would also undertake to see that the figures of *verses* are right which are prefixed to the notes. The printers will proceed a little more rapidly now. . . . I am profiting by Miss Irving's kind help (to whom give my love), in writing out part of St Matthew, and hope to have the whole of that Gospel in the printers' hands before we quit London.'[1] The first volume of the Commentary was published on 22 October 1856, and the last on 6 June 1870, a year and a half after the move to Lincoln. The whole labour of Elizabeth and the other members of the family is summed up in a letter[2] from her father written when the great work was nearly finished, and the cares of the bishopric were beginning to press on him:

Holbeach

3 April 69

My dear Elizabeth

Would you kindly look at the enclosed, and then examine all the *copies* you can find of Parts i and ii of the Holy Bible either that have notes of *emendanda* by me or your dear mother, and make a collection of them, for the Printer, and let me have the benefit of them and of any remarks that may occur to you for our adoption in the proposed reprint of the Pentateuch? You will find my copies, in the Study, and in the Library; and you will find my emendations, and those proposed by others, at the beginning of the Volumes. I hope that this will not be very troublesome to you—if you knew how much I need your help in these things now that I have no time for them myself; and I am never unthankful, my dear daughter, to Almighty God for the great blessing He has given me in your help, in these important matters. The

---

1. Letter lent by Mrs Leeke.
2. From the Bishop of Lincoln to E.W. (lent by Mrs Leeke).

success with which it has pleased Him to give to our united labours (and when I say *ours*, I mean your dear mother's also and your Aunts' and your sisters) on His Holy Word will, I am sure, be ever thankfully remembered by us all.

I am

my dear

Elizabeth

Your affectionate father

C. Lincoln

The work led to constant discussion of difficult points, and the children learnt a good deal from informal conversation in the family circle. In the same way their father's preoccupation with the condition of the Church at home and abroad meant that ecclesiastical problems were always to the fore. But it is remarkable how with Elizabeth as with her father there was no temptation to put religiosity in the place of religion, or to substitute ecclesiasticism for churchmanship. There was a complete absence of sentimental emotion; no personal gossip concerning the clergy was tolerated; no substitution of interest in the preacher for interest in his message. The Services of the Church were never degraded to a means of spiritual dissipation, nor, in the words used by a recent writer, were the adjuncts of religion pursued for the 'sheer fun'[1] they afforded under the guise of pious devotion. Theological questions might be and were discussed at meals; passages from the Greek Testament were construed and interpreted on Sunday evenings and there was gentle teasing of Mrs Wordsworth for saying ὁ παρθένος instead of ἡ παρθένος, supported as she was by one of the girls who thought it very strange that the Virgin should be a 'he'(ἡ); the household assembled morning and evening for prayers, but it is inconceivable that the grown-

1. Osbert Sitwell, *Two Generations*.

up daughters of the house ever stood up to repeat passages of Scripture at dessert as did the daughters of Archbishop Tait, or that the family and their friends should join in singing 'Rock of Ages' during a picnic beside a waterfall in the south of France.[1]

An important part in her daughter's education was taken by Mrs Wordsworth. Elizabeth's love for her exquisite mother was a profound emotion, but it had its roots in an admiration which came near to veneration, rather than in mutual understanding. Just as she knew that she herself never understood the Freres, so she felt that the mother, who was like a '*very* soft cushion' in the firm support she gave to husband and children, never understood her eldest daughter and her intellectual life, although that mother was a woman of education and intelligence.[2] The certainty of her affection was always present, although there was little outward demonstration. Mrs Wordsworth never gave way to spoiling or petting her children; a formal curtsey accompanied their good-night kiss, and in ending their letters they were 'affectionate and dutiful'. There is something consciously didactic in the admirable lesson in good manners which Elizabeth received from her mother for her twelfth birthday:[3]

Cloisters Westm
20 June 1852

. . . Your Birthday as indeed I may say all your Birthdays makes me think much of your dear Grandmama who soon came to see us and to help nurse me when I was not very strong. I wish you could remember her as she was before sickness weakened her and then you would remember as I do the many instances of her tender love to us all—One thing you can do and that is to take all opportunities of showing

1. Osbert Sitwell, op. cit.
2. Note supplied by Miss E. Frere.
3. Mrs Wordsworth to E.W. for her birthday (lent by Mrs Leeke).

attention and love to the one whom she loved best in all the world and who by God's great mercy is still spared to us. And this reminds me to ask you whether you have written to Grand-papa or to Aunt Lissy since they were staying with us. While I am from home I should wish you to do so once in a week or ten days as they would I know be pleased to hear from you and it is almost the only means you have in absence of showing that you are mindful of them.

The following letter shows that Elizabeth and Priscilla had in fact the Christmas before (1851) remembered their Grandfather who wrote this charming letter[1] in reply:

> Bedford Square
> Christmas Day 1851

My dear Elizabeth and Priscilla

I must thank you both for the very handsome Bag which you have worked for me and which will remind me most agreeably of my two dear Grandchildren whenever I take from it a handkerchief sweetly scented with Flowers of their Gathering; for we need not confine ourselves to violets which pass away with the early Spring but may find various flowers throughout the year which will supply their place; though none perhaps may be quite so delicately and deliciously sweet as the promised Violets.

The sweetest perfume however will be the fragrant affection of their little hearts whose fingers have been so diligently and so successfully employed upon the work and hers more especially whose pen has indited her very neat letter of Introduction of it to

> My dear little Girls
> affectionate Grandpapa
> Geo Frere

1. Lent by Mrs Leeke.

The lesson was assimilated and Elizabeth showed her gratitude all her life in fulfilling the duties of family correspondence and in sending the promptest thanks even for such trifles as Christmas cards.

She was grateful also for the infinity of pains which her mother took to make her children speak plain and to read aloud intelligibly. This was an accomplishment of practical value in a family which spent much of the evening in reading aloud and listening to reading, and which was accustomed to the best. Mrs Wordsworth's own reading, like her husband's, was a thing of beauty, and through it her children had been made very early to know good literature. One of Elizabeth's greatest gifts was the rare quality of her speaking voice and her power of using it with a natural modulation to bring home to her hearers the fullness of her meaning, whether she spoke with a very human wit, or with an inspiration that had in it something divine. Besides the training in speech, Mrs Wordsworth saw to it that all her children wrote firm and clear hands, not indeed with her own incredible fine elegance, but certainly not with their father's fantastic curving illegibility. Elizabeth's writing grew larger and freer as she grew up and in its vigour and decision was an index of her character.

It was Mrs Wordsworth's responsibility also to see that her daughters were taught to do plain needlework, and Elizabeth was proud that she could cut out and make a serviceable shirt, although it was a task somewhat against the grain. Her mother used to groan over her buttonholes and gathers, and later in life Elizabeth felt sure that she would have reprobated her underclothes with their marks of cobbled mending. The needle was not her chosen tool, but her wits enabled her to use her fingers for all practical needs. She was a good improviser, and would run up a period dress for theatricals or make scarlet flowers for decorations all on the spur of the moment.

There was always music in the family, for Mrs Wordsworth,

like her sisters Lissey and Anne Frere, had musical gifts of a high order and had received a sound training from Dr Crotch. Her rendering of Handel's songs and of airs from the *Messiah* in a remarkably true and pure soprano was an unforgettable experience. Priscilla and Susan Wordsworth had charming voices and Elizabeth could always take a part, and played the piano as well. It is on record[1] that in October 1855 she played as a duet with Miss Irving the Overture to Rossini's *Il Barbiere di Siviglia*, and 'Chi Vive Amante'; she also sang Handel's 'Verdi Prati', and took a part with her mother and governess in a trio 'Dark Shades of Night'. She owed much to Miss Irving, the possessor of a 'delicious contralto voice'[2] and a knowledge of modern music, who enlarged the scope of a musical taste hitherto nourished chiefly on Handel and Mozart. Later on there were lessons from music-masters in Brighton and London; but with all her love for music Elizabeth found her instinctive means of expression in drawing and painting.

Canon Wordsworth had a keen pleasure in pictures as well as stained-glass, and he made her happy on her fifteenth birthday by the offer of a paint-box. She wrote with much naivety and more humility on this occasion: 'I rather hope Miss Irving will be able to go and make a sketch today, and then I can go with her, and if we go to Eastbourne it will be very nice to carry away some recollections of it in a sketch-book, but I shall need a good deal of practice first and I suppose the sea is as difficult to draw as anything, but Miss Irving, I dare say, will help me a little.'[3] There is something reminiscent in this of the ambition of the young lady who exclaimed to Ruskin on a moonlight night how much she would like to sketch the scene; and of his devastating reply: 'My dear young

1. Note by Canon Christopher Wordsworth.
2. *Glimpses*, p. 22.
3. E.W. to her father, 23 June 1855 (letter lent by Canon Christopher Wordsworth).

lady, how can you with your HB pencil and your bit of india-rubber hope to portray the moon in all her glory?' But Ruskin's influence was very strong when Elizabeth Words-worth was a girl. Her imagination was fired by hearing him give a lecture (about the year 1856) on *Illuminating and Medieval Art* in which he read out Longfellow's lines from the *Golden Legend* about Fra Pacifico. His *Elements of Drawing* (published first in 1857) was one of the books to which she owed most, answering as it did her questionings on the principles of art; and she had the benefit of the teaching of Miss Eliza Hobhouse on lines that he would have laid down. Miss Hobhouse, tall and dark with beautiful hands, was an old family friend of the Freres; she set up Elizabeth and her sister Mary 'with big drawing boards and crayons, and made [them] do studies nearly as large as life, of pitchers, white arum lilies, and other things.'[1] At school Elizabeth learnt the really useful elements of perspective, but the style of drawing inculcated was slick and insincere. 'We copied blacklead pencil drawings on Bristol board, we did sketches with ready-made sunset and moonlight "effects" of pink and grey respectively, which looked really imposing when touched up with Chinese White by the master's steady hand . . . and we filled pages on pages with "touches" as they were called, done copy-book fashion. The master did a little scribble on the top left-hand corner, which was supposed to be typical of the foliage of oak, birch, elm, willow etc., and we repeated it (*non passibus equis*) over and over again! Well might Ruskin inveigh against such methods as these.'[2] Elizabeth came out of the process un-scathed: her study of the *Elements of Drawing* and Miss Hobhouse's teaching left a permanent impress on her bold draughtsmanship and firm line.

1. *Glimpses*, p. 41.
2. *Glimpses*, p. 37.

While the foundations of education were laid by her parents, the influence of her governesses and of her school were important. She owed a great deal to the succession of able, cultivated and well-bred women who filled the office of governess in the family, and who, as a letter already quoted shows, took practical charge of household and children at Stanford, when Mrs Wordsworth was away in Westminster or elsewhere with her husband. Anything less like the typical governess of nineteenth-century memoirs and fiction it is hard to imagine, and their presence bears witness to a standard of education and character among the women of certain sections of upper middle class society which has been too often over-looked, alike by the feminists of the last century and by the would-be humorists of the present in their desire to exploit the less agreeable aspects of Victorian home life. Kind Miss Emmett was in charge of the Wordsworth children at Rydal in 1850; Miss Margaret E. Irving, whose brother was in a position of some importance in a government office, was with them at Stanford at least from 1852 till 1857 and was the friend of all the family: Aunt Wordsworth ends a letter with love to Miss Irving, and the Canon sends messages of love and thanks for her help in the Commentary. Another dear and life-long friend was Miss Murray (afterwards Mrs Wood).

More in accordance with the general view of girls' education in the fifties was the school at Brighton to which Elizabeth went in January 1857 for a year, coming home again when she was seventeen-and-a-half. Her parents' chief motive for sending her there was the expectation that besides acquiring accomplishments herself, she would be able to pass them on to her sisters on her return. She was always sceptical of the success of this part of the scheme, but none of her sisters, except the youngest, ever went to school. Much of the teaching was superficial; enough has been said of the religious instruction and the drawing lessons to show how far the standard was below that

to which she had been accustomed at home. Still, she learned
to speak French with some fluency and to read German.
Dancing and music were good; and to Mr Philips, a visiting
master who was a well-known figure in Brighton, she owed a
new independence of judgement in literature and history, and
the awakening of the desire and capacity for writing. In
another direction, too, the lessons learnt at school were to
stand her in good stead. She gained an insight into human
nature outside the bounds of her own family circle, and in
particular into the ways of girls living in a community. She
came to realize that it was not always the girls she liked best at
first sight that she liked best in the long run,[1] and this gave her
the capacity for suspending her judgement and for finding the
real values beneath the outer crust. The school did not omit
to pay attention to health, according to its lights; Elizabeth
had a fire in her room in winter, but exercise and fresh air
were limited to occasional dancing lessons and 'crocodile'
walks along the roads of the town, not unfrequently enlivened
by a visit to the pastrycook's. This was all very dull—only a
few girls had the good fortune to go riding on the Downs—
and the energy of healthy young women could find an outlet
only in a premature interest in dress and foolish flirtations, of
which the Italian singing master was the object for a certain
set of the girls. This experience made Elizabeth Wordsworth
an ardent believer, later on, in games for girls, and she advocated hockey at Lady Margaret Hall when it was looked on
askance by many people, and defended early morning swim-
ming in the Cherwell. She herself took a walk every morning
of her life, and learnt the new pastime of bicycling when she
was nearer sixty than fifty. But the real significance of her
school-days lay in their effect on her own development. She
was removed for the time from close contact with her family

1. Letter to her sister Dora at school, 22 April 1868.

and her father's compelling personality; the very facts of mutual affection and common interests tended to restrict the growth of her own individuality. In fresh surroundings she had the opportunity to possess herself more completely and to start on the path which led to the full freedom of her spirit.

Part II 1858 – 1878: Expanding world

Travels and visits 1858–68

During the next ten years the 'seriousness' which had oppressed the child and the school-girl began to give way before the lightness of heart and power of humorous observation which Elizabeth developed during the ten years of her 'young-ladyhood', together with a conscious love for the unexpected. She liked Herodotus 'because you never knew where to have him. Just as you think he's settling down to give you a long-winded history of a man, he flies off with something or other about his great-grandmother.'[1] She liked riddles too, because of the surprise in the solutions, and she filled a MS book with riddles she had collected from various sources;[2] she also experimented in their invention. Life expanded with ever increasing fullness and interest in the companionship of friends of her own age, in travels abroad and visits at home. She was beginning to try her hand at writing, and sketching and painting were a constant means of expression. Westminster and Stanford still formed the background, with the emphasis on Westminster, where the elder girls often spent the spring and summer with their parents. Their father made very little use of 'his position as a Canon of Westminster, with a considerable reputation as a preacher and a literary man, to

1. *Thornwell Abbas*, ff. 140–1.
2. Album given her by John Wordsworth in 1859 (or later).

enable him to "get into society" as the phrase is. Never was anyone who ran less after great people or celebrities';[1] but that is not to say that he and his family were not brought into constant relations with notable men in the political and still more in the ecclesiastical sphere, and also with foreign clergy who visited England either to consult libraries or to promote reform in their own countries. Yet these contacts, interesting as they were, had less significance for Elizabeth than the circle of intimate friends who lived round them in the Abbey precincts;[2] Dean Trench and his daughters at the Deanery; Canon Nepean and his large and pleasant family, their next-door neighbours in Little Cloister; Mr F. H. Rivaz and his daughters at 19 Cowley Street; Mr and Mrs Edward Harnage, their daughter Mary, and Mrs Harnage's niece, Anna H. Drury, author of *The Blue Ribbons* and other tales. They lived at 7 The Terrace, Dean's Yard, now pulled down to make way for the Church House, and their house was the centre of much agreeable society.

The air seemed to be filled with sunshine in those summers in the early sixties, and London offered that sense of exhilaration which is peculiar to it on fine days and nights, whether Elizabeth went in the morning freshness with her sister Mary and Mary Harnage to copy old masters in the National Gallery, or to make sketches of tombs and chapels in the Abbey; or whether they strolled with the Canon, or played croquet with each other in the long hot evenings in the College garden, for all the world like Millais' illustrations to *The Small House at Allington*. Even visiting the patients at the Westminster Hospital with the Trench and Rivaz girls lost its implication that there was something wrong with the world and took its place among the pleasant occupations of the day. There were

1. J.W.O. and E.W., *Christopher Wordsworth*, pp. 40–1.
2. *Glimpses*, pp. 43–7.

dinner-parties too, and visits to the play and even to the opera, on one occasion with Mrs Harnage, when Thackeray was to be seen in the audience. On her side, Elizabeth made herself felt for her varied talents; she was racy, talked a good deal, and showed a keen sense of humour.[1] Her gift for conversation like her father's was in strong contrast to her mother's quietness, which she found something of an embarrassment when they were paying formal calls. Conversation seemed to be demanded, and yet it would have been discourteous for her to rush in when her mother maintained a composed silence.

It was at Little Cloister that Elizabeth kept her twenty-first birthday alone with her parents:[2] her sisters, who were away at Bournemouth with Aunt Lissey, and her brothers at school had to be content with sending their wishes for many happy returns by post. Their letters[3] showed a complete equality of approach; although Elizabeth devoted careful thought to their different needs, there was nothing 'elder-sisterly' in the relationship.[4] This was so, partly no doubt because Mrs Wordsworth was always the controlling factor, and partly also because the family was guided by the idea of 'Liberty, fraternity and equality'. Most of all it was because of Elizabeth's essential youthfulness; she couldn't have been 'elder-sisterly' if she had tried. John was in his last term at Winchester and his birthday letter put the circumstances of the occasion in a nutshell: '"*In nidum servas*" (excuse Latin, it is an exercise for you) I believe, whilst the others go about the country. You do not I suppose do any Latin, though perhaps you are become an accomplished painter. Do you try oils as well as watercolours?' There was no birthday party, but Anna Drury came in to spend the evening, and the beauty of the full midsummer

1. Mrs Wayne's 'Reminiscences' (Mary Harnage).
2. *Glimpses*, p. 43.
3. Letters from John Wordsworth and Susan Wordsworth.
4. Mrs Wayne.

moon flooding the house remained the sharpest memory of the anniversary.

This tranquil happiness was broken three days afterwards by the death of Mr Harnage suddenly at his club. It was a great shock to the Wordsworth household and especially to Elizabeth for whom it was the first loss of a familiar friendly figure after she had come to years of discretion. At the time she was reading the *Pensées* of Pascal, a book which took on a special significance at this moment of grief, and book and sorrow combined for a time to give a renewed seriousness of reflection to her thoughts. A number of poems written between May 1861 and August 1863 bear witness to this. The earlier pieces were copied out fair in an album given to her mother in November 1862, but others were added during the following year. A sonnet[1] for All Saints' Day 1861 is inspired by remembrance not of saints in glory, but of:

> Dear friends, whoe'er and wheresoe'er ye be. . . .
> What though a vast expanse of land or sea
>   Divide us? With united voice we sing
>   The praises of our Father and our King;
> One is our hope, one heart, one aim have we,
> And what if some have past the waves of Death?
> Is sweet communion e'en with them denied? . . .

Sometimes, there are traces of Pascal's thought in musings on the insignificance of man, even the greatest contrasted with the universe; but, on the other hand, she asks, 'Can *he* be small to whom Eternity is promised?'[2] And a year later, she wrote:[3]

1. Album, p. 14.
2. Album, pp. 31–2, 'Thoughts in a Train', written at Genoa, 26 May 1862.
3. Album, 'Daisies', written at Stanford, May 1863.

O strange, divine Infinity
How little man can fathom thee,
Present alike in rolling orbs,
In insect wings, and tiny flowers,
Thy contemplation quite absorbs
And quite exhausts our fallen powers;
Yea, Human Nature is too grand
For man himself to understand.

But the dominant notes are a passionate delight in earthly beauty, yet 'ever subject to decay', and at the same time 'a pledge of immortality to man'; and a prepossession with the passing of human life—'The noblest names of old are like a dream.' The only solution of the mystery is to be found in the Christian hope of life and peace eternal.

These themes received a particular emphasis during her travels abroad in the spring and summer of 1862; they were nourished by the religious and political situation in the countries visited, especially Italy, and the poems written at the time form a diary of the tour. In April Elizabeth set off with Mrs Harnage, her daughter and her niece for Dresden. The journey from London is recounted in three cantos[1] beginning with 'The cab all lined with straw' which took them to the station 'on Monday morn'; the victim of the Channel crossing 'too weak to eat, too sad to joke'; the 'well-cushioned train, of all soothing things the most soothing' which took them to Brussels, and Charlemagne's Aix; and

Then, O Farina! came the town
Which owes to thee her wide renown.

After this, Brunswick, Minden, Hanover, Leipzig, Magdeburg

1. Album.

and finally the Victoria Hotel at Dresden, 'In luxury of perfect rest.' She was fascinated by Dresden: 'The picturesque old town with its beautiful bridge, and the glorious sunsets and moonrises to be seen from it, the quaint figures of women with baskets on their backs; the lovely neighbourhood which we visited in steamer excursions; the opening leaves and buds of Easter; the masses of white cherry blossom, all threw me into an ecstasy, as did the glorious Rembrandts in the gallery, the San Sisto Madonna, the crowds of other art treasures, not forgetting the great Holbein Madonna'[1]—so she wrote many years afterwards. At the time, one of those same excursions on the Elbe, to Pilnitz, inspired a long poem in blank verse which celebrated 'The exceeding beauty that around us lay,'[2] not forgetting the woodland flowers which 'we beheld, And plucked our fill, and paused and plucked again.' Another expedition to see the 'Dresden China' manufactory at Meissen was described in a letter to Aunt Lissey,[3] and the prose has it every time over the verse for the simple vigour of the phrasing: 'We went into what used to be the Bp's garden in the good old times. It looked down from the ramparts over such a lovely view—and now it was looking its very best, for the lilacs etc. are in full bloom and if we had jumped off the wall, we should have fallen in the middle of the lilac bushes which grew underneath. Then further on you saw old houses and the Elbe was beyond. It was worth some trouble to see anything so beautiful and so uncommon.'

Many hours were spent in the Print Room of the Dresden Gallery; the party had an introduction to Professor Gruner, who had superintended the erection of the Mausoleum at Frogmore, and he allowed them to make copies of the sketches. His wife was a charming woman, 'French by birth, German by

---

1. Glimpses, p. 48.
2. Album, p. 16, 'Pilnitz', 28 April.
3. Letter from E.W. to Miss Frere, from Dresden, 2 May 1862.

marriage and English by naturalization.'[1] There were pleasant acquaintances, too, in the English colony—Mrs Hamilton and her daughters. There was also the enjoyment of visits to the opera without fuss or parade for a trifling sum, and to the play. By way of refreshing themselves after moving to lodgings at No. 4 Mozinsky Strasse, they went to see Goethe's *Iphigenia in Tauris*, which called forth a youthful essay in dramatic criticism from Elizabeth: 'it was strictly classical, only 5 actors. We had a stick of a king, a respectable Pylades, a very good Orestes and an excellent Iphigenia . . . she posed herself after the manner of a Greek statue. . . . Iphigenia is such a high-minded honourable creature, one gets quite fond of her. I am sorry to say the house was not half full. If we go to see Flick and Flack, which is the rage here just now, I daresay it will be different.' So the letter runs on, a letter which emphasized the writer's enthusiasm for natural beauty and her interest in people whether in real life or the drama. She impressed Mary Harnage with her whole-hearted enjoyment of the Galleries, the opera and the rest, and with the width of her interests and her liking for anything that was good of its kind. She left her friends to travel under the escort of their footman, George, for Frankfurt A/M where she joined her parents and Priscilla on 13 May for a six-weeks tour in Italy via Switzerland.

These Italian travels come before us in vivid detail through Elizabeth's diary of poems, supplemented by the two volumes of her father's *Journal of a Tour in Italy*. He had undertaken the tour with the express purpose of investigating the religious situation and the chances for reform at a moment of extra-ordinary interest, political as well as ecclesiastical. With the support of Napoleon III, Victor Emmanuel had been pro-claimed King of Italy in February 1861, the price of French

1. See previous note.

adhesion being the cession of Nice and Savoy. 'En criant pour l'Italie, V.E. a perdu sa voix,' as the current witticism had it, to Elizabeth's keen delight.[1] Venice and Rome, with the surrounding remnants of the States of the Church, were alone outside the union, and their incorporation was the burning question of the day, together with the attitude of Pius IX in view of the threat to the temporal power: 'Can Rome become the Capital of Italy?'[2] a query which received the neat reply, as Elizabeth recalls, 'Non piove' [Non Pio, V.E.]. But so acute an observer as Canon Wordsworth was forced to conclude that time alone could give the final answer, for 'with all its melancholy appearance, dilapidation, dirtiness, decay and desolation, which fill the heart with sadness, on the first entrance into Rome, especially from Città Vecchia, Rome has still a position in the world which no other city can boast.'[3] This was true no less for the northern pilgrim of the nineteenth century than for his medieval predecessor, although the former no longer had his first taste of Rome from the heights of Monte Mario but, as the Canon notes,[4] from the waiting-room of the Trastevere Railway Terminus.

The party had entered Italy from Canton Ticino on 30 May, having driven over the St Gothard Pass with its scenery 'orrida e selvaggia',[5] and continued by boat down Lago Maggiore and finally by train to Milan. At Canobbio they had heard of the arrest five days before of a hundred Garibaldians under Colonel Nullo, who had planned, with the King's support, to rouse the populations of Tyrol, Eastern Lombardy and the Veneto against Austria; but at the last moment his minister Ratazzi lost heart and disowned and arrested the

1. *Glimpses*, p. 48.
2. *Tour*, II, p. 223.
3. *Tour*, II, p. 6.
4. ibid., p. 4.
5. *Tour*, I, p. 48.

volunteers. Undismayed, indeed stimulated, by all this political excitement, the Wordsworths spent six days working hard at the sights of Milan, and the Canon made contacts with persons of varied points of view and engaged in discussions on Church government and doctrine. The determining factor in the religious situation was the opposition of Pius IX to the policy of Victor Emmanuel, which had brought about a deadlock in ecclesiastical matters. No fewer than thirty-four episcopal sees were vacant and the bishops, acting under orders from Rome, forbade the celebration of the new national 'Festa dello Statuto' in their cathedrals. The general decay of discipline and learning was a matter of grave concern to all, clergy and laity alike, who had the welfare of the Church at heart, and they worked for a reformation from within, founding in every city a 'Società Ecclesiastica' to promote clerical learning and morals, and to protect those who were loyal to the new government from the despotism of the Curia. With all this Canon Wordsworth was in ardent sympathy, and he hoped that it might succeed in countering the excessive claims of the papacy, both temporal and spiritual.

From Milan the party went by way of Pavia to Genoa, and then to Leghorn, Pisa and Florence. They reached Florence on 31 May in time for the Festa dello Statuto, and after spending Ascensiontide and Whitsuntide there, took ship at Leghorn for Cività Vecchia, and went thence by train to Rome. The humours of the journey were recorded by Elizabeth's pen and pencil. A couple of sketches illustrate 'our night on board the *Provence*',[1] the boat from Leghorn. The first is called 'Silent Suffering' and shows a lady lying in a berth with baggage beside her labelled 'Cività Vecchia' and 'Napoli'; the second illustrates the troubles of an Italian lady, in a berth adjoining, who is sitting up with an infant and appealing for help to the

1. Sketch-book.

silent sufferer and the steward, in a deliciously characteristic monologue:

> Ecco, Bimbo, caro mio, stai quieto Bimbo.
> Ho lasciato il mio ventaglio
> Signorina, Lei sta bene—Lei può dormire
> Cameriere, cameriere, date mi dell' acqua,
> Cam-e-ri-ere.
> Ah mi duole la testa
> Signorina Lei dorme, ma non posso dormire io,
> Mi dogliano le gambe.
> Ecco Bimbo stai tranquillo
> E spento il lume—Cameriere!

The subsequent train journey produced a poem[1] describing, in the manner of Chaucer's prologue to *The Canterbury Tales*, the carriage full of fellow-travellers ('Hard were its boards the seats were far from wide And painful was our posture at the best'). There was a Zouave, 'A trusty servant of the Pope was he A brave defender of the Holy See'; there was a Frenchman young and gay, 'He gave not for the Pope a pullet hen And said that Priests were worse than other men'. Next came a dainty lady with her children twain, 'Constant at church her errors to confess, But yet a little overfond of dress.' Beside her were two German sportsmen, 'With gun, and pouch on back, and broad brimmed hat.' 'A sister, hight of charity was there Gentle and meek her eye, her face was fair; Her well-starched cap projected o'er her brow Spotless and white as lily flowers or snow. . . . Beside her sat a friar with shaven crown And sandalled feet and garments thick and brown. Well could he turn to anything his hand A welcome visitor throughout the land Could mend the chairs and make the clocks to go Could

1. Album.

tinker up the pots and horse's shoe.' The company often was completed by the Wordsworth party:

> A good man was there of religion
> The humble parson of an English town
> The name whereof we may not here record;
> ('Twas in the diocese of Oxenford).
> Within his bags full many a book had he
> Dearer to him than manors, gold, or fee,
> Than robés rich, rebeck, or psaltery.
> A wife he had besides and daughters twain
> Who oft to speak the Italian tongue were fain
> Learnt from the guide-books I must freely own
> For speech of Rome was to them unknown.
> Now history of them no further tells,
> Save that their coat of arms bore three church bells.

The first sight of Rome is celebrated in verses written in recollection at Stanford, in more serious mood. Rome, so long the subject of thoughts and dreams, is 'Not wholly new, nor altogether strange.' 'Those antique towers . . . yon grand-grey dome . . . That massive castle, the yellow Tiber' all in turn are recognized. Her mind wanders to the ancient legends of the city; and then comes to rest not in Petrine memories, but in the image of St Paul called up by the vision of his great basilica as the train passes it close by.

The Wordsworths reached the city on 11 June, just after the canonization in St Peter's on Whit Sunday of the Japanese Martyrs, which had brought hundreds of foreign bishops to Rome—the bishops of the new Italian kingdom were denied passports by the government. The great ceremony was generally regarded as the pretext for a demonstration of Papal authority and Catholic solidarity, in view of the attacks on the temporal and, to some extent, on the spiritual authority of the Roman Pontiff. The historian Gregorovius wrote of it: 'This religious comedy is the greatest theatrical spectacle which the Church has displayed for a long time.'[1] It demanded for its setting decoration and drapery on a colossal scale in defiance of every canon of taste. The marble pilasters were concealed with coloured paper: the great arches of the nave were filled with columns made of lath and canvas covered with marbled paper against a backing of silk and velvet. Gilded festoons supported the lunettes in which were pictures representing the acts and sufferings of the Martyrs. At a time when the Pope's departure from Rome was freely debated,[2] Pasquino had it that he was packing up St Peter's in paper— 'gia incarta S. Pietro'. But it was the process of unpacking that met the eyes of Elizabeth Wordsworth when she stood silent and awestruck by the curtained door waiting for the first vision of the vast interior:[3]

> Clad in the summer golden light of Noon
> O majesty! O richness! Art sublime!
> O consecrated memory of the Past!
> O spirits of the mighty dead around!
> O Rome, thou mistress of the western world.

and then the swift revulsion:

> Are *these* the triumphs of thy later days?
> These mimic columns, tinsel ornaments
> These puerile (not childlike) decorations
> The tawdry mushroom splendours of an hour! . . .
> Now piece by piece, the pageant is dissolved
> How silently, how swiftly torn away!

1. F. Gregorovius, *Roman Journals*, tr. Hamilton, 1907.
2. ibid.
3. Album.

One hollow pillar lies beside our feet. . . .
Oh! fallen pillar, emblem all too true
Of them who neared thy transient eminence,
Of Rome, degenerate City of today
Hollow and vain, with falsehood veiling Truth,
A splendid Lie, fiction Ephemeral.

The city was quieter than it had been for some time, what though the Pope was a pensioner of France, and Rome but a suburb of Paris, in spite of the partial withdrawal of the French garrison.[1] In the lull, Pius IX followed up the canonization with a Consistory in which some 399 bishops presented him with an Address explaining the *dominium temporale* as a necessity to ensure independence in spiritual matters, and Canon Wordsworth visited museums and collections and discussed problems of MSS and antiquities with curators and librarians. With his family he attended ceremonies and sermons—the Pentecostal ordination in St John Lateran; the Corpus Domini procession in St Peter's; the eloquence of Padre Toeschi in the Gesù. And they were indefatigable in sight-seeing: the Vatican picture gallery gave Elizabeth the opportunity for an exercise in art criticism, for there is good internal evidence that the notes contributed by one of the party to the *Tour in Italy* are from her pen.[2] Very characteristic is the passage: 'There are some small early pictures by Raffaelle, little gems in their way, the colour so pure and bright, and the drawing so delicate, as to remind you of the pictures in an illuminated prayer book or missal, in the golden age of illuminating. In his early pictures, the figures are more or less in the costume of the day; the classical draperies belong to his later style. Anyone who will compare the *Sposalizio* at Milan with his last great work will

1. *Tour*, II, p. 85.
2. *Tour*, II, p. 141.

see this at once, and I think most people will confess, that though they may not be so grand and bold as those he afterwards executed, there is something more delightful about those simple early figures.' Elizabeth's twenty-second birthday, a Sunday, was spent in Rome: after service at the English Church a long visit was paid to the Catacombs of S. Callisto, the return being made by way of the Ghetto situated beside the lovely Ripa. The next day the party went in the summer evening to the Palatine to explore the ruins of the Palace of the Caesars; and thence to S. Paolo fuori le Mura. They walked on the Appian Way; perhaps, as Canon Wordsworth hoped, on some of the stones which were trodden by St Paul as he came with the brethren 'from Appii Forum and the Three Taverns' on his first visit to Rome 1800 years ago;[1] and they watched the fading of the sunlight and the lengthening of the shadows over the Campagna.

Looking back after fifty years Elizabeth could say that, to her sister and herself, 'this tour will always be full of memories of surpassing beauty both in Art and Nature, for when all is said and done, one comes back to the exquisite charm of the Italian soil and climate as *the* thing to which the country owes her wondrous enchantment. But to our elders the political and religious situation was even more interesting.'[2] So she wrote half a century later, but her poems and letters at the time show no less a preoccupation with the events and personalities of the day than with the loveliness of Italian country and Italian painting. Her strong sense of the contrast between the beauty of the scene, the greatness of the Roman past, and the disillusion of the present runs through all her thought. This was all the more marked because she was in Italy in the early summer, from 20 May to 2 July, a season unknown to most English

1. *Tour*, II pp. 214–15.
2. *Glimpses*, p. 49.

travellers when 'the days are long and the mornings and evenings are delightfully fresh.'

The Wordsworths had taken an apartment with high airy rooms in Palazzo Parisani in the Piazza San Claudio.[1] It was close to the Fontana di Trevi, that queen of Roman fountains, and they enjoyed in the hot summer days the splashing of the clear water into the wide shallow basin beneath. The Rome they learnt to know was a Rome still unexcavated, with the Campo Vaccino a peaceful pasturage for cattle and goats, and the Palatine a broken ruin festooned with trailing plants; the Rome they lived in was a Rome still bound by tradition, the Senator and the Conservatori still dwelling on the Capitol, the Pope and the Cardinal still driving in their carriages about the city; a Rome of picturesque dilapidation beside all the magnificence. Moreover, although journeys were long and uncomfortable, with constant change from carriage to steamer, and steamer to train, there was the thrill of passing St Barnabas' Eve on the Mediterranean with the full moon streaming on the calm sea; or of dashing down the zig-zag road of the Mont Cenis in a diligence drawn by twelve mules and two horses, while the starlight gave place to the first gleam of the sun gilding the mountain peaks and revealing the enamelled bosses of wild flowers in the rocks above the road.

Rome was left behind on 25 June, and Turin was reached on the twenty-eighth. Canon Wordsworth thankfully absolved himself from sight-seeing in a town which had few artistic or historic monuments, but he found compensation in the absorbing interest of the reactions of the Parliament to the episcopal manifesto issued at the recent Consistory in Rome, and in calling on distinguished personages who played a part on the ecclesiastical stage. Chief of these was Carlo Passaglia, the celebrated theologian who had been chosen by Pius IX to

1. *Tour*, II pp. 53–4.

expound the doctrine of the Immaculate Conception at its promulgation in 1854; but in 1862 he was living in Casa Cavour at Turin engaged in collecting 9,000 clerical signatures to an Address framed by himself in which the Pope was implored to lay aside his temporal power and unite with all loyal citizens in making Rome the capital of Italy. Before the year was out, Passaglia had suffered excommunication, but the ban had not been imposed when Canon Wordsworth was seeing him in Turin.

Another ardent reformer was an ex-priest, Signor Pifferi, who desired the overthrow not only of the temporal but also of the spiritual authority of the papacy. He translated into Italian the Canon's *Three Letters on the present conflict between the Court of Rome and the Kingdom of Italy*, which were published with great effect this same year in Turin, and as the presumed author of the *Letters*, he was offered a pension by the Archbishop of Ferma if he would promise to desist from future writings. Elizabeth Wordsworth was keenly interested in the vicissitudes suffered by Passaglia and Pifferi, and a letter written by her to her sister Susan throws an interesting light on the visit to Turin as she saw it.[1]

Turin
30 June 1862

My dear Susan,

Many thanks for your kind letter and good wishes. We found quite a large collection of letters here, all of which we were much pleased to get, including a nice long one from Aunt Anne to me. We could wish there was a better account both of her and Uncle John in it. I hope when you get fine weather, he will feel stronger. Turin is a modern business-like town—the streets as straight as possible, and

1. Letter from E.W. to S.W. (lent by Mrs Leeke).

the map very like the pattern of a checked plaid. In fact one
street is so like another that it is not easy to help losing ones'
way. Yesterday, we went to the English Church, a poor
little place, with nothing to recommend it, except the fact
of its being a church, and one of the right sort. It does seem
a great pity that they cannot have a little more to attract
strangers in the way of music and architecture—for though
we may feel that those things are not of much consequence,
if we have the more solid and important ones, yet it must
make a great difference to people who are only just beginning to make acquaintance with the Ch. of England.

There is one very excellent Italian here, named Pifferi,
who interests himself very much in our Ch. and in the cause
of Reform. He came here last night, and speaks English
very fairly well. I believe he has sacrificed his worldly
prospects (for he was a Romish priest) to his principles. He
makes a little money by teaching, but it must be a hard life.
Papa is just gone to try if he can see Passaglia. He had to
escape from Rome, on account of the offence his writings
had given, and the Inquisition has still got his papers. Mr
Severn tried very hard to get them, and that Papa might
bring them here to Passaglia, but the other party was too
strong for him. Mr Aubrey de Vere, whose name you may
have heard, and who was our fellow traveller in the steam-
boat, and has come across us two or three times since,
thinks there was a good deal of personal feeling and disappointed ambition in the case of Passaglia as well as of
Liverani. Everyone speaks of him as being a man of extraordinary learning and abilities, and of the influence and
authority he had a few years ago at the Court of Rome.

We are in a beautiful Hotel here, and I believe have for
fellow lodgers a good many deputies to the Turin parliament.
Victor E. generally lives, when he is in these parts, in a palace
a little way out of town . . .

K

We are well—Papa a little tired—but he has had a fair
night, and feels less so than yesterday. As he truly remarks,
'It is not a bad thing to be in a place where there is nothing
you *must* go and see.' But goodbye, with much love to all

Ever yr aff. sister

Eliz. Wordsworth

The day before leaving Turin, Elizabeth summed up her
thoughts in a poem entitled 'Changes and Chances',[1] suggested
by the present state of affairs in Italy. The dominant idea is
once more 'our human mutability' and the career of Passaglia
its particular illustration:

He, who a few short years ago,
Was honoured, praised, and harkened to,
In Rome's great city sought, caressed
By Pontiff, priest, and mitred guest,
Degraded now, abused by all
Who were his flatterers ere his fall
Tastes all the bitterness of shame
More keenly, following hard on Fame. . . .
Doomed, like the exiled Greek to find
His enemies than friends more kind
The shelter that their roof bestows
His safest refuge from his foes.

The influence of the Italian Tour was deep, and continued to
make itself felt after the return to England. A poem written
at Westminster in July has for its title: 'On Memory, and the
Responsibilities it brings with it', and seems to recall Italy in
one of its stanzas; and a whole series of sonnets in September
were devoted to Raphael's cartoons. In November, the Corpus

1. Album.

Domini procession seen in Rome in June provided the subject of a long poem; and again, as late as 30 March 1863 at Stanford, a sonnet on the Catacombs, which she had visited on her birthday, shows the persistence of her Roman memories even after the state entry of Princess Alexandra of Denmark on 9 March had called forth another poem. In it the notion of the essential equality of men is illustrated, thus completing the trinity of which liberty and fraternity had been celebrated in the Italian poems:

> O wondrous human sympathy, to bring
>   Lofty and low together in accord!
> To link the humblest peasant with his king,
>   To charm us with a look, to thrill us with a word.

Liberty had been evoked in thought by the sight of the Tiber with its memories of the heroism of Horatius and Clelia, and of St Paul, who was brought a prisoner to its shores,

> Yes! liberty is sweet, but love can make
> A captive glad, who suffers for *her* sake . . .

And at Florence, on Whit Sunday, fraternity had been conceived as the mutual brotherhood of all creation in which:

> Each member, with his place content,
>   Or be it low, or high;
> Joined to the rest in firm cement
>   Of Love and Charity.

The thought of *Liberté, Egalité, Fraternité* continued to haunt her, and in 1866 she made a sketch of Marie Antoinette in the Conciergerie, with this legend on the wall above her head. Throughout 1862 and 1863, in spite of the lively descriptions of journeys and delight in the humours of travel, 'seriousness' had it, and only towards the autumn of 1863 did it once more begin to give way to lightheartedness when new friends and scenes changed the current of her thought and association.

In the next five years Oxford began to play its part in Elizabeth Wordsworth's life, and to exercise an ever-increasing influence. Stanford indeed was in the Oxford diocese, and a close bond linked Canon Wordsworth to his bishop, but Oxford itself was not so easily accessible from Stanford as were Reading and London, and for their first ten years in Berkshire it had not much significance for his children. Now, in October 1861, John Wordsworth went up to New College. He was fortunate in having his home so near, and there was to be much coming and going between Oxford and Stanford. His friends came often to stay at the roomy vicarage for dances— one year there were as many as eight in neighbouring country houses—or for hunting, or summer picnics on the Downs. For Elizabeth a further link was forged two years later, when Mrs Coxe, the wife of Bodley's Librarian the Rev. Henry Octavius Coxe and an old friend of the Freres, wrote to Mrs Wordsworth saying that her daughter Susie (Susan Esther) was laid low with an injured knee, and would Mrs Wordsworth spare one of her daughters to come and stay and cheer Susie up.[1] Mr Coxe was also the rector of Wytham, and so in October 1863 Elizabeth went off on a visit to the rectory and found Susie on the sofa. The two girls fell in love with one another at first sight, and a friendship began which was broken only by Susie's death in 1893, when she had been for many years the adored wife of John Wordsworth. Elizabeth maintained that the only useful thing she had done on that first of many visits was to pick the leaves of the flaming Virginia Creepers in the

1. *Glimpses.*

village and arrange them on the invalid's table, but she enjoyed to the full the charm of the whole household in its simplicity and lightness of heart. Mr Coxe, with all his cultivation and learning, had a fund of humorous stories, and Mrs Coxe recounted her happy recollections of an earlier generation of Freres. She was the daughter of Sir Hilgrove Turner and his French wife; her daughter inherited her rich dark hair, and big near-sighted dark eyes, her gaiety of temperament and unconscious originality. 'Susan Esther', as she was known to distinguish her from Susan Wordsworth, won all hearts with the quick sympathy, racy talk and social *savoir-faire* which came to her from her father, together with her literary and artistic feeling. A gift for musical interpretation was all her own, and her charm was revealed in a special way in her dancing, with its gliding even movement and the look of absolute enjoyment on her face. The spell was cast not only on Elizabeth, but also on her brother John, just turned twenty, to whom Wytham Rectory and the Coxes' house in Beaumont Street were always open. In repeated visits Elizabeth came to know Oxford well, Oxford 'between the Commissions' of 1850 and 1870, when the structure of the University was changing, but only as yet very slowly, and the attendant social revolution which was to make of Oxford a great residential city was hardly envisaged. The charm of a society of which *Alice in Wonderland* was the fine flower still lay upon the place.

The feminine community consisted only of the wives and daughters of Heads of Houses, professors and university officials, and the advent of young married women, the wives of fellows of colleges, was still in the future, although it was in the very near future that the marriage ban on fellows was to be lifted. Party feeling in Oxford ran very high; the rift between academic liberals and conservatives generally followed the parallel cleavage between the political parties, and invaded even social relationships, so that opponents did not care to meet at the same dinner-table. Mr Coxe's happy disposition set him to a certain extent outside these animosities of the sixties, and won for him the friendship of both sides. Elizabeth Wordsworth had therefore the good fortune to be spared a full introduction to this cramping state of things, and as time went on she came to have strong links with men and women of most diverse points of view, without ever compromising her own.

The visits to the Coxes were returned, and Susan Esther and her brother Hilgrove came to Stanford for Christmas dances at the vicarage. The Wordsworth sisters had for their own a big room at the top of the house, which was in consequence known as the 'Con-sistery'. Here all the preparations were made; dance music was practised by the home musicians, who took it by turns to play the valses, quadrilles, galops and lancers; programmes were drawn by Susie with fabled animals arm-in-arm on dainty pink polished cards, or adorned by John who sketched a jackdaw with peacock's feathers within a lace-like border stamped on the ivory boards; wreaths of ever-greens and paper decorations were confected by the girls, John the while reading Browning aloud in the true fashion of the 1860s. Young Oxford had been carried away by Browning, who was causing an amazing furore in England, and the under-graduates of the day gave much time and thought to essays in interpretation of his poems. They wrote poetry too, and John came under the influence of A. H. Clough and Matthew Arnold. Just at the time when Elizabeth was writing the series of poems on Italy, her brother composed a long poem in the manner of Cowper on the Visitation of the Sick. Together they were responsible, but in very unequal proportions, for a small volume of *Ballads from English History*, which was published anonymously in 1864 by the National Society. Of the twenty ballads Elizabeth wrote seventeen, and John two, while one was contributed by their Aunt Anne, the widow of Captain

Frere. Canon Wordsworth wrote the preface to the ballads which, he said, had been communicated to him in MS.

The same year, 1864, Elizabeth wrote some lines on the white pigeons flying round the spire of St Mary's at Oxford, and a certain number of poems have been preserved which deal with events of the moment, public or private. There are not very many of them, and letters and journals also took their place. Her sketch-book seems to have been the vehicle for notes and comments on life; and she provided the pen-and-ink drawing of Stanford church which was lithographed as the frontispiece to the Rev. L. G. Maine's *Two Lectures On the History and Antiquities of Stanford-in-the-Vale, Berkshire*, (published in 1866).

In 1865 John Wordsworth's friend W. J. Courthope, the future author of the *History of English Poetry*, won the Newdigate Prize, and a party from Stanford went to Oxford to hear him read his poem in the Sheldonian. The next year was an Annus Mirabilis for New College, when its members carried off the three Chancellor's prizes; the Latin Essay fell to John for his composition on the 'Comparison of Thucydides and Tacitus', and his family went up in force for a very gay Commemoration. The vivid impression made on Elizabeth by the sight of the ancient buildings serving as the background for solemn ceremonial and lively diversions in the summer sunshine is recalled in her novel *Thornwell Abbas* which was written a little later, and published in 1875 under the pseudonym of Grant Lloyd, combining the names of her two grandmothers. The action takes place in the years 1861 to 1867; it is set in the surroundings of Westminster and the life of a country parsonage which the author knew so well, and the book contains much of her characteristic thought and comment at this period. Two girls, the daughter of the squire and the niece of the vicar, go to Oxford for Commem; the details of the journey by train with a faithful maid, the arrival at the station, the description of the Head of a House and his wife with whom they stay, all are finely observed, as are the humours of dinners, luncheons, balls and river picnics. 'The popular prima donna puts her head in its Parisian bonnet out of a mullioned window, the nineteenth century is playing croquet on the old shaven lawns of retired Leisure, strains of Gounod and Wagner come floating along cloisters and quadrangles sacred to Croft and Aldrich, to Greene, Boyce and Purcell. Old Latin terms are jumbled up with modern slang. Young Oxford may be caught smoking a cigar under his trencher cap. Muslin dresses and pink ribbons flit about among the brown shades of the Bodleian, and Rimmel's perfumery mingles with the scent of old leather bindings and worm-eaten paper. The staircases are flowing with champagne, the tables groan under strawberries and cream. The old founders and benefactors look down on us in all kindness.' Here the picture is lightened by a flash of true understanding, which the author was to make her own; 'A really great mind is always one to make allowances. Would Archbishop Chichely have grudged us that delightful luncheon in All Souls? Would William of Wykeham have wished to turn those lovely geraniums and lovelier young ladies out of New College Gardens? Would Cardinal Wolsey have shaken the tassels of his red hat at the Christ Church ball?' And what perfect satisfaction she received from the sight of scarlet geraniums against the grey walls of her brother's college; and the thought of the cardinal's robes of the founder of Christ Church, his friend Edward Talbot's Alma Mater; as happened so often she renewed that earliest pleasure conferred by a nasturtium bed at Harrow, and the great red wheels of a carriage.

Elizabeth's taste in dress, always a matter of keen interest with her, is revealed in the detailed description of the gowns worn by Dot and Irene for their Commem ball. 'Dot really looked very nice—a little over-dressed—in pink silk, trimmed with white lace, and some pearl ornaments (family heirlooms), and a wreath to match her dress.' Here the limitations of wealth and the convention proper to a very young lady of position are neatly touched off; while Irene, refusing to be hampered by her own lack of means, turns her need into the obedient servant of her taste. She 'had indulged in a new white tarlatan, as the cheapest thing she could get. Mademoiselle, who loved making bargains, had let her have some French flowers, every whit as good as new, at half price. They were Austrian briars, and their rich audacity of colour suited well with the wearer's dark locks, brilliant eyes, and changeful complexion. A piece of black velvet, fastened by an old miniature round her throat, and an old black and gold fan, lent her by Mrs Amberfield, gave a piquancy and effectiveness to Irene's dress which made Dot's carefully-arranged and expensive toilet seem tame in comparison.' There is more than a reminiscence in this description of Susan Esther Coxe at the ball. A spice of malice enters into another picture: 'a dashing female figure in blue and silver, with conspicuous shoulder-blades and frizzy hair' which suggested the comment 'what a loss she is to a music-hall somewhere or other.'

Besides the delights of Commemoration, 1866 had brought other pleasant experiences.[1] In the early spring Archdeacon Wordsworth (he had become Archdeacon of Westminster in 1865) was delivering a series of Sunday sermons in Cambridge, and that led to weekends spent with various Heads of Houses whose hospitality included Mrs Wordsworth and Elizabeth and Mary. The visit to Trinity Lodge stood out from the rest because the parents had many social engagements and the field was left free for the daughters. Dr Whewell had lost his wife not long before, and their presence 'was almost the first bit of cheerfulness that had come to the house since this sad

1. *Glimpses*, pp. 57–71.

trouble.' The kindly Master laid himself out to entertain his guests, and the hale old giant might be seen with a girl on each arm doing the round of sights: the kitchens with the turtle shells put up on various occasions; the library with the busts of famous men and the MS. of Milton's *Lycidas* and *Sonnets*. The Master declaimed, and announced his liking for, 'Methought I saw my late espoused saint', while Elizabeth stuck out for 'Euclid and Archimedes'. Then they went to Caius and Jesus and St John's, admiring the new chapel, and finished up with the Round Church. Throughout the stay at Trinity there was much light persiflage and literary talk. Elizabeth was reproached one morning for not appearing at 8 o'clock chapel; another time when the party was capping Jane Austen she was asked, 'What was the name of Emma's governess?' a question she countered with 'Can you tell me Mr Knightley's Christian name?' They discussed Scott's *Antiquary*, and Charlotte Yonge's *Clever Woman of the Family*, Wordsworth's poetry and the *Rejected Addresses*; 'Why,' exclaimed Dr Whewell, 'I had no idea such little chits as you are (I don't mean Mrs Wordsworth, of course) knew anything about them.' They looked at landscapes and portraits and listened to Handel, and they were all very gay and lighthearted; so that the shock was great when the news came that the Master had been thrown from his horse. He died less than a fortnight after he had kissed them goodbye, with the parting words, 'I am so glad to have seen you; we shall meet again.'

A good deal of time was spent in London. Archdeacon Wordsworth now sat in Convocation *ex officio* and not as the representative of the Chapter; consequently he had greater freedom in expressing his personal views. Many important subjects were under discussion; the Conscience clause for Elementary Schools; Ritualism; the Colenso Controversy; and in all the debates the Archdeacon took a vigorous part. The presence of many clergy in London gave occasion for episcopal dinner parties on a vast scale in which wives and daughters had a part. There were other diversions, such as Fechter's interpretation of Hamlet, and the entirely feminine pleasure of criticizing other people's clothes and choosing one's own. A letter from Elizabeth to her sister Susan in the country serves up with observant humour and witty phrasing a slice out of the varied life at Westminster, 'breakfast table chat for you and Mary'.

Cloisters
May 3. 1866

My dear Susie,

I believe the others wrote to Mary today, so I will begin a letter to you. On Tuesday we went to a large party—there were 23 to dinner—at Ely House—Mrs Beresford Hope was next Mamma—I was opposite, between Archdeacons Moore and Bickersteth, with Mr Browne at the right of the latter, and the Dean of Canterbury of the former. Mrs Browne is delightfully hearty and kind—at the same time such a ladylike lady of the house—I never was at a party of the same size which had less stiffness about it. After dinner we saw Arch^n Sanctuary and numbers of others, and Miss Jeune (Susie Coxe's great friend on the strength of which I ventured to introduce myself). She seems constant in her allegiance to Oxford. Mrs Sanctuary is so much better as to be able to visit her son in Dorsetshire. Mr and Mrs Kemp were there and very friendly. Poor Mrs Kemp in some uneasiness of mind by reason of what I shall call a Donna Rodriguez cap (it reminded me so of the duennas in Don Quixote) with a sort of long tulle veil coming to the waist which the 'florist' had assured her was the correct thing (as it certainly was, for another lady had one just like it), and which always caught behind whenever she sat down— People are getting so theatrical in their dress now, some at least, and very often no doubt those who care least about it are most victimized.—The next morning a good many 'dignitaries' came to breakfast—afterwards to a Committee on Ritualism. A second session is going on in the drawing-room (Thursday) and I hear the voice of the Dean of Ely pronounce the well-known words 'by the Authority of Parliament in the 2ᵈ year of K. Edward VI.' The Wife's Sister bill was thrown out by the Commons yesterday, by a majority of 18. Who cares for the Reform Bill after that? Some movement is being, or going to be, made in Convocation for the repeal of the Divorce Act, and for the Increase of the Episcopate. Altogether I think the world is improving. It was really a very interesting sight to see the audience at 'Hamlet' last night—the pit was full, numbers of middle class tradespeople etc. whose behaviour was just what one would like to watch quiet and very attentive—the men more so than the women perhaps. There was nothing out of the way in scenery or dresses—quite a contrast in that respect to the last play we saw here—the Master of Ravenswood. Fechter's acting was as nearly perfect as one could expect that of anyone, not born on purpose for the part could be—and his being a German was not so distressing in a Dane as it would have been in an Englishman. There's an Irish sentence!—but I daresay you will understand. Miss Leclerc made a very good Ophelia, though not quite pretty or sylph like enough. She has got pretty hands and beautiful hair, and makes the most of both and sings prettily with a good deal of pathos those scraps of songs at the end. The ghost was very ghosty till he began to speak— but the voice was such as could only have come from a healthy pair of lungs—quite incompatible with the ethereal essence of a spirit. Altogether we (Chris and I) were much pleased, and want to persuade Papa to go. We hope he will go to the National Portrait Gallery—which Chris and I also went to, in preference to the Royal Academy. We are glad you enjoyed being at Oxford. Today is turning out very bright at last. Chris leaves us this afternoon. We saw Lady Orde and Cousin Anna and Charlotte Frere yesterday—all well. Annie is gone to Hove today. The Photographs were in time for the Cape parcel. There are 2 copies of the Ballads in my right hand corner drawer done up in brown paper, if you want them for anyone and I have plenty more in the cupboard here price 9*d*. It seems funny to be here quite out of the Reading atmosphere—pray write and tell us all that goes on with regard to it. We have got the 'Dove in the Eagle's Nest' I think it very pretty. Pris and I got some bonnets at Gomm & Harts, in a style of great simplicity, for fear of corrupting the minds of our Sunday Scholars at Stanford—hers is to be white straw and mine white aerophane, both trimmed with pink crape. I was so amused with the lady abbess of the establishment who came in while mine was being discussed and the evident relief of mind with which she said—when I suggested a little bit of pink *outside* as well as in—'*that* would make it a very pretty bonnet!' Most of the trimmings were what Signor Morelli called tourmentés—all wriggled about and frittered away. Priscilla got herself a new hat and white feather—so I think Messrs Gomm & Hart ought to be much beholden to us. We are in hopes John will come on Saturday. Convocation seems like to sit on Friday. Papa is very well and Archd[n] Bickersteth remarkably so. Now I must write a line to Charlotte, so goodbye. We are very glad Cousin Emily has taken to Sophy Toller. I hope she won't make invidious comparisons between her two mistresses—for I cannot fancy anyone more goodtempered than her present one. Mrs Conway is still far from well and wants a superior governess. I am afraid Aunt Lissey is scarcely likely to know of one 'finished' enough. Much love to all Ever y.a.s. Eliz.

Wordsworth. This is a gossipy letter and need not be handed about—and is meant to be breakfast table chat for you and Mary.

Another letter to Susan describing a visit to Roffey Park near Horsham in April 1868 must find a place here, because of the light it throws on the activities of a wealthy young woman of the period who occupied herself with amateur farming— half in the manner of Marie Antoinette and half in that of a modern owner of a pedigree dairy herd. It illustrates, too, the conventions of the day which might be shocked when two young women of twenty-eight and twenty-three were taken by their hostess to tea in the rooms of a charming bachelor curate, before an S.P.G. meeting!

Roffey Park
April 30, 1868

. . . arrived here at 3.44. We met Mr Sanctuary, just arrived from Chichester, and walked beside his horse up to the house, where we met with a very kind welcome; and after washing our hands and 5 o'c dinner, were carried off by Lizzie to an S.P.G. meeting in Horsham but first of all (don't mention it to the critical world at large!) to tea with Mr Mount, a most charming bachelor curate, and a great admirer of Mr Burgon's, and of course in his turn, greatly admired by the Horsham ladies. However I don't think either Mary or I are the worse for it—we sang some trios out of the Elijah etc. Mr Towers spoke, and spoke very well at the meeting—yet it was rather sleepy work, after so many hours railway. (May 1.) Yesterday afternoon, when this *ought* to have been posted, Lizzie took us out for a drive through the Forest, you can imagine how lovely it all was— then we met a fairy-like pony carriage with two little brown ponies with bells round their collars driven by a young lady, not quite pretty enough for a fairy queen, but with a very good-natured face. (a Miss Peters, daughter of the great Banker (Masterman & Peters) and of course rolling in riches) who insisted on our going round by their house to 5 o'c tea, and franking us through two turnpikes. Mrs Peters gave us a kind reception. Mr Peters is said to be a very shy man much given to the pursuit of chemistry and photography in his own rooms, (so we did not see him). The young lady does all the farming and took us through four or five conservatories and a pretty garden to her dairy—all inlaid with marble and painted with wreaths of roses, in honour of her name—she sells a good deal of butter in Brighton at 1/6 pr. lb! Then to a farm yard full of Alderney cows—and the most lovely little fawn-like calves, quite the creatures one would like to pet and keep on a lawn! As to the dogs and cats they were almost countless—besides a hall full of stuffed birds and live ones in her bedroom, and a pet pony that she rides round the farm every morning—it would have been a paradise for Landseer. All the people about here seem to have more money than they know what to do with—really it is quite an uninteresting prosperous place. The very cottages have a well-to-do look about them—but the country itself is much rougher and wilder than ours, and the soil so peaty that rhododendrons and even camellias grow out of doors all the year found. I am glad to say all our kind friends here seem pretty well and happy—and very kind they are to us. I hope you had a pleasant day in London. We want very much to hear from home, especially about the dear party at the Rectory. It makes one almost ashamed to be so idle when we think how busy you all are. I wonder how the Working Party went off, but [here the letter ends, the next sheet being apparently lost].

Behind all this pleasant dining and visiting and travelling there was the steady background of Stanford-in-the-Vale, an *obbligato* of parish work and Bible commentary accompanying the variations on life played in country houses and Little Cloister. Elizabeth had a class of girls which was successful and popular;[1] when she was away her parents took the girls in her stead—and very promising girls they found them—and noted how eagerly sixteen of them arrived, long before the hour fixed, to welcome her, when her return had been expected. She and her sister Mary were appointed at a meeting in the village school-room on 13 December 1867, to collect for the S.P.G. in the district of Red Row, Clayponds and Faringdon Road.[2] She would accompany her father when he went to administer the Holy Communion to old and sick parishioners; she would help to prepare for the ruridecanal conference at the vicarage, and rejoice in the excellent reports on the school submitted by H.M. Inspector. There were village weddings and village concerts to attend; Sunday school with a class to teach; and 'churchyard politics' during the American Civil War to smile over.[3] Feeling ran high in the Vale, and Farmer Spooner might be heard addressing an elderly countryman in smock frock: 'Mr Wilkins, it ben't no use arguing. I only says what I've been saying all along, that if them Northern fellows was to be made slaves of themselves 'twould just serve them right.'

There were endless small duties to be done, small kindnesses to be thought out, and small humours to be enjoyed, and Elizabeth was happy with the tranquil happiness of a healthy and dutiful young woman in the midst of a united family and provided with congenial friends and occupations; but her

1. Letter from C.W. to E.W., 27 November 1865 (lent by Mrs Leeke).
2. Note by Canon Christopher Wordsworth from the *Stanford Parish Magazine*, No. 1, p. 3.
3. Sketch-book, 29 April 1863.

emotional and intellectual life was not fully satisfied. There are signs that for the moment she had come to a dead end, and was growing tired with the continuous activity which yet did not claim the highest effort of her powers. In the spring of 1868 Mary Wordsworth, away on a visit, wrote to Susan at Stanford: 'E. looks all the better for the change. Still I fear that our share of work falls rather heavily on your shoulders.' At the moment only Susan of the sisters was at home, and even when Elizabeth and Mary were there as usual, they felt that they were a very small party. A good many changes were happening in the family. Dora had gone to school at Brighton after Easter, and Priscilla, the year before, had taken up the profession of nursing at King's College Hospital. Miss Frere was becoming increasingly infirm and helpless, and needed much care on the part of her nieces. Elizabeth wrote to Dora at school:[1] 'We have got Aunt Lissey on the new couch in the drawing-room, which is certainly a nice change for her, but she does not attempt to sit up'; and she ends the letter 'Time to read to Aunt Lissey—more love than opp' to write it in, Yr very aff. sister, E. Wordsworth.'

The young Christopher had left Winchester, and was following in his father's and grandfather's steps at Trinity College, Cambridge. John, after brief periods as a master at Harrow and Wellington was elected in 1867 to a fellowship at B.N.C. and settled down to an academic career. He was at length to realize his dream of becoming engaged to Susan Esther Coxe in May 1869, but because marriage involved the resignation of his fellowship this did not take place until Innocents' Day, 1870. So far none of his sisters had married, although there was always much pleasant male society. Not only were there plentiful opportunities for meeting distinguished men in London, but the dances and picnics in Oxford

1. E.W. to D.W., 22 April 1868 (letter lent by Mrs Leeke).

and Stanford often brought young people together. There were many occasions for tête-à-tête conversation and the real exchange of thoughts and ideas—a stroll up the High during Commem; the opportunity for talk enjoyed by dinner and dance partners; the long hours of boating, driving or walking. Elizabeth recalled in particular what proved to be the last picnic to the White Horse Hill, an occasion which was significant also for the future.[1] A party of John's Oxford friends had come over to the hospitable vicarage for Whitsuntide 1868. Among them was Edward Stuart Talbot, then a young student of Christ Church, who was within two years to be the first Warden of the new foundation of Keble College, and before the decade was out to call Elizabeth Wordsworth to be the first Principal of Lady Margaret Hall. But all this development was still in the future, and at the time the most important member of the party was an older man, John Conington, Corpus Professor of Latin in the University of Oxford, and translator of Virgil. There were besides A. O. Prickard of New College and T. L. Papillon of Merton and later of New College, editor of Virgil; altogether a Virgilian party.

On the Sunday afternoon they all went for a long walk in Buckland Woods where the rhododendrons were most lovely and the Professor talked about Jane Austen and modern novels, and also about Cowper, who had been intimate with the Throckmorton family to whom Buckland had belonged. Next morning the conversation turned on Harriet Martineau and her courteous reception of Mr Conington, unusual in view of her character of reserve. 'Afterwards a party of us went to the White Horse Hill,' as Elizabeth recalled many years later. 'All the gentlemen but Mr Talbot walked up through Captain Butler's grounds. A lovely day; had lunch on the hill-side.' There was all the interest and movement of the company of

1. *Glimpses*, pp. 107–9.

young men and women walking and driving to the summit of
the Downs and following the green road; and there was also
the message of past and present evoked by the wide-spread
landscape, motionless under a blue sky or mobile-seeming
under wind and cloud with crests and hollows like a swelling
sea. It was to become part of her remembered treasure. Her
thoughts in England, no less than in Italy, were disposed to
dwell on the true element of permanence in any situation
within its apparent mutability, and to give a subjective colour-
ing to the message:

There you see, on the White Horse Hill, the well-marked
remains of an entrenched camp which with its artificial
outlines and earthworks reminds you of a time when fierce
fighting went on along those ridges, and down amid those
hollows. You can think you hear the shouts and cries and
shrieks of warfare; you can, in imagination, see the weapons
flashing and the missiles flying, the blood-stained figures,
the wounded and the slain. All this passes before your mind
like a vision. You look again; there is stillness everywhere—
a still sky above you, looking all the bluer and stiller for the
black presence of one or two rooks, slowly hovering over-
head; turf cropped smooth by the sheep, at your feet, delicate little flowers, milkwort, wild thyme, eyebright, yellow
cistus; or lady's slipper exquisitely inlaid among the grass.
Nature has regained her ascendancy in this spot, once
desecrated by the strife of human passions; God's creatures
are doing His will, living their quiet lives once more in the
old way. What has become of the fierceness of man? Down
at the bottom of the valley are the little villages each grouped
about the village church—usually the one building that has
lasted where camp and castle have had their day and gone to
ruin—just because man's need of religion is something that
endures, while his wars and strifes are but for a time and

soon forgotten. 'Blessed are all they that put their trust in Him.'[1]

This vision is recorded in a Commentary on the Easter Psalm, *Quare fremuerunt gentes?*, but it must have been seen in high summer, because the flowers are summer flowers. Lady's slipper will have been Birdsfoot Trefoil as it used often to be called, although the name is formally given to a very different plant.

On Whit Monday 1868, the quietness and permanence of the Vale seemed to include the vicarage as well as the Church of Stanford. Archdeacon Wordsworth never considered seeking further preferment; he had sufficient scope for the cure of souls; he had sufficient means for his needs and his family's; he had sufficient leisure for his work on the Holy Scripture and sufficient opportunities for urging the causes he had deep at heart; he was becoming known as a speaker, a preacher and a writer of weight. The summer passed in the usual occupations, and declined into autumn. Early in November, Elizabeth went with her parents to stay with their old friend Miss Watson at Langton Green, and from her house they called on the Oswells—Mrs Oswell was the daughter of their Westminster neighbour, Mr Rivaz—and on Mr Saint in the moated house of Croombridge Place.[2] Old links were strengthened and the past impinged sharply on the present. Then at the end of the month the future asserted itself. Two events happened which made a revolution in the steady routine, and changed the life of the whole family. For Elizabeth a turning point was reached under the direction of new affection which brought its liberating force to bear on the development

1. Elizabeth Wordsworth, *Psalms for the Christian Festivals*, 1906, pp. 56–7. Ps. II (for Easter Day).
2. *Glimpses*, pp. 100–3.

of her personality, and of new circumstances which gave the needed scope for her re-created energy.

On Saturday, 13 November, Archdeacon Wordsworth received from the Prime Minister, Disraeli, a letter[1] telling him of his intention to recommend the Queen to raise him to the episcopal bench on the ground of his abilities, learning and shining example.[2] That same day, with the matter still pending, he and Mrs Wordsworth joined Elizabeth and Susan at Wellington College on a first visit to the Headmaster, Edward White Benson, future Archbishop of Canterbury, and his wife Mary Sidgwick, called Minnie, who was also his cousin, the sister of William, Henry and Arthur Sidgwick. The acquaintance was due to John Wordsworth, who for a short time had been sixth-form master under Dr Benson. The coincidence of the offer of the bishopric and the visit to Wellington was one of a whole group of coincidences possessing true significance, and through it the decision to accept the episcopal office was indissolubly bound up with the beginning of a great friendship. At first it seemed probable that Ely would be the vacant see; including as it did the University of Cambridge, it had strong attractions for Archdeacon Wordsworth. None the less he wrote a first letter declining the offered preferment, because he felt that his life had been too much one of study for him to make so fundamental a change when he was already over sixty. Dr Benson used all his powers in urging the duty of acceptance and promised himself to give up his work at Wellington before long and come to help the new bishop in his see. By the Sunday evening the letter of refusal was recovered and a second one was sent to the Prime Minister accepting *any* post to which her Majesty might be pleased to call him.

At Reading on the journey home it was learnt that the see in

1. *Christopher Wordsworth*, pp. 202–14.
2. *Glimpses*, pp. 103–5.

question was Lincoln, not Ely, and *terra incognita* to the Wordsworths. Characteristically, when they got back to Stanford that evening they sought information from Camden's *Britannia*, in which the natives of Lincolnshire are said to walk about perforce on stilts; and further enlightenment came from the Rev. T. Mozley, one of those natives, who sent a sketch consisting of a single horizontal line, with the legend '*nil nisi pontus et aër*'. With greater knowledge they learned of many links with their old life. St Hugh had been consecrated Bishop of Lincoln in St Catherine's Chapel, the old infirmary chapel of the monks of Westminster, which had been incorporated in the house in Little Cloister; St Hugh's Day fell on 17 November, the very day on which Archdeacon Wordsworth had accepted the nomination to Lincoln. It was also the accession day of Queen Elizabeth, the second foundress, so to speak, of Westminster. St Hugh was to mean much to his latest successor, and he was always held in affectionate honour by Elizabeth Wordsworth. The formalities of election and confirmation were quickly concluded; at Stanford the heartrending farewells were said and the touching presentations were made, and the home of nearly nineteen years was left on Wednesday, 17 February 1869. In the peace of Mr and Mrs Coxe's hospitality at Oxford the few days were passed until it was time to go to Westminster for the consecration. At dinner in John Wordsworth's rooms in B.N.C. friends were gathered who helped to bridge, for the bishop-elect and his family, the passage from the old life to the new; Mr Burgon, Mr E. S. Talbot, and Mr Conington. They all knew Stanford well; Mr Conington, whose mother lived at Boston, could tell them much about Lincolnshire, and Oxford served as the cement which joined the two.

On St Matthias' Day, 24 February, before the High Altar of the Abbey, Christopher Wordsworth was consecrated bishop of Lincoln, as his predecessor William de Bois had been in

1203. A last walk in the College Garden; a melancholy inspection of book-cases in the study at Little Cloister; a day spent in doing homage at Osborne; and another in taking his seat in the House of Lords; and on the 27th the new bishop with his wife and daughters 'arrived in Lincoln just in time to see the Minster in its afternoon beauty.' They settled into the episcopal mansion at Riseholme a few miles from Lincoln, since to the bishop's keen regret there was no house for him in Lincoln. For his daughter Elizabeth it was the beginning of a more spacious way of life; freed from the petty details and engrossing parish cares of Stanford, she was constantly brought into contact with wider public interests, and came to understand the problems which face a statesman and administrator. It was the beginning also of the deepest friendship of her life. The affection, free, equal and fraternal which grew between her and Edward and Minnie Benson satisfied the needs of heart and mind. Because of its explosive force she was impelled forward on the road to maturity and possession of herself.

Index